AN HISTORICAL SURVEY
OF SCOTTISH LITERATURE
TO 1714

AN HISTORICAL SURVEY

OF

SCOTTISH LITERATURE

TO 1714

BY

AGNES MURE MACKENZIE

M.A., D.LITT.

[signature: Agnes Mure Mackenzie]
[Edinburgh. 18.7.37]

" *Le temps n'est plus où l'on considérait tous les siècles
qui ont précédé [l'Union des couronnes] comme indignes
d'attirer l'attention de la critique, comme occupés par de
vagues et informes productions qui ne méritaient pas d'être
classées dans la littérature nationale, et où on les aban-
donnait à une érudition dont les recherches n'intéressaient
que ceux qui s'y livraient.*"

GASTON PARIS, *adapté.*

LONDON
ALEXANDER MACLEHOSE & CO.
58 Bloomsbury Street
1933

PRINTED IN GREAT BRITAIN BY ROBERT MACLEHOSE AND CO. LTD.
THE UNIVERSITY PRESS, GLASGOW

IN PIAM GRATAMQUE MEMORIAM

GULIELMI ELPHINSTONE

ABERDONIAE EPISCOPI

DEI ET PATRIAE ET MUSARUM SERVI

MCDXXXI—MDXIV

PREFACE

I HAVE tried to give a brief continuous sketch of the history of that part of our literature which is written in language descended from one form or other of " Anglo-Saxon," for the period from the end of the Macalpin dynasty, to which the first surviving fragments belong, to the end of the Stewarts as a reigning house : from the death of Queen Margaret Eiriksdotter to the death of Queen Anne. I did not venture farther, since the admirable but too modestly named *A Scottish Man of Feeling : Henry Mackenzie*, by Dr Harold Thompson, has recently given an account of the eighteenth century Risorgimento, from Hutcheson to Burns, so lively, scholarly, and comprehending that it would be an impertinence on my part to attempt to supplement it. From Burns to Scott's death the ground has been fully covered, and for the last century, there is scarcely material to be worth a history.

I have attempted to suggest behind my story an adumbration—there is no room for more—of the development, and retrogression, of Scots culture in that time, and its relation to Scottish history in general and beyond it to British and to the affairs of that Europe of which Scotland, for the first three of these four centuries, was very much more a part than it is customary, now, to remember. If I have seemed to overload my account with history (and I have made it discursive of set purpose) it is for the reason, which I deeply regret, that my country's history is so little known. That may seem untrue at first sight, for the Scot, like the Frenchman and unlike the Englishman, has a sense of the past : it is always, to him, a vital part of his present, and although his outlook is frequently parochial with regard to place, it has very rarely the more serious fault of parochialism with regard to time. Unlike the Frenchman, however, he has rarely an accurate knowledge of that past, and as many of the factors commonly eliminated from the current version of our country's story have a vital connection with my immediate subject, I am forced to handle them with a certain fulness.

I must thank Mr J. H. Lobban, my sometime chief, and Dr Dan Mackenzie, for the kind loan of many valuable books : neither gentleman, however, is responsible for the use I have made of them, nor for any of the opinions expressed hereafter.

St John's Wood, *April,* 1933.

CONTENTS

(The author) has done as well and as much as he could, that whatever was worthy of a mention might have it . . . and now he hath done, he hath not pulled up the ladder after him : others may go on as they please with a completer composure.

COTTON MATHER, Decennium Luctuosum

PROLOGUE

Scotland in space and time—the growth of the nation—the confusion of tongues—mediaeval culture in Scotland—Scotland in Europe—the end of the Macalpins—the new age

THE oldest extant piece of literature known to have been produced by a man of these islands is the work of a sixth-century monk of Dumbarton. It is not without significance, perhaps, that this senior work of all Scottish, and British, letters is a tale of disaster, of the shattering of a culture that seemed immortal, and that its author was to die in exile. It is worth noting that St Gildas uses the Imperial tongue, for Dumbarton was never within the Imperial frontier, not even a part of the loosely-held, quickly-lost province of Valentia, between the Forth and Clyde and Hadrian's Wall.

Yet though our literature carries back so far (1), a mediaeval literature of what is now Scotland, in any language related to the common speech of the whole modern Scottish nation, Highland and Lowland, has left very scanty remains. There are several reasons for this scantiness. One is the simple one that much has perished : we know that for certain. Another is a point very often forgotten, that even modern Scotland is very small. In actual territory she is rather more than half the size of England with Wales, but in population—and history is of men and not of miles—the constant ratio of the developed kingdom to her neighbour has been roughly as one to eight : she has about three-quarters the man-power of Portugal, rather less than three-quarters of that of Holland, and about two-thirds that of Belgium. If for something like half a millenium this small country should be called upon to withstand, successfully, her neighbour's continual attempts at armed annexation, against these odds, we might expect the fact to have a certain effect upon her output in the arts. Artistic creation is, from one point of view, the using of energy not demanded by mere living : and a man with his back to the wall of his burning house, and eight well-armed enemies in front of him, seldom finds himself with the leisure to write sonnets. That a century and a quarter of active literary production should come as soon as this menace was even partly removed, is perhaps not altogether without meaning.

Further, and no more commonly realised, Scotland, in any modern sense of the word, is not only a small nation, but a very new one. The statement is startling to a foreigner. It is probably even more startling to a Scot, who is accustomed to such facts as that a Highland professional man, of no special rank or riches, and not notably " well-connected," as England would put it, can often trace descent to, say, Sigurd the Volsung, with collateral (and legitimate) female lines to the royal houses of Bruce, Macalpin, Capet, and Plantagenet. (These illustrations are not invented ones.) Lowland pedigrees seldom run so far, but a considerable number of Lowland gentlefolk—a very much larger proportion than in England or even France—must have a descent going back to at any rate the thirteenth century. Indeed, one of the differences between Scots and English social values, and one that means more than may appear on the surface—that the Scot defers to, say, the Duke of Buccleuch as to the head of an ancient family, and the Englishman as to a Duke—is significant of this sense of a long past.

Scotland has a long past. But she is a new nation. It is not merely that the modern kingdom of Scotland does not come into being till the mid-thirteenth century—strictly speaking, indeed, not until the late sixteenth, for Orkney and Shetland were not finally ceded until 1590. The lateness of growth of the *kingdom* would, in itself, scarcely matter. Italy and France, for example, were *nations* for centuries before they existed as kingdoms. England shows the same order, with a shorter gap. But although what we mean by the present kingdom of Scotland is older than the kingdoms of France and Italy, existing from the time of Alexander II, what we mean nowadays by the Scottish nation is not older than the late eighteenth century. Less than two hundred years ago—at the time, say, when Scott's father was a boy—our Scotland was still two completely different nations, differing not as Gascony does from Artois or Devon from Yorkshire, but as France does from Germany—differing in language, in social organisation, in laws, dress, *mœurs* generally, and very considerably in religion, the only bridge being the common central government (rather dubiously effective north-west of the Line) and the fact that the Highland gentry have from Bruce's time onward belonged more or less, sometimes fully, to both of them. Earlier still, she was not two nations, but several.

It is interesting, and instructive, to compare her growth with that of her neighbour. Certain sharp contrasts are obvious : Scotland, like France, suffered from a capital too near her frontier, and from the fact that her wealthiest districts were precisely those most open to invasion. Leaving out that of 1745, which most carefully did no damage, the last large-scale invasion of England to touch anything below the extreme north edge of Yorkshire was in 1066. The last in Scotland were three together in 1544-5-7. The first of these destroyed the capital : the butcher's bill for the second included seven monasteries, sixteen castles, five towns, two hundred and forty-three villages, and three hospitals, in the richest of the country, sacked mainly by Spanish mercenary troops, the most ruthless in Europe: the third included a battle as slaughterous as Flodden. The three together did not succeed in achieving the aggressor's purpose, but in spite of the fact that they also distributed Bibles to the natives, they cannot have helped Scotland very much.

A more significant and less obvious comparison, however, is that of the different growth of the two kingdoms. England as early as the seventh century was already a nation, in the sense that Italy was a nation in 1820. She was split up yet in several separate kingdoms, but was homogeneous culturally, more or less racially, and fairly, though rather less so, linguistically : a Wessex man in Alnwick would be no worse off than a modern Buckie trawler might be in Bideford. By 802 she was an actual kingdom : the later oscillations of her frontier and her later annexations by Denmark and Normandy did not alter that, though the latter profoundly affected her culture, and for some time her language. Scotland, on the other hand, at the beginning of the ninth century, was partly a piece of England, speaking English, partly a Norwegian colony, speaking Norse, and the rest three separate independent kingdoms, speaking three separate Celtic languages. The only quality all five had in common was an extremely lively pugnacity. It was not until 844 that by the same sort of dynastic accident as was later to unite Scotland and England, Kenneth Macalpin, King of Scots, succeeded to the Pictish crown and by joining the two most important states, laid the foundations of the united monarchy that was to take, for its accomplishment, four centuries and a quarter of strenuous time and the work of eleven generations of his descendants, twenty-seven of whom were actual sovereigns. It was not until 1018 that his great-grandson's grandson, Malcolm II, won Northern Northumbria from Canute of England, and made it the provinces of Lothian and the Merse. In 1034 Malcolm's grandson, Duncan I, succeeded, by another chance of pedigree, to a fourfold realm that now included the old Welsh kingdom of Strathclyde. The North and West were not annexed from Norway until in 1263 Duncan's great-grandson won that wild battle among the foam and the broken ships at Largs. Carham and Largs rank next after Bannockburn, and like it are no victories of aggression, but of justified self-defence against an invader. " Une nation qui se défend ne périt pas."

Hibernian and Caledonian Goidel-Celts, Welsh Brython-Celts, Scandinavian Norse, and Teuton Saxons —the salad, with Celtic for its dominant element, was at least in the bowl when the Dark Ages were ending, and long before Largs, and just in time to benefit by the awakening that follows the First Crusade, the new Scotland was taking her place as part of Europe. What chiefly brought about that important advance was a piece of wild imprudence on the part of Malcolm III, conveniently a widower of his Norse queen. He married a shipwrecked and penniless princess-errant, was her devoted lover to his death, and in that, did his country magnificent service. It is as edifying as Perrault, which presumably is why, in Scottish schools, one hears little of the match and of its results. The lady was both a genius and a saint—a combination frequently most annoying to those who dislike the theology of the saint and are anxious to prove it must be bad for " progress." She had also been bred at the courts of two other royal saints, her kinsmen, one a scholar and the other a fighting statesman, the latter in close touch with Byzantium and the traditions of the Empire, the former with the new strong life of France, already by tradition playing in the North the part of Byzantium in Southern Europe. Through her mother, Agatha of Hungary, she brought the blood of the Caesars to her sons.

St Margaret was not only the greatest personality that the House of Cerdic had produced in the seven generations since Alfred : she was also an excellent European, at the time when the conception of what we call Europe and her age called Christendom was clearer than it has been since the thirteenth century. Malcolm was wise enough to comprehend her wisdom, and to support her unfalteringly in its use, to the great gain of his kingdom. They left a strong dynasty. Three of their sons were Kings of Scots, their daughter and their grand-daughter Queens of England, another grand-daughter Empress, their nephew Duke of as yet independent Brittany. Alexander I was a great king, his brother David a greater, and though David's two grandsons were indifferent monarchs, their successors were not. The house does not rot, but keeps its vitality to the end. If Alexander III's son had lived, even if Margaret of Flanders, Princess of Scotland, had borne him a son to take the place of his niece, the story of Scotland might have been less unhappy.

It is in the time of the last two Alexanders that the literature of our language had its real beginning. The various branches of what is called Old English had produced a literature of merit before Northern Northumbria was ceded to Malcolm II, or the rest of England annexed by Normandy ; and until the Danish invasions of the ninth century, the Northern dialect was the chief literary speech. Before Lothian and the Merse were ceded, however, the literature of Old English, of " Anglo-Saxon," was drying up in decadence. Beyond a thin trickle of monastic chronicle, there is nothing in either country, in anything corresponding to its modern national speech, between Carham and the thirteenth century—nothing, that is, in any form of English during the great Renaissance of the twelfth century, one of the most brilliant ages in the history of culture, and little surviving—next to nothing in Scotland—from the thirteenth century, the full and splendid tide of the Middle Ages. Mediaeval vernacular literature in both countries belongs in the main to a time of decreasing spiritual and mental vitality. It comes after the noon of its age, though the last of it, in Scotland, reflects as does no other literature the gorgeousness of the mediaeval sunset, of the age of fan-vaulting and the " flaming " Gothic, of plate-armour and head-dresses like spires and wings. We are apt to forget, however, that although in the true Middle Ages neither country has much to show in what corresponds to our modern tongue, this does not mean that either was bereft of letters. In the eleventh, twelfth, and thirteenth centuries, Englishmen, and English-, Welsh-, and Gaelic-speaking Scots alike, if they were men of learning, spoke and wrote the international language, Latin, that transcended national barriers and even as late as the late seventeenth century put the science and learning of all Europe on an international basis. Dr Helen Waddell, in a book that wears its astonishing scholarship like a rose in its cap, has taught us the charm and vitality, on the purely literary side, of that Latin culture even in the Dark Ages, whose work generations of post-Renaissance learned have damned in procession without reading it.

The Scottish culture of the true Middle Ages was trampled practically out of existence by the century of war that followed the death of Queen Margaret Eiriksdotter, twenty years after that of St Louis in the last Crusade ; and that of the early Renaissance was wrecked in turn by the disastrous invasions of Mary's minority and the century and three-quarters of religious war that followed. But, for Scotland, the Middle Ages began well : Margaret and Malcolm had set her upon her feet, in the full tide of European life, brought her out of her position as a stormy border state between England and Scandinavia, in constant and enduring danger from both. We had no Norman Conquest to organise the whole kingdom as a unit, but those inveterate emigrants achieved a good deal of peaceful penetration : indeed, the head of the northernmost of the Highland clans is of Norman descent. David I in special favoured them, a little oddly perhaps for his mother's son : but he had close Norman connections by marriage, for though his own queen was of high Saxon-English stock his sister was wife of the Count of Boulogne and stepmother of the first King of Jerusalem, the greatest of the Crusaders : his other sister had married the Norman King of England, and he, as a young prince, a seventh son, unlikely to succeed to the throne, had spent much time at his brother-in-law's court in England and Normandy (2). His statesman's vision realised the Norman heirship of the Roman genius for organisation and the value of their intimate relations with France and Italy at a moment, between the first two Crusades, when the re-awakening life of Europe in general and of these two countries in special was being newly fertilised from the East. In fact, it was well for Scotland that he did, for the descendant of his great-granddaughter's Scoto-Norman husband was Robert Bruce, Earl of Carrick and King of Scots.

By the time of the last two Alexanders, South-east Scotland at least, Central and North-east Scotland to a lesser extent, were wealthy and well-organised. Farming increased in prosperity, and was not serf-labour : the abandonment of villeinage in Scotland (3), long before it died out in the two countries most closely linked with her fortunes, left room for the growth of the free peasant class that gave troops to roll back Plantagenet aggression. Trade flourished, with Flanders, the market of the North, with England, France, Scandinavia, Italy. Berwick, the wealthiest city, was a great port, whose colony of Flemish merchants so identified themselves with Scottish interests that in the hideous sack of 1296 they fought gallantly side by side with their hosts, and died to a man in the ruins of their Guild-hall. Edinburgh under the last Alexanders was a more spacious and civilised city than the Edinburgh of the Union of the Parliaments. There was much building, and noble : but the great silver bell called Mary and her twelve brothers called for the Apostles do not sound now from Lindores across the Firth, and the great abbeys—there were six in Fife alone—are pitiful shards, the few cathedrals left no more than stripped and mutilated carcasses. The ruin is not all the work of the Reformers. Balmerino, for instance, was sacked by Hertford on the Christmas morning of 1547, on his way to ravage the nunnery of Perth, at the head of his Greek and Spanish mercenaries : but Arran's Protestant lords had opened his way.

There was active and increasing provision for education. By the early twelfth century there appears to have been a school of some fame at the great international pilgrim-port of St Andrews, and although we have lost touch with the thirteenth century we know that besides the older monastic schools the borough grammar schools were beginning : those of Perth and Ayr were in existence at the beginning of the century, and that of Aberdeen—something of an outpost—a generation later. It is not uncharacteristic, however, of our wandering nation that when the modern European university begins to take shape, about the beginning of the thirteenth century, the first Scottish foundation for university teaching should be established abroad, and incidentally, by a woman. In 1262, thirteen years after the founding of University (the first) College at Oxford, and twenty-two years before Peterhouse was founded at Cambridge, the Celtic Countess of Galloway, Devorgilla, founded a Scots College there, and called it after her Scoto-Norman husband, John Baliol : it is still distinguished traditionally by a hard intellectual edge, a turn for abstract philosophy, and a certain arrogance. Though the connection with Baliol still exists, the wars in which Devorgilla's unpleasing son was to be prominent, if scarcely active, broke it for a time, and another Scots College was founded in 1326, by the Bishop of Moray, this time in Paris, the great mother-university of all the North. Paris, by the way, much earlier than this had a Rue d'Écosse, which is said to take its name from Scottish students : and in 1324 it had two Scots booksellers.

In the early thirteenth century a Border man, Michael Scott, taught at Oxford, Paris, and Toledo, and was a prominent figure at the brilliant Sicilian court of the dazzling Emperor, Frederick II, *Stupor Mundi*. By his translation, partly from Greek and partly from Arabic, of Aristotle's works on mathematics and ethics he made an enduring mark on Western thought, and his reputation in the sciences was sufficiently enduring for an Italian of a hundred years later to mention him casually in a vernacular poem, as Mr Aldous Huxley might mention Darwin. A little later Richard, called "of St Victor," had scarcely less contemporary fame as a scholar-theologian.

The foreigneering tradition, which to judge by French comments was already established by the thirteenth century, has never been lost, and has probably had a good deal to do with perpetuating the broader outlook, both socially and in their degree curricula, of the Scottish universities as compared with their English neighbours. Even when the

Reformation caused Scotland, politically, to turn her face to England rather than to the Continent, a continuous stream of Roman Catholic and Episcopalian Scots (4), who found life at home too exciting for peaceful study, kept up the old habit, though not all of them kept it quite so extensively in their individual persons as a seventeenth-century sub-principal of the Collège de Beauvais, one Dempster, who held office, at various times, at Louvain, Rome, Douai, Tournai, Navarre, Toulouse, Montpelier, Pisa, and Bologna ! All through the sixteenth and seventeenth centuries, until Latin fell out of use as a spoken language, there were Scots teachers and scholars from Coimbra to Copenhagen. Scots Latin is still comprehensible abroad, as English for long was not : but the disuse of it as currently spoken speech put an end to this free trade in teachers, since not all Scots scholars had the talent of the Admirable Crichton for academic dispute in twelve languages. (One is hardly astonished that the gentleman, though equally handy with more concrete weapons, got himself stabbed before he was out of his twenties.) There are indeed still traces of the tradition, in such institutions as the Collège écossais at Montpelier, and the fact that the chief exports of Aberdeen are still given as " fish, granite, and professors of classics " (5).

The stream of scholars was only one of the tides that washed back and forth across the North Sea. The influx of Scots into foreign trade may be gauged by the fact that in the sixteenth century it was estimated that there were thirty thousand Scots in Poland alone, organised in Scots Brotherhoods, powerful enough to stand up to the Polish government. And Scotland has always exported fighting

men. In Italy, a Scot was in command of the troops
of Genoa in 1120, and in the next century there were
Scottish lords of Piacenza : in Spain, the Marquès
de la Motilla is descended from a Scots knight who
distinguished himself at the intaking of Seville in
1247, and Douglas and his knights in 1329 left an
enduring tradition. Further north, the Danish earldom of Orkney was held in 1379 by a Scotsman—
whose father, by the way, had been killed fighting the
the Moors in Spain. In Prussia at the same time,
there were Scots fighting side by side with the Knights
of the Sword, and a Douglas was Prince of Dantzig,
a city which even quite recently had a quarter called
Little Scotland, and whose present Art Gallery and
Academy of Commerce were founded, a hundred
years ago, by a Scotsman. The great theatre of
foreign service was France, where the tradition was
immemorial : the Emperor Charles the Fat had a
Scots wife. Even when Scotland as a nation ceased
to be France's ally, it continued until the Revolution
and past it : and many Scots soldiers bear witness that
when the alliance was renewed, very practically, in
1914, the old friendship had not been forgotten. As
Duruy puts it, " La France chercha et trouva toujours dans l'Écosse des amis dévoués." Everyone,
even in Scotland, has heard of the famous *Garde
écossaise*, whose descendants the Royal Scots count as
senior regiment in the British Army, though their
nickname of Pontius Pilate's Bodyguard was first
applied to their other, younger, parent, Turenne's
Régiment d'Hébron, by French troops who were
jealous when Louis XIII gave these the right of the
line whenever they should be in action. According
to Eginhard, the tradition goes back to Charlemagne.

Scots shared with St Louis the desperate business of the last two Crusades, where he made them his guard. The Lorraine branch of Clan Macleod goes back to a soldier of the fourteenth century. The great period of Scots service in France begins then, when the Garde écossaise was formally constituted by Charles V. Jean Fouquet painted them in a Book of Hours, drawn up behind the King, with the forget-me-not badge upon their shields ; and some of the faces look like lively portraits. When in 1420 Charles's pitiful son signed away his son's birthright at Troyes, the Guard reneged his service to a man, and marched out to join the disinherited Dauphin, who later, in recognition of their service under St Joan, gave them precedence over all the troops in France, though it was his son again who gave them the most distinguished C.O. on record—Our Lady, no less ! Until the Revolution their Captain stood at the King's right hand at his crowning : they did their devoir to deserve the distinction, for when Francis I was taken at Pavia there were only four of his Scots Guard left alive. The Guard were not all of their countrymen to serve in Charles VII's wars : a Scot of the royal house was Commander-in-Chief of France in 1421, and in the four following years over thirty thousand Scotsmen entered French service. As late as the seventeenth century there were daily masses in both Tours and Orleans for the souls of Scotsmen killed serving with the French colours—masses founded, perhaps, by that Scots Bishop of Orleans who received St Joan when she rode in as victor. Even as late as 1878, a Scots colony, descendants of these soldiers, existed near Tours, and Orleans has still a Street of the Sword of Scotland (6).

It is perhaps worth considering what might have happened to Scots civilisation if these articles of export had always been in double circulation. Before 1540, at any rate, there was no bar against that, and as the tradition, even if we disregard Eginhard, goes back to the twelfth century at least, one may gather that the mediaeval Scot had an excellent chance of transcending insularity of outlook, in the arts as in other things.

The fact that (until the B.B.C. renewed some interest in music at any rate) Progress has robbed the modern man of any regular contact with any art save those of architecture and literature, has caused us to take for granted that any man who cannot read is necessarily a barbarian. But the mediaeval gentleman who could not read—even, apparently, that degraded animal the mediaeval peasant—would appear, in general, to have been more capable of appreciating the statues of Chartres or the glass of the Sainte Chapelle than the cultured moderns who created Oxford Street and built the North British Hotel in Edinburgh, although these latter could certainly read and write. And the proposal to blazon Popple's Pills on the face of heaven presupposes a populace who can not only read and write but will enjoy that entrancing spectacle—projected by men with at least a secondary education. Even in the matter of literature itself, we forget that those mediaevals who could not read took it as much for granted to be read to as we do to be played to by the B.B.C. The mediaeval Scots gentleman was read to fairly often, and as we should expect from the mixed nature of his country and its foreigneering habit, in several languages (7). It is rather amusing that he should apparently have spoken more English than his English contemporary equal did. The English gentleman of the thirteenth century would be able to understand English, often to speak it : but his habitual tongue was French : he thought in French. His Scots contemporary spoke, as his common vernacular, most often Gaelic, but increasingly English, and as the Norman element strengthened, French, while learned men of all classes (some Popes were serfborn) spoke Latin. There was not so much class distinction of speech as in England, though the upper classes probably spoke French or Gaelic rather more than English. Alexander III took his Coronation Oath in Latin and French. The fact that so many languages were in common use in a country where even in the mid-twelfth century a royal charter addresses itself to " the Normans, English, Scots (8), and Galwegians of the realm," made for a rather polyglot upper class. In the thirteenth century a French *Roman de Fergus,* whose setting is partly in the Mearns, and which tells of an Arthurian knight who is son to Somerled of the Isles, is dedicated by its author, Guillaume le Clerc, apparently a Picard, to Alan of Galloway, a Celt whose native vernacular would be the Welsh-Celtic of old Strathclyde or the Gaelic of the Goidel enclave in the extreme Southwest. If a speaker of one of these languages wanted to be on dining or marrying terms with his neighbours (and Alan's son-in-law was the Norman Earl of Winchester) he had to be intelligible in the others.

The polyglot tradition was sufficiently firmly established to be long-enduring. The Scottish pilgrimship whose forty passengers were massacred by an English pirate in 1320 has a French name, appro-

priately *La Pelaryn*, and even in 1400 a letter from
the Scots Earl of March to his second cousin Henry IV
of England is written in English but has the signature
(Le Count de la Marche d'Escoce) and the address
and the King's honorifics in French. Even in a poem
written in the fourteen-fifties, long after English had
become the Scots legal language and the Lowland
literary speech, an English soldier, chaffing a Scotsman, is made to address him in a weird mixture of
English and what is meant for French and Gaelic.
Indeed, the tradition persists in a fashion yet. Most
Scots of the educated classes are more or less bilingual,
and that naturally and without self-consciousness.
This extends even beyond the use of Scots or Gaelic,
to the national differences in the use of standard
English. Not long ago in Dunbar, I was amused to
notice I had asked a scavenger, " Can you direct me
to the station ? " The phrase would simply not have
come to me in England, where I have spent almost a
third of my life. And I invariably notice that a return to my own country greatly increases the extent
and precision of my *speaking* vocabulary, *in English*.
It is probable that the persistence of an at least bilingual habit has something to do with the remarkable adaptability of our race, that coexists with such
tenaciousness of identity.

Now, in the Middle Ages, naturally, and especially
in the true Middle Ages, where there is most of it,
this casually polyglot habit goes with that of thinking
in European terms rather than national. A man's
adherence was not to a place but to a culture, to
Christendom ; and to a person, his feudal lord or
tribal chief. When place began to cut across this,
there was intricate trouble, and nowhere more than

with us. The thirteenth century Scots King quite naturally did homage for English lands to the King of England, the King of England for French ones to the King of France. A baron might hold in Carrick, Lincoln, and the Vermandois, doing homage for his lands to three different kings, and when his overlords were at loggerheads supporting whichever his principles, or his interest, might suggest.

It was then in such a setting as this that somewhere in the thirteenth century there begins in Scotland as in England a " literary " literature in English—not a folk-literature, but one using the forms and based on the subject-matter of that already written in French or Latin. But the oldest surviving piece of Scottish literature in the common tongue is a lament for a national disaster. The last Alexanders, continuing the work of Alexander I, David I, and their parents, had made Scotland powerful, prosperous, and civilised, and established her in the European comity. Then the Queen, Margaret of England, died as her sons had done, and the King married a young French wife at Jedburgh. They say that Death was seen to dance at the wedding. Queen Yolette was young and lovely, the King infatuated. He galloped along the Fife cliffs, an eager lover, and next morning, instead of a wise and gallant king, the sovereign of Scotland was a child princess of Norway, next heir through her dead mother, King Eirik's queen, to the direct line of the strong Macalpin house, that had served Scotland nobly for nearly half a millenium.

Little Queen Margaret never set foot in her kingdom, and the first Scots-English literature that has survived is a popular lament for the lost age. Lost it was : one need not go far into that. After a hundred

18

years of comparative peace, Scotland tasted again what she had already known under the grandsons of David I, what was to be the curse of her history, a central government represented by a child, in a country of fierce arrogant nobles and difficult communications, with the enemy at the door of her wealthiest provinces (9). This was the worst of all the nine minorities that were to trouble the next three centuries, partly because the young Queen's death and the end of the recognised dynasty meant a scramble for the Crown among equals none of whom would accept another, partly because the notion of national entity—certainly that of the nation as a unit —was scarcely developed anywhere, and was least so, precisely, in that Estate of the Realm that gave natural leaders to secular affairs. In the uncertainty, these took a disastrous step. We must be careful, however, how we blame the men of 1290 in the light of later facts. The situation was much more difficult than it appears to the modern eye. The principles of primogeniture were still not clearly defined, as can be seen in France even a generation later, in the closely parallel situation that followed the death of the infant John I : and in Scotland the situation was further complicated by survivals of the tanist principle, and by the past recognition of the elder Bruce as heir-presumptive in the event of Alexander II's failure of issue. Very clearly, some arbitrator was required, and in the absence of a representative assembly, the most obvious one was a friendly monarch. Now, the Queen Dowager's father, the Comte de Dreux, was a much more powerful person than Philip of France : but he was not technically a sovereign prince, and Philip himself was a lad barely out of his teens. Eirik of Norway, the late King's son-in-law, was an allied sovereign, but he was himself a claimant, and by feudal conceptions, one with a strong case. Edward of England, on the other hand, was brother-in-law of the late King, and himself of royal Macalpin descent through Matilda of Scotland, mother of the Empress Maude, through whom he held his throne. He was head not only of the nearest kingdom, but of one with which Scotland had for a century been on terms of friendship and increasing commercial and social intimacy. He was a man of proved ability and force of character, and in close personal and feudal relation with most of the claimants, nearly all of whom held English lands of him (10). Altogether, he was in the circumstances so obvious a choice that—as Barbour was to point out after the fact—they over-looked his past dealings with Wales and Ireland. Edward also was aware of some elements of the obvious : he saw a chance to make up for his grand-father's loss of the vast French inheritance of the Plan-tagenets, a loss that rankled in England for centuries. Scotland found herself in the case of Belgium in 1914.

Yet, as Cardinal Mercier said of the latter country, " des provinces occupées ne sont pas des provinces conquises." Scotland submitted at first, bewildered from lack of leading by her barons, most of whom, if they owed allegiance to an unidentified King of Scots, owed it also to a very definite Edward for English estates. But perhaps a little curiously—though French history would supply some parallels—that inter-national body, the Catholic Church, has always, in Scotland, been as nationalist as the Episcopalian one was to be later (11). It kept Scots spirit alive in that dreadful decade, till Wallace rose like a banner, and the revolt blazed up—a movement of the Church and of the Commons, for Wallace himself was only a poor knight. Wallace was broken, tortured to death at Smithfield in 1305. Next year, Robert Bruce had cleared the clouds from his mind, and was in the field. There was eighteen years' struggle against all conceivable odds. Scotland emerged from it beggared and bled white, but conscious—intolerantly and sometimes intolerably conscious—of herself as a nation. Her people were no longer subjects, more or less loyal, of the King of Scots. They were *Scotsmen*. Even the Highlands felt themselves to be so, however they might clash with their Lowland neighbours : my own clan country is far enough to the north-west, but our chief, Iain Mòr, my lineal ancestor, led a detachment of his people at Bannockburn, and had followed Bruce's fortunes since 1306. By 1320 the Council spoke with one voice for what had been " the Normans, English, Scots, and Galwegians of the realm," in that famous letter to Pope John XXII, that has some claim to be part of Scots literature :

" (King Robert) like another Joshua or Judas Maccabeus, having endured toils, misfortunes, the extremity of want, and many perils, has rescued his people and inheritance out of the hands of their enemy. . . . In defence of our liberties, by reason of his deserving and of his rights, we are his men, for at his hand salvation was wrought upon us. If he should desert our cause, if he should subject us or the realm to the power of England, we would instantly cast him out as our common enemy, traitor to our rights and to his own, and choose another to rule us. For so long as but a hundred of us stand, we will never bow down to England. We fight not for glory, riches, honours, but for freedom, lacking which no man of virtue may survive."

And that, as our generation puts it, was that.

THE MEDIAEVALS

*Scotland under the Bruces—lost work—the romance—Hucheone—the comic poems
—Barbour—Wyntoun—Blind Harry*

SURVIVING Scots literature, in a language that can
be called English (or Scots, if one prefers, though
Scottis, to a mediaeval Scotsman, meant Gaelic (12))
begins for practical purposes in the fourteenth century. That time was a stony seed-bed, although, God
knows, there was blood enough to enrich it. The
roots of the old culture were starved with war, and
that pious son of the Church, Edward I of England,
had found his piety somewhat overborne by resentment towards the politics of the Scots clergy, with
expensive results to Scottish monasticism, and consequently to Scottish education. King Robert's
death, followed by those of his great generals, Douglas
and the Regent, Randolph of Moray, plunged the
kingdom in another minority, not redeemed by the
rule, grown up, of a worthless fribble. Edward III
considered that a scrap of paper could really not be
allowed to stand in his way, and swept down upon his
brother-in-law's still crippled kingdom. Things were
very bad for a while : the barons who had backed
the wrong horse in the preceding war, and consequently lost their Scots estates, were eager to help
Edward. The seven-year-old King and his Queen,
Edward's young sister, ironically known as Joan
Make-peace, were sent to France for safety, and on his

return David's own folly made him prisoner in England, released at a cost he was far from being worth. And in 1350 the Black Death struck Scotland, carrying off a third of what population was left after sixty years of almost unbroken war on Scottish soil, and dealing the Church, especially, a blow from which, in Scotland, she never recovered.

Mercifully for Scotland, if not for her great ally, Flanders in 1336 quarrelled with France, and had enough economic hold on England to be able to order her into a French invasion, on a dynastic excuse whose cynical thinness is usually masked, in English histories, by the omission of part of the Capet genealogy. Successful at first against the hot-headed Philip VI and that romantic incompetent, John II, Edward found himself faced with a cock of another feather in Charles V, backed by generals like Clisson, Boucicault, and Du Guesclin. England, having let herself in for a disastrous losing war to the south, had no leisure for large-scale aggressions to the northward, and as Norway had long ceased to be a menace, Scotland after about 1360 had more peace than she had known for seventy years.

It is natural that literature should have made some recovery. In fact, by this time, our knowledge becomes more than inferential. We know a good deal about it, and have—some of it. It is still, however, a tolerably difficult subject. Much that we know certainly to have existed has perished, and it is difficult in the first place to know exactly what it was that was triumphantly banished to the grocers' shops in the general wreck of libraries at the Reformation, or perished under the intermittent trampling of armies between 1290 and 1547. For example, we know definitely that one of the popular romances of the late Middle Ages was *Sir Eger, Sir Grime, and Sir Graysteill.* But the oldest extant copy of it is of 1681. A modern book may have more copies than readers, but a mediaeval one, of " pure " literature in the vernacular at least, might be known to many people who had never touched a copy, or even, thanks to the trained memory of the professional reciter, seen one. We are so used to thinking of a book as essentially a bundle of printed paper that we find it difficult to realise the implications of the fact.

Not only are the actual copies few. They vary so with different copyists that there arises another difficulty, immaterial in itself but inconvenient for our present purpose—the difficulty of distinguishing Scots from English, and *vice versa,* a difficulty increased by the fact that until after 1400 there was little difference between the English of Scotland and that of Northern England. Again, it is often difficult to relate book and author. Right up into the sixteenth century we have authors without books and books without authors, and furious scholarly wars of attempted alliance. As Hill Burton put it cheerfully, " there are some topics which the temper and reason of the human race seem not to have made strong enough to encounter," and the attribution of anonymous works of art, and sometimes of signed ones, is certainly one of these.

It is generally agreed, however, that in Scotland as in England and in the France from which, in the long run, the literature of both derives, the principal vernacular forms are the song, the long narrative poem called the romance, and the more or less meditative or didactic poem of some length, which sometimes develops a lyrical quality, or again may have a (generally allegorical) narrative element, while separate from all these is the fabliau or short story, generally either farcical or didactic.

The Scottish song of the true Middle Ages is " sunk without trace," or very nearly. There are scraps of three, two of which may be and one pretty certainly is older than 1300, while the third, surviving in the work of an Englishman of the fifteen-eighties, is on Bannockburn. But the hudibrastic gallop of *Colkelbie's Sow*, in the latter part of the century, gives a riotous list of over fifty songs, whose names or first lines a popular audience was expected to recognise familiarly. Some of them, probably, can well be spared, but others have attractive openings like " Late, late in evening," and " The sun shone in the south." We have not, so far as is known, a line of any of them.

The romance in English uses two kinds of form, the *metrical*, rhythmed on the French base of counted syllables and rhyme, and the *alliterative*, rhythmed on a pattern surviving, or reviving, from " Anglo-Saxon," with counted accents, divided by a heavy caesura, and the stresses marked not by rhyme but by alliteration. The history of this alliterative verse is a queer business. It seems to have revived in Northern Middle English, from which a peculiarly Scots speech is yet scarcely differentiated, about the middle of the fourteenth century, after at least a century and a quarter of apparently complete disuse. Which seems very odd, for your mediaeval poet was not given to deliberate archaising. Had the general *saccagerie* of the south of Scotland anything to do with this puzzling and unreasonable blank ? If not, what carried the tradition, and made it raise its head high enough to last into the sixteenth century, and to produce work like the intricate jewellery of *The Pearl* and *The Twa Maryit Wemen*—the latter a court-poem, the former a piece of intricately, even abstrusely, " literary " work ? It certainly had a strong hold upon Scots poets, for the most characteristic Scots work of the *late* fifteenth century shows a sort of fusion of the two forms, alliterative and metrical, that has no analogue in England, and produces, in such things as Dunbar's *Ballat of Our Lady*, an intricacy of form unparalleled in any other form of English, or in Northern French, and handled, at its best, with an astonishing mastery.

I have already spoken of the enduring popularity of *Sir Eger*. This was shared by others of its class, now lost. *The Complaynt of Scotland*, in 1548, gives a list of forty-seven popular tales, which includes *Sir Eger* itself and several others which are clearly of the romance type. Some are Arthurian, others are classical stories : some of the lost ones sound like folk-tales of the kind that were to survive in the Highland ceilidh, and these may conceivably have been of Gaelic origin. The list (see note 53) includes known French and English work—the first item, in fact, is *The Tailis of Cantirberrye*—but it also includes a good deal of surviving Scots, including two courtly and rather " highbrow " allegories, and of the lost pieces there are several whose titles (sometimes most enticing ones) show them to have been certainly or probably native, like *The tail of Sir Waltir the bauld Leslie* or *Skail Gillanderson the kyngis sone of Skellye*. The dozen classical ones also were probably known in Scottish recensions mediaevalised into romances, in the manner of the extant *King Orfeo*.

We have enough information about the romance in Scotland to generalise, and speculate, so far. But in dealing with individual specimens of the actual romance, we find ourselves on less certain ground. For example, we know that there was a Scots *King Orfeo*. And there is a *King Orfeo*, a graceful fairy-tale version of the legend, with a happy ending, less like a classical legend than like *Tam Lin* with the parts of the hero and heroine reversed. But its language is too southern to be a Scotsman's, and it is in octosyllabic couplet. It is difficult to be sure exactly how far these points are evidence. Barbour, not long after the middle of the century, and a most indubitable Scot, was writing fluent octosyllabic couplet, and the southern forms may be the copyist's. It is impossible to pronounce either way.

The earliest named Scots writer of romances belongs to the thirteenth century, before the time of the lament for Alexander III, since he saw that king's last years at any rate. He lives in tradition as Thomas the Rhymer, Thomas Lermont (13), Thomas of Ercildoune, who kissed the Queen of Elfan and took the consequences ; and (whether by virtue of that affair or not) it is he and not Barbour, whom he antedates by about a century, who can claim to be the Father of Scots Poets. But we know little about him. We know that he existed, and (roughly) when, and that he wrote a *Tristram*, and so took his part in the great international fabric of the Arthurian Legend : Gottfried of Strasburg quotes him, within his own century, as the supreme authority for his *Tristran und Isolde*. Whether his inspiration was the other, Norman, Thomas, or Béroul, Chrétien de Troyes, or Marie de France, we do not know. But he was an ancestor,

27

apparently, of an even more magical namesake, Thomas Malory, for one of Malory's *Frensshe bokes* is not French at all, but an English *Tristram*, one of the earliest of the English romances : it is pretty certainly before 1300. And this *Tristram* is avowedly derived from Thomas of Ercildoune, of whom it speaks as of a famous authority on the story. Indeed, the Englishman Robert Mannyng of Brunne says of Thomas's *Tristram* in 1338, at a time when Scots were not popular in England,

> Over Gestes it has the steme [esteem.
> Over al that is or was.

There are some extant alliterative romances on Arthurian themes which are certainly or probably Scots. One is a *Golagros and Gawaine* of the late fourteenth century, by a named author, one Clerk of Tranent. A *Mort Arthure*, of considerable merit, is sometimes attributed to Hucheone, but is unlikely to be either his or Scottish. There is also a sort of short story, *The Awntyrs of Arthur at the Tarne Watheling*. It also is rather uncertainly Scottish, though more likely to be so than the *Mort Arthure*. The setting is Cumberland, but that does not prove anything much as to provenance, since several indubitably French romances have Scottish settings : its climax, the appearance of the very gruesome ghost of Queen Guenevere's mother, is of a type, grotesque yet genuinely eerie, that suggests Scots work rather than English, and the language is undoubtedly Northern. This also has been assigned to Hucheone, but the attribution, though not certainly wrong, is at least doubtful.

I have already referred to *Sir Eger, Sir Grime, and Sir Graysteill* as surviving in a copy made three hundred years after it had been fashionable contemporary literature. Indeed, it was actually reprinted later, in a chapbook version of 1711. It is metrical, not alliterative, and a lively affair. Our text, which belongs to a time when it was offered for popular consumption much as the once-esteemed *East Lynne* can still be bought nowadays in small country stationers', is vulgarised and clumsy in places, but the chivalrous spirit of the mediaeval original comes through. There is some excellent fighting, described by a man who knew something about it, and a practical and lively heroine. The personages, in fact, are not dummies, and the main interest, significantly, is as much in their relation as in the adventures.

These are all typical of their time, and they are work, in their kind, of considerable merit. The principal surviving work of the fourteenth century, however, that may have been or certainly is Scots, is on the one hand the long narrative, not romance but serious and scholarly biography, *The Brus*, by a definite personage, John Barbour, Archdeacon of Aberdeen, and on the other a group of poems, assigned to a rather shadowy author, Hucheone of the Awle Ryale (Aula Regalis), who is identified, plausibly enough, with a Sir Hugh of Eglinton, known to have died in 1381, in the reign of Robert II, and therefore Barbour's (possibly elder) contemporary.

There has been much critical war over Hucheone. But at all events, there is as much evidence for his existence as there is for that of most mediaeval authors. By the same evidence, he wrote *The Pistyle of Swete Susane*, and handled certain other subjects. Now the *Pistyle* (epistle) shows much individuality : and another poem on a subject that Hucheone is known to have treated shows what looks like common authorship. Thus when other work, with the same strong individuality, resembles that of the author of these pieces, it may not unreasonably be assigned to him. If Hucheone wrote *Gawaine and the Green Knight* and *The Pearl*—and the weight of evidence is that he did—he was the greatest Scots poet before Dunbar, and though not such a master of technique was no mean artist, and capable of a power of poetic emotion of which Dunbar was not (14). It is also, not probable, but quite certain (though I have never seen the fact remarked) that whoever wrote *The Pearl* was, far more than Chaucer, the forerunner of the fifteenth century Scots poets commonly but for the most part absurdly known as the Scots Chaucerians. Dunbar and the author of *The Pearl* are as unlike, temperamentally, as Dryden and Thomas Traherne : but their *literary* methods, and tastes, are closely alike, and do not at all resemble those of Chaucer except in one or two points that they and Chaucer share with their age at large. *The Pearl* anticipates the " aureate " poetic diction of fifteenth century " literary " Scots poetry, with its strong infusion of French and Scandinavian—the latter not very likely in English work. Like the Makaris, again, it has a very characteristic union of frank homely realism with delight in splendour, in gorgeousness of decoration, and an eye to the fiercer aspects of nature and to their decorative quality which is not found in work known to be English between the Conquest and Spenser, nor indeed, in the same temper, between the Conquest and Wordsworth. The extraordinary intricacy of form in *The Pearl* has no parallel in known English work until Swinburne, but plenty in Dunbar, and finally, though the argument is one that never convinces anyone but the arguer, I recognise in it that indefinable but perceptible quality, the mentality of a countryman, as I do in *The Testament of Cresseid* and not in *Troylus and Creseyde* (15).

Of the poems attributed to Hucheone, two are narrative, and to these are sometimes added the *Mort Arthure* I have mentioned—pretty certainly not his, though we know he did write a *Gest of Arthur*—and *The Awntyrs of Arthur at the Tarne Watheling*, which might be his, though doubtfully. Of the others, *The Pistyle of Swete Susane*, which is assigned to Hucheone by his younger contemporary Wyntoun, is a sort of short story, a graceful version, in elaborate stanza that blends rhyme and regular metre with alliteration and the changing rhythm associated with it, of the earliest of detective-stories, the tale of Susanna and the Elders, from the Apocryphal continuation of the Book of Daniel. It is a charming thing, with a genuine and touching emotion, and a garden-background like the flowered borders of a mediaeval book. *Gawayn and the Green Knight* is a longer Arthurian story, not known elsewhere : it may be the *Awntyre of Gawane* Wyntoun refers to, the more as it tells of a single episode in that many-adventured gentleman's career. Using alliterative verse, not rhymed but in *laisses* or groups divided by the *bob* of rhymed short lines that ends each stanza of the rhymed *Susane*, it takes an old folk-tale theme as a start, and goes on to make out of it a story whose interest is practically that of a novel, in the interaction of character and event. It is one of the best of the Arthurian poems, with a lively humanity, shrewd and yet that of a man to whom the chivalric spirit is a real thing—a man who enjoys a hunt both as a sportsman and as an artist with an eye for the decorative, who knows the life of palaces that he is describing, and who under his appreciation of its colour has an interest in the principles of conduct. His whole outlook, in fact, is not unlike that of Scott. He is scholar by taste, though probably not a professional, gentleman by instinct and breeding, and man of the world by habit.

The same temper shows in the three non-narrative poems assigned to him. Two of these, *Patience* and *Cleanness*, in unrhymed alliterative verse, are moral discourses. They show, on subjects sufficiently testing, the work of a man well-bred by both nature and nurture, his outlook generous and lofty, but his feet on the ground of actuality. Both reveal a sweet, sane, and noble mind, free from the common tendency of mediaeval ethics (in their artistic presentment at all events) to exalt one virtue separately from and at the expense of the rest, as in the notorious example of Griselda. *Cleanness*, which is a discourse on chastity, has a noble passage on honourable love between man and woman.

The third of these, a very lovely thing, is *The Pearl*, which is semi-lyrical narrative—not romance, but an allegorical vision-poem of a type popular from the thirteenth century onward until well into the Renaissance. It is a great poem, and a deep one—deeper, intellectually and emotionally, than anything in Chaucer. It has less than the perfect finish of Chaucer's best work, partly, perhaps, because the greater passion and more intellectual texture have in places been too much for the extreme intricacy of the form. It gives a side of the Middle Ages that in Chaucer is almost entirely absent, harking back in spirit to the great age of the twelfth and thirteenth centuries, that culminated in Dante : indeed it is not at all improbable that the latter cantos of the *Purgatorio* did not merely suggest its imagery but were part of the catena of emotional experience that eventually crystallised in its creation. Hunters of *quellen*, not being as a rule men and women of profound human experience (16), are apt to forget that an experience of art is an experience like another, and may affect a man's subsequent creative work in more ways than merely as something from which to copy.

That *The Pearl* is far less well known than Chaucer is unfortunate, but inevitable, for even to someone who reads Chaucer or Barbour currently, it is difficult going. It is in the gorgeous " aureate," or rather enamelled, diction that was to grow into the language of Dunbar, inlaid with French and Scandinavian words like foreign jewels, in an intricate pattern of form that almost enforces an enormous vocabulary. Its 101 stanzas combine metre and alliteration in the manner of *Susane* or of Dunbar's *Ballat of Our Lady*, but more elaborately : a four-accent metre, not, as is usual, strictly iambic, but with a *ripple* in it deriving from the freer alliterative rhythms, has its structure marked by a sort of descant of very rich but irregular alliteration, and by a strict stanza-form of rhymes arranged *abababbcbc*. These stanzas are linked in groups of five whose *c*-rhyme is constant and whose last line is repeated, with variations, so as to make a refrain, with always the same concluding word, which recurs in the first line of the next verse, but not as its rhyme : and these groups are themselves linked by the use of the refrain-word of each to open the group that follows, while the whole is rounded by giving the last group, for refrain, an echo of the opening line

c

of the poem. It sounds desperately artificial, but in fact there is so much spirit and sincerity, so living a movement in its union of supple rhythm with strongly marked structural outline, that it does not strike one so at all. The pattern of imagery to which this intricate music provides an accompaniment is (like so many Scots poems in the next two centuries) in the line of descent from the allegorical dream-pageantry of the thirteenth century *Roman de la Rose*, that is one of the nodal points of mediaeval literature, and parent of a tradition that was to last into the eighteenth century and include *The Divine Comedy*, *The Faerie Queene*, *The Pilgrim's Progress*, and *The Dunciad*. It has been suggested that the poem derives from *The Boke of the Duchesse*. There is nothing in the dates to forbid it, but apart from the fact that both poems are memorials of a dead lady, one might almost as well say that *The Brus* derives from the *Duchesse* because it uses the same form of verse. After all, Blanche of Lancaster is not the only dead lady in mediaeval letters ! And the whole mental and emotional attitude of *The Pearl* is nearer that of the close of *Il Purgatorio*, where Beatrice in the mantle the colour of flame comes through the strange garden of the Earthly Paradise, to be her lover's guide to the vision of Heaven. I have no doubt that the author of *Gawayn and the Green Knight* would have liked *The Boke of the Duchesse*, and it is quite possible that he had read it : if he did, however, it does not show in *The Pearl*. But it is more than likely that he had read *Il Purgatorio*, and found healing in it. The lost lady here is his daughter and not his love, but her function is the same, and his spiritual process is that of Dante : grief at her loss drives him to accidie, the paralysis of the soul, and

34

then vision of her fulfilled, in more glorious life, leads to the vision of *L'Amore che muove il sole e l'altre stelle.*

The poet mourns his Pearl (probably enough *Margarita*) lost in a garden—

> O mool, thou marrest a merry jewel,
> My privy pearl withouten spot.

He sits, mourning, in an *erbere*, at the time of Our Lady's Assumption into Heaven, and, although " my wretched will in woe aye wraught," he falls asleep among its scents, and his spirit " springs in space."

> My goste is gon in Godeʒ grace,
> In auenture þer meruayleʒ meven.

He comes between crystal cliffs to a strange forest, whose leaves are silver and boles like the precious blue from the East. The little stones of the earth are orient pearl, and birds the colour of flame make unearthly music. Then in the midst of it, the sound and jewelled colour of a swift river :

> Swangende swete þe water con swepe   [rushing.
> Wyþ a rownande rourde raykande aryʒt :   [murmuring : running.
> In the founce þer stonden stoneʒ stepe,   [bed : glittering.
> As glente þurʒ glas þat glowed and glyʒt,   [gleam : shimmer.
> As stremande sterres, quen stroþe men slepe   [safe.
> Staren in welkyn in wynter niʒte,
> For vche a pobbel in pole þer pyʒt   [placed.
> Watʒ emered, saffer, or gemme gente,   [noble.
> þat all þe loʒe lemed of lyʒt,   [water.
> So dere watʒ hit adubbement.   [adornment.

(þ=th. ʒ=(in Northern) the modern *ch* of Scots. ʒ at the end of a word=z, initially=*y*. *u* initially or between consonants=*v*.)

The next division is full of this water-music. He longs to cross, for " Lovelier is the farther land." Then, as he seeks a ford, under the crystal cliffs on the

far bank is a maiden in gleaming white, and the
stabbing line, in the strangeness, " I knew her well,
I had seen her ere." He is filled with a " gladdande
glory " that has long been lost to him, and yet it is
troubled because " I saw her in so strange a place."
Silent, he gazes : the vision of the lost Pearl is in
terms of pearls—" precios perle " is the overword of
its canto, whose climax is the great flawless pearl on
her breast. He finds words at last, and cries to her,
and she lifts her grey eyes to him under her crown of
pearls, and rebukes him gravely as Beatrice does her
lover when " Gli occhi mi cadder giù nel chiaro fonte,"
and he waits for the ice at his heart to be breath and
water of tears. She is stern at first, with the *pietate
acerba* of Beatrice, for his grief is sin, because it is
selfish and lacks faith. Before he can cross the water
he must win to other counsel. He begs mercy humbly,
of God and of her who has been his bliss and his bale.
She is tender then : he who loves her shall learn her
joy. She is Bride of the Lamb, in the train of the
Queen of Courtesy—that lovely epithet of Our Lady
is another refrain. He cannot believe in such fortune,
but she counters with the parable of the Vineyard,
and through her expounding of it he comes to vision :
the refrains sway on through " þe innocent is ay saf
by ryȝt," and " perleȝ maskelleȝ " (17) to " Jerusalem," the City of the Passion and of the Triumph of
the Lamb, and so to the glory of Apocalypse. From
the jewelled walls the gates of great pearl lead him on
to the light—the overword is " moon " here—and
then suddenly out of it,

> Ryȝt as þe maynful mone con rys
> Er þenne þe day-glem dryue al doun,

he sees the gleaming procession of the Virgins, all in

the pearled livery of his own Margarite, and bearing each on her breast " the blissful pearl with great delight." They pass on led by the Lamb, glorious with His wounds, and now he sees among them " my little queen "—the tender intimate word, among all that splendour—and at sight of her forgets all else and plunges in the dividing stream. But " it was not my Prince's will." He wakens, to find himself in the green arbour (18) where he had slept, with his head on her grave-mound, and grief floods him again, the grief of a man who has dreamed of the lost, and now must waken. But the vision, though nothing can change his grief itself, has changed him towards it. He will not strive and cry now for more than is given, and because he is willing to be poor, behold he is rich, in Christ's dear blessing that (no longer in the Pearl but in the white disc of the Host) he can see every day in the priest's hands.

I have described *The Pearl* at length, not only because of its intrinsic beauty and the fact that it is one of the noblest examples of a favourite and characteristic mediaeval literary form, but because its author's work is technically, so far as we know (19), the earliest example of the type of verse and of poetic diction associated with Scots literary poetry in the next century, though for English descendants he had to wait until Swinburne. And although anyone who has tolerable acquaintance with modern Scots and the English of the Authorised Version of the Scriptures will find little difficulty, once he gets his eye in, with the contemporary work of Chaucer and Barbour, the diction of *The Pearl* is rather formidable. I still remember the emotions it roused in a Senior Honours English Language Class, on their first encounter with it.

The Pearl has taken us over one border of the romance, for its narrative element is of the slightest, and deliberately put aside, one might say, by the convention of the dream, until the tone is nearer both lyric and the germ of poetic drama. But there are other directions in which the romance shades into other forms. One, at the opposite extreme, is parody, where the subjects of romance and the methods of the romancers are seen with an eye set for the humorous " realism " of the fabliau. There is little extant trace of actual Scottish romance-parody corresponding to Chaucer's *Sir Thopas*, but we do find examples where as in the French *Roman de Renart* the formulae of the romance are used for comic ends, as in *Colkelbie's Sow*, or where the romance turns into broadly comic adventure, as in *Rauf Coilȝear*. (Ralph the Collier.) *Rauf* is a late offshoot from the Matter of France, the Charlemagne cycle of the Gestes, with the Emperor as a sort of Goodman of Ballangeich, on the text that *charbonnier est maître chez soi*. It uses the alliterative metrical form, like *Susane*. *Colkelbie's Sow* is further from the romance, but its comic point can only be taken by an audience familiar with the romance-convention. It begins with pure parody in the vein of *Sir Thopas*, a take-off of the third-rate professional, in a pompous prologue to the nobility and gentry, with a promise of *some solasing* and orthodox rhetoric about " amusement combined with instruction." Then it drops solemnity and plunges with a wink and a grin out of its broken-winded riding-rhyme —the state verse, for it is after 1400—into a dancing breathless three-accented couplet. The Sow is sold for three pennies, and the three divisions tell what happened to each. The second and third return to a (deliberately ?) broken riding-rhyme, and one is a sentimental novelette, highly moral (if one seems to see the writer's tongue in his cheek), while the third deals heroickally with high descent in the hen-run. The first part is the main one, however, and the best. The first penny buys a little pig, who is stolen by a local lady of light virtue. She gives a party on the strength of it, and the list of guests is a headlong hudibrastic like a dance of the stone grotesques from a cathedral. The pig objects vociferously to being killed, and the local pigs organise a rescue party : there is another catalogue, disclaiming, with a wink, all the orthodox display of learning from the *Bestiaries* that an audience might be expected to look for as surely as an audience of a 1920 novel would look for some of the theories of Herr Freud, or of an 1870 one for something or other about heredity. Their owners come in chase, with much mock-heroic patter, but all ends happily in dancing and deray, with the famous and tantalising catalogue of lost songs. It is worth remarking that the poem survives only in a single copy made at least a century and a half after it was written, by the invaluable Bannatyne. *Rauf Coilʒear* survives in a single printed copy of 1572. And yet the number of allusions to them in the fifteenth century show both to have been very popular. In fact, they have a good deal of the headlong and reckless humour that is one of the permanent notes of Scots letters and assuredly of Scots music : the essence of it is in the wicked tune of *The Soutar of Fife*. It is something quite different from its English equivalent. The Englishman is swept off his feet by the grotesque : the Scot smacks his bonnet on his head and plunges overboard. The distinction, in self-abandonment, is not confined to the emotion of mirth.

Nor are the modifications of the romance. In another direction, it shades into the history proper, from which in fact the original French form of it derives. Scottish examples of the fourteenth century include a *Troybook* and a very large collection of *Lives of the Saints*, both sometimes attributed to Barbour, who may quite possibly have written some parts of the latter. Barbour, or a pupil of his, may also be responsible for *The Buik of the most Noble and Vallȝeand Conquerour Alexander the Gret*, an anonymous version of three French romances from the *Cycle de l'antiquité*, based on the pesudo-Callisthenes. It has a strong likeness, in spirit, diction, and handling, to *The Brus*. Its single manuscript is of 1438, nearly half a century after Barbour's death : but the senior of the two MSS. of *The Brus* is half a century later again than that. The great mediaeval vernacular example of the history-romance in Scotland, however, and one of the best anywhere, is that same *Brus*, which is one of the type that come closest to history proper. Indeed, it comes so close to that, in both method and purpose, that it is rather misleading to class it with romance at all. At first glance, perhaps, its superficial appearance inclines one to do so, especially if one is that type of scholar that German influence, before the War, made a pest in England and America and even, though fortunately to a lesser extent, in Scotland : and it is sadly too obvious that most of the gentlemen who have written on Barbour have never got very far beyond the first glance. Yet although *The Brus* is narrative, and excitingly adventurous narrative, and uses the eight-syllable couplet—a regular mediaeval metre-of-all-work in France, Scotland, and England alike—it is no more " romantic " in the modern colloquial sense than Duruy, Macaulay, or J. R. Green, and certainly no less accurate than the two latter, though that, perhaps, is not an extensive claim.

It is serious history, by a scholar. Verse seems, to the modern reader, incongruous with that, but its own age would not have thought so. It was not until fairly late that prose was considered a suitable medium for serious literary work, and for history the two appear to have been regarded, for some time, as interchangeable. Villehardouin, in the thirteenth century, uses prose, but Barbour's own contemporary, Froissart, began his *Chronique* in verse, although he refashioned it later in the more elastic form. When Barbour calls his book romance, he does not intend to imply that it is fictitious, but that it is primarily a narrative about a hero. He is writing a *Life and Times*, a *Faictes et Gestes*, and he is in method and temper an historian—not a " scientific " one, of course, but after all the scientific historian is a liar by nature from his professional birth, while the literary historian, so long as he does not set out to be literary, is a liar merely by accident or on purpose. Barbour, indeed, as historians go, is honest. He omits Bruce's discreditable waverings as a young man, his failure to back Wallace : but this, after all, is less unscrupulous than it can be made to sound, for it is his purpose, not to write a complete life of Robert de Brus, but to give an account of the glorious reign of Robert I, with only so much of antecedent event as may be necessary for comprehension. He also, for instance, omits Wallace's rising, and assuredly not from any lack of sympathy : it is not relevant to what he is doing. In what he does do, he is obviously trying to get at the facts. When his sources provide different versions of the same incident, he says so, and gives them, and in spite of his strong and sincere national feeling, he is never an ungenerous enemy, and has none of the jingoism Dr Gregory Smith appears to wish to impute when he goes out of his way to scoff a little ponderously at the fact that in *The Brus* the Scots are invariably victorious against odds. The jeer, in fact, does tell, but not against Barbour, for in the first place, the Scots in *The Brus* are *not* invariably victorious : and if they generally are, it is simple historic fact that under Bruce's leading they generally were, and against considerable odds of men and material : had they not been so, Scotland would have ceased to exist, and neither Bruces nor Stewarts, nor presumably His present Majesty (whom God preserve) would ever have sat on a throne. It is very sad for the professorial mind, but events have a disconcerting trick at times of resembling the kinds of fiction that aren't in fashion. No fashion, indeed, is quite so fluctuating as that in what is considered possible.

What we know of Barbour, outside his poem, is little, but we have the main outline of his life. He was born about 1320, studied at Oxford and in France, became archdeacon of Aberdeen, and wrote rather copiously, all his work being history. We know that *The Brus* was finished in 1375, under the first Stewart king, and that Barbour himself died in 1395, in the reign of the unhappy Robert III. A *Brut* of his, presumably the early history of these islands, and what is more regrettable, a *Stewartis Oryginalle*, presumably the early history of the house that in Barbour's middle age succeeded the Bruces, have been lost : the *Brus*, which appears to have been as popular as its subject, and merits, would lead one to expect, exists in two MSS. of the next century, one incomplete, and was reprinted again and again as a popular chapbook into the eighteenth century. Modern Scottish schools ignore it, by the way, confining their reading of mediaeval literature to Chaucer, though Barbour's language is easier even to a pupil who does not speak Scots, since his accidence is closer to modern English, and the final -*e*, being already silent, does not complicate the metre for a beginner.

The Brus is not, as sometimes seems to be thought even by men who should know better, " folk-poetry " as the ballads are, nor yet is it " literary " in the sense in which *The Pearl* is " literary." Its very precise modern equivalent would be, say, the *Montrose* of Mr Buchan—work that the scholar can read with pleasure and profit, but with nothing difficult for the intelligent unlearned. Barbour in fact makes it clear from the beginning that he is not addressing himself to the *conoscenti*, to the limited, trained, public of Dunbar's court-poems, or of *The King's Quhair*. He sets his note at once, with the opening lines :

> Storys to rede ar delitabill,
> Suppos þat þai be nocht bot fabill :
> þan suld storys þat supfast wer,
> *And þai war said on gud maner,*
> Have doubill plesance in heryng.

One observes that he grasps the importance, to an historian, of a competent narrative style : not all his modern successors are as wise. He keeps his promise, for he can tell a story, with admirable force and liveliness, and modern research has shown that he took

43

pains over his facts. Indeed, he had excellent opportunities : he was born in his hero's lifetime, and saw the whole reigns of Bruce's son and of the son of that Walter Stewart who had so distinguished himself at Bannockburn. Just as the young Scott knew men who in their youth had fought at Culloden (20), so the young Barbour would know men who had been all through Bruce's campaigns : in one place indeed he says expressly that he had his tale from Sir Alan Cathcart, who was there and saw cheerful reckless Edward Bruce charge Amery St John's men out of the fog. Some other passages too have the mark of the eye-witness—the knights on the crossing to Rachrin blistering their hands on the unaccustomed oars, or Douglas's men fighting in silence at Bannockburn, or Randolph's, disappearing from sight among the main body of the English, " as þai war plungit in þe se," and the cloud of dust and of the steam of sweat rising above the skirmish at St Ninian's, when Randolph's schiltroms threw back the pick of the enemy's heavy cavalry on that burning Midsummer Eve, before the great battle.

He had more than memory to depend on, however. Froissart's Flemish predecessor, Jehan le Bel of Liége, remarks in his chronicle that Robert I had caused histories to be made. These are lost, like so much else, but they would hardly be lost in one generation. And he obviously knew Gray's *Scalacronica*, written in Norman-French just after 1355 by an English knight, prisoner in Edinburgh Castle, who says he had access to Scots, French, and Latin histories in the Castle library. Gray was the son of one of the most distinguished men on the English side of Bruce's War, who had seen Bannockburn as Randolph's prisoner.

Barbour, who by this time was in the middle thirties, may have known him personally, and would certainly have had access to the same sources, both men and books. He can further be tested by various official records, Scots, English, and French, and by contemporary historians : and they show him to have been careful. He may sometimes transpose the order of events : the siege of Perth, for instance, comes out of its place, an easy mistake to make in the long series of captures of *lieux-forts* between 1307 and 1313. It appears also that he is certainly wrong in blaming Comyn for the betrayal to Edward of Bruce's intentions. But the most famous of Barbour's mistakes, one that is pounced on joyously by nearly every historian of letters who writes of him, is one that, as it happens, he never made. The legend of it—it is one of the things every pass-man knows about Barbour—throws an interesting if disconcerting sidelight on the way in which histories of literature are written. There were, as everyone knows, three Robert Bruces—(21) the original claimant of 1290, grand-nephew of William I and once heir-presumptive to that monarch's son ; his son, Earl of Carrick by marriage ; and *his* son, the King : and (alas for my trade !) it is regularly stated that Barbour takes them all for the same man, or at any rate confounds the King and his grandfather, as if a modern historian should remark light-heartedly that Edward I and VII had been Duke of Kent, married a widowed Princess of Leiningen, and had one daughter, Queen Victoria.

In cold fact, Barbour does nothing so surprising : some worthy gentleman, unfamiliar with Middle Scots, mistook a passage rather compressed to be lucid, and the historians who came after him . . . it

ought not to happen, of course, but it does, and as our
neighbours across the Atlantic say, then some. What
one actually finds, when one looks at the text, is that
Barbour begins by saying he is going to tell the story
of the King. Then, since he is writing in the thirteen-
seventies, he has to devote a preliminary book to a
sketch of the factors which produced the condition of
affairs when Bruce assumed the crown in 1306, and
of his claim to it, before he can settle down to his
main job of telling about " This lord the Brus I spak
of ar " (*ar*=before) as the hero of the coming story.
Now, it does happen that when he reaches the King,
and uses that phrase to indicate the fact, the last
Bruce he had mentioned was the Claimant. But his
last reference to him was in l. 153, and anyone reading the narrative currently and coming in l. 477 on
" this lord I spak of ar," takes the *ar* to refer back to
l. 25, which announces the subject of the book to be
King Robert. The astonishing confusion is a mere
mare's nest, built by gentlemen so learned that they
can only read one word at a time, with pauses between to write elaborate notes—scarcely, perhaps, the
public at which Barbour was aiming. It is just possible, however, that Barbour may really have confused
the two elder Bruces : he does certainly call the
Claimant Earl of Carrick. But it is at least as possible
that he did nothing of the sort, but merely assumed
that a man who died sixteen years before he himself
was born had inherited his earldom, as the King had
done, instead of marrying it—or according to tradition, being married by its heiress, a spirited young
Galwegian who knew what she wanted.

Barbour gets over his preliminaries as briefly as
possible, and comes to the character of Edward

Plantagenet, as revealed in his previous dealings with Wales and Ireland, and then to the ugly business of the English Occupation. His indignation warms him to one of his few but effective moments of rhetoric, and the climax of the preliminary book is, not irrelevantly, the famous little excursus upon freedom and " foul þryldome."

> A noble hart may haiff nane es,
> Na ellys nocht þat may him ples,
> ȝyff fredome failȝhe. . . .
> Na he, þat ay has levyt fre,
> May nacht knaw weill þe propyrte,
> þe angyr, na þe wrechyt dome
> þat is cowplyt to foule þyrldome,
> Bot ȝyff he had assayit it :
> þan all perquer he suld it wyt,   [par coeur.
> And suld þink fredome mar to prys
> þan all þe gold in warld þat is.

Remembering that the lines were written soon after the wretched reign of David II, saved, very barely, by the younger Randolph, by his sister Agnes of March, and Christina Bruce—written soon after the crowning of Walter Stewart's son and the great Bruce's grandson, " worþi, wise, and leil," but too old to cope with danger, one can see a warning, and perhaps as well one inspiration of that stirring resistance of the thirteeneighties, whose gallantry culminated in Otterburn.

His theme stated, Barbour gets down to it, with the young Douglas as a penniless student in Paris, and Bruce's first riding north, a desperate outlaw, and so through his reign to his death as a strong king and the gallant epilogue of the Heart and the death of his friend and general, Douglas. He takes room to move now, to go into the detail of those wild adventures, that sound so improbable to the little literato—still more to the literata—of Bloomsbury or Morningside, and so much less so to anyone who served on one of the eastern fronts of the War, or even to anyone who knows Scots country and some actual (not scientific) history.

He tells them well, too. It is customary to remark, with an air of superiority, that Barbour was no poet. Neither was Boswell. Is there any reason why either of them should be ? Barbour, of course, wrote in verse. But he was a man of the fourteenth century. He wrote verse for the reason that made the nineteenth century historian write Gibbonese, or the twentieth century simper à la Strachey : it was a suitable and becoming thing to do. It probably would not have occurred to him that the use of verse obliged him to be poetic : he was accustomed to verse treatises on medicine or astrology. In fact, he does not try to write poetry : what he did set out to do was more like philosophy—to give a narrative of adventure and the portraits of certain men, with a unifying idea behind the portrayal. He had seen the whole unhappy reign of David II, the disasters of the King's captivity, of Dupplin, Halidon Hill, and Neville's Cross, and the coming of Robert Stewart, gentle, kind, dignified, too old to grip. He knew the miracle of Bannockburn was not an end, but a beginning, and desired the inheritors of that beginning to be worthy, and not falter, whatever might appear to be the odds,

> For gude begynning and hardy,
> And it be followit wittely, [intelligently.
> May gar oftsis unlikly þyng
> Cum to full conabill endyng. [satisfactory, *convenable.*

He is seldom sententious, but when he is he talks sense, and courageous sense, and means it.

He does more, in his narrative, than mean. He achieves, and considerably, with no sort of condescending handicap-allowance for a well-intentioned primitive. His pure narrative, as undecorated narration of events, description of actual persons, has never had its due. It is different in kind from Chaucer's—Chaucer was writing fiction, to begin with : but in its own fashion it is not behind him. It is straightforward stuff, that moves—moves in both senses, for Barbour has a sound liking for the manly virtues. His great episodes, after the full and admirable description of Bannockburn, are Douglas's last battle and young Walter Stewart's gallant defence of Berwick : and it was no clumsy writer who could make us, in so few words, see that siege in detail, from Sir Walter's defence of the burning Maryport to the women gathering the spent English arrows and running with them to their men on the low walls.

Yet, though he loves gallant action as Scott loved it, the action is no more his primary interest than it was Scott's. *Arma virosque canit* : and the emphasis is on the second noun. He is not the type of historian who believes that battles are fought or countries freed by Influences in a vacuum. His subject is not *dedys*, but

> þe dedys
> Of stalwart folk þat lyvyt ar . . .
> And led þar lyff in gret travaill,
> And oft, in hard stour of bataill,
> Wan richt gret price of cheualry.

His portraits, little set-pieces in the manner of Dutch painting, are excellent : that of Douglas makes you

see the man, his tall figure, sallow face, and gentle
manner, his slight lisp, and the force and intelligence
and steely courage that underlay them. His slighter
sketches can hit off a personality in a few lines, as in
that of the old lady to whose house Bruce comes when
he is a hard-pressed fugitive in 1306. He tells her he
is a traveller, and is answered :

> " All þat travelland ere
>   For saik of ane, ar welcum here."
> þe Kyng said, " Gud dame, quhat is he
> þat garris 30w have sic specialte
> Till men þat travalis ? "   " Schir, perfay,"
> Quod þe gud wif, " I sall 30w say.
> Gud Kyng Robert þe Brus is he
> þat is rycht lord of þis cuntre."

The gallant old lady, and her sturdy offer of her two
sons when she learns who he is (she does not take time
to be sentimental) is a type that has been a considerable factor in our history.

The central figure, throughout, is the King. It is
the King as king and not as man he is drawing, but
with that limitation (which, in its place here, is an
artist's) he does him admirably. Bruce is not simply
a hard hitter on the watch for sporting exploits :
Edward Bruce, in fact, who *was* very much that, is
used as something of a foil to him. Barbour appre-
ciates the King's qualities as a general, his eye for
country, his strategic skill, his uncanny resourcefulness
at a pinch : but what interests him most is Bruce's
extraordinary gift of leadership, the rare quality
that wrought the miracles of Montrose, or, in larger-
scale action, of Caesar or Napoleon, all leaders who
could make the common man attempt, and achieve,
the plainly impossible. *The Brus*, indeed, is very

largely a study of leadership : Barbour fully under-
stands the part played by sheer personality, and in fact
discusses it in one of his few digressions out of narrative;
and he contrives to give us, not Bruce's meditations
before Bannockburn or after Greyfriars Kirk, as the
fashionable modern would find incumbent, but the
Bruce his men saw, telling tales at the crossing of Loch
Lomond, showing royal courtesy to the French knights
taken at Biland, or to the poor laundress at Limerick,
wading up to his neck in the dark moat at Perth,
wheeling his pony for the perfectly-timed axe-cut that
slew the mailed De Bohun on his heavy destrier,
or, the controlled fire showing, knocking down Colin
Campbell for charging too soon against his explicit
orders. Barbour's real theme, in fact, the whole
point of *The Brus*, is very much the question of morale.
It was that, above all, under the mercy of God, that
won those impossible wars, and set us free. Bruce, all
through his career, had to face an enemy with greater
resources, almost invariably in greater numbers, certainly with enormously greater reserves to make good
losses of personnel : and though strategy had much
to do with those amazing victories, it was less strategy,
in the long run, that brought them to pass, than his
power of keeping up the morale of his own troops and
playing the devil with that of the enemy's. One can
see the same qualities in his great lieutenant Douglas,
whose name in England was a kind of bogey.

It is this sense of what won Salamis and the Marne,
held Thermopylae and Verdun against crazy odds,
that makes Barbour's work so little obsolete. The
priest of the fourteenth century is worth reading, for
professional reasons alone, by any young subaltern of
the present day. The depth, too, of Barbour's under-

standing is revealed in his feeling for the other side of leadership, the " leadable " quality in the men of the command. He has nothing of that lofty contempt for the *roturier* that shows in Froissart, whom he quite possibly met about the Scots court in 1365. That worthy bourgeois of Flanders was also a priest who liked tall men of their hands, but charming person as he is, he is the snob that Barbour never was, and especially, (and un-Flemishly, after Courtrai) with regard to courage. Barbour, being a man of sense, knows that the common soldier does as a rule need leading, but he gives him full credit for his response to it when he gets it : and when he can lead himself, like Binnock at Linlithgow, or Sym of the Ledhouse who shares the credit of Roxburgh with the great Douglas, he has " his place in the story," without condescension.

That sense of the deep human dignities pervades *The Brus*. It is a rough world Barbour draws, but not a world of brutes. These hard-bitten soldiers are in fact as much more civilised than Smollett's fighting-men of the seventeen-fifties, as Barbour's language is cleaner : and there is hardly a coarse phrase in the whole of *The Brus* : the few that there are are straightforward (and completely relevant) references to plain natural facts. The fundamental tests of a civilisation are, first, its attitude towards the Ultimate Powers, however it conceives them, and secondly, the attitude of its men and women towards each other. Barbour's God is a God of Battles, undoubtedly, a God who bids men sell their cloaks to buy swords : but the Deity to whom his knights give thanks after action is not the Neronian tribal demon of Calvin, and their attitude towards him is that of gentlemen to a Gentleman. The eighteenth century attitude to women is (outside avowedly "sentimental" fiction)

a good deal less " civilised " than that revealed in the
King's care for the poor laundress or Douglas' for the
little group of ladies who followed that tattered court
through the woods of Deeside—Queen Elizabeth and
the young Princess Marjorie whose sad short life, eight
years of it in prison, ended before they cut from her
dead body the first king of the haunted line of Stewart,
and the gallant Countess of Buchan, who had left husband and kin and her good name sooner than yield the
ancient right of her house to set the crown on the
King's head at Scone.   It is a world where the spirit
of chivalry is still real, in spite of horrors like the Sack
of Berwick.   (Perhaps after all no Plantagenet was
quite sane.)   Barbour himself shows its high courtesy.
He never rails at the English : when he condemns, it
is simply by letting their actions speak for themselves.
He contrasts, indeed, rather remarkably with Minot's
attempt to assume, simultaneously, that Bannockburn
was an English victory and that, of course, the Scots
won by a foul.   He never grudges honour to a gallant
enemy like Aymer de Valence or Gilles de Argentine,
counted in Europe the best knight of his day after
Bruce himself and Henry the Emperor.   One of the
most heart-warming things in the whole *Brus* is
Argentine's noble end at Bannockburn.   His praise is
not only for knights, for he finds room for the exploit
of a nameless English soldier in the raid on the Fife
coast—an episode which, as he says himself pretty
roundly, did the Scots no credit, for they broke rather
badly until they were rallied by the fighting Bishop
of Dunkeld, Bruce's *awn bischoppe*, he who as Abbot of
Inchaffray had blessed the army before Bannockburn.
Even a renegade like Ingelram de Umfraville has his
due for courage, and in fact is given the superb retort

53

to Edward's " ʒhon folk knelis till ask mercy," on that same morning—a retort that reminds one of the French *émigré* officer when the Emperor Joseph told him triumphantly how the Austrian troops would cut through the *sans-culottes*, and was answered drily, " C'est ce qu'il faudra voir, sire."

It is difficult to read Barbour and not feel a personal liking for the man : one likes him as one likes Joinville, though Barbour was " bigger " than that very lovable person. Certain critics, apparently, have achieved the feat, but I can only hope, for the sake of their manhood, that he was one of the people they took as read, or that they had some conscientious scruples about any approval of a Catholic priest, however scholarly and patriotic, and however competent in authorship.

The surviving work that may be grouped, somewhat loosely, with Barbour's, is that of Andrew Wyntoun and " Blind Harry." They inherit each an aspect of *The Brus*. Wyntoun is the historian pure : save Barbour himself, the oldest of surviving Scots historians in the Lowland vernacular. He also was a churchman, Prior of St Serf's in Loch Leven, and a generation younger than Barbour, born under David II, about 1350, and dying somewhere about 1420, shortly before James I returned from exile. His *Oryginale Cronykil of Scotland*, in Barbour's metre, is *original* in the sense that it handles our country's affairs since the Creation, and, in its earlier portions, in some others. When it reaches the eighth century, however, he begins to have real value as an historian, having obviously had access to some of the monastic records that were regularly kept, sometimes for centuries, to become waste paper after 1560. Some of his sources for the later periods are extant, as when he, avowedly and with modesty, borrows from Barbour. For his own time, the reigns of David II, Robert II, Robert III, and the subsequent regency, he is one of our best authorities. For the customs and point of view of his own time, he is most enlightening, as in such passages as the description of the great international tournament at Berwick in 1338, an appreciative account of hard knocks and high courtesy : it is here that we have the famous episode of William Ramsay's shrift in his helmet, his brother's rough but efficient surgery, and the admiring comment of " the good Earl of Derby." From the literary point of view he is Barbour's inferior : he is a scholar, and can quote to the point from Aristotle, Cicero, Livy, or Josephus, but though he writes straightforwardly and with vigour, his gift of narrative is less, and his subject-matter is less manageable.

It is customary to class with Wyntoun and Barbour a third man known as Blind Harry, who lived in the latter part of the fifteenth century, in the full tide of a very different school of letters. He was certainly alive in 1492, under James IV, and the sole MS. of his work, which is of 1488, thus comes in his lifetime, though it can hardly be the original one, as according to the Latin historian John Mair or Major, *The Actis and Deidis of the Illustre and Vallʒeant Campion Schir William Wallace* was written about 1450, under James II.

Harry is commonly put alongside Barbour, and in fact his *Wallace* is meant as a pair to the *Brus*, and fully shared its popularity. In spite of the frank discipleship, however, the two works are not really of the same class. *The Brus* is a serious " Life and Times." *Wallace* is semi-popular *biographie romancée*—rather freely *romancée*, in fact, in dealing with some of the larger incidents, though it is fair to add that we now have good evidence for the truth of stories that have been impugned, such as that of Wallace's journey to France. Harry does make a show of authorities. There were *Gestis* of Wallace : Wyntoun alludes to them. There was also, undoubtedly, much oral tradition. Harry says that there was a Latin life of Wallace, by his chaplain, Arnold Blair, and although no one has ever come across any other trace of it, that is no proof that it did not exist. But none the less the display of sources becomes a little reminiscent of the Yellowed Document in the Secret Drawer that opens so much late-Victorian fiction, and Harry's attitude to whatever they were seems to have been light-hearted, to say the least of it. With a calm worthy of Hollywood he stages a march of Wallace's to St Albans, and a touching scene where Queen Eleanor comes as envoy.

It is very shocking, especially to professors. But if one is not a professor, one may remember that novelists do at times treat history with freedom : and a novelist is exactly what Harry is. Barbour was a scholarly historian, writing with a definite political purpose and a keen interest in social ethics. Harry certainly meant to appeal to patriotic feeling—his own is plainly sincere : and he took an interest in the values of conduct, as does every novelist who is one at all. But he was a professional story-teller, aiming primarily at entertainment. This does not imply that he was uneducated, for though he is careful to announce that he is no highbrow, as a popular novelist he is more like Mr John Buchan than Mr Edgar Wallace. (I hasten to add that I do not mean to accuse that gentleman of Harry's casual attitude towards fact !) He is a competent, even a skilful, craftsman whose writing is neither clumsy nor amateurish, and he is obviously well-read. In fact, he is far more a disciple of Chaucer than any of the so-called Chaucerians, except King James : and unlike James, he follows the Chaucer of the Tales, not of the Visions. He uses Chaucer's riding-rhyme, and is much more successful with it than its English imitators of the period. I give Wallace's lament over Sir John Graham.

> Quhen thai him fand, and gud Wallace him saw,
> He lychtyt doun, and hynt him fra them aw
> In armis vp. Behaldand his pale face,
> He kyssit him, and cryt full oft, " Allace,
> My best brothir in warld that euir I had,
> My aefauld freynd quhen I was hardest stad,
> My hope, my heill, thow wast in maist honour,
> My faith, my help, my strenthiest in stour.
> In the was wyt, fredom, and hardines,
> In the was treuth, manheid, and noblesse,
> In the was rewll, in the was gouernans,
> In the vertu withouten varians,
> In the lawte, in the was gret largnas,
> In the gentrice, in the was stedfastnas. . . .
> Martyr thow art for Scotlandis rycht and me ;
> I sall the venge, or ellis tharfor de.

The resemblance is even closer when he permits himself a lyrical interlude in stanza-forms that Chaucer, though he did not invent them, sometimes used, as in the apostrophe before Lady Wallace's death :

> Now leiff thi myrth, now leiff thi haill pleasance.
>   Now leiff thi bliss, now leiff thi childis age,
> Now leiff thi zouth, (now) follow thi hard chance,
>   Now leiff thi lust, now leiff thi mariage.
>   Now leiff thi lufe, for thow sall loss a gage
> Quhilk neuir in erd sall be redemyt agayne.
>   Folow fortoun and all her fers outrage.
> Go leiff in wer, go leiff in cruell payne.

Fy on Fortoun, fy on thi frewall quheyll.
Fy on thi traist, for her it has no lest.
Thow transfigowryt Wallace out of his weill,
Quhen he traistyt for till haiff lestyt best.
His pleasance her till him was but a gest.
Throw thi fers cours, that has na hap to ho,
Him thow ourthrew out off his likand rest,
Fra gret plesance, in wer, trauaill, and wo.

I have said that *Wallace* was extremely popular. In fact, it went into more editions than any Scots book before the poems of Burns. It was printed as early as 1508, and a Revised Version, carefully Protestant-ised, appeared in 1570. One in modern Scots comes in 1722, at the early dawn of the Risorgimento, and it was popular as late as Burns's day. Yet it is worth noting that for all this large and enduring popularity, the sixty years between its writing and the first printed text are represented by a single MS. The equally popular *Brus*, for twice that period, has one MS. and a portion of another, one of which is by the same copyist as the unique *Wallace*, John Ramsay, whose name, since his country has so neglected Barbour, I give *honoris causa*. That any of the three survives is a mere chance. What perished?

I have called Harry novelist. He is so in more than the sense that he tells a story, which after all (as I was lately informed by a very young gentleman) is a thing no decent novelist would do. He is interested not only in his hero's adventures, but in his hero—a thirteenth century man seen from the fifteenth, certainly, which is rather as if Boileau should describe Bayard : but Harry was not setting out to be Really Modern. The adventures do not simply happen : they happen to Wallace. And they happen with considerable verve.

Take the opening episode, of the gay dagger. It may not be fact, but it has a lively truth. One can *see* the lad knocking out the insulting Englishman and bolting through the crowd to his uncle's lodging, where a resourceful housekeeper crams a gown and mutch on him, sits him down at the fire with distaff and spindle, and then, all civil readiness to oblige, shows the English military police over the house. There is the same gift of sheer narrative in the Irvine fishing episode, when Wallace " left his sword at home, but he never did that again." We see him quietly fishing on a good rising morning : " happy he was, took fish abundantly." Then a group of Percy's grooms turn up, and there is excellent dialogue : the lad answers courteously when they ask for fish, and in a manner not uncharacteristic of their race, they take the courtesy for weakness, and begin to bully, until his temper flies (22). The subsequent scrap is a good one, and Harry is sufficiently just to make Percy a sportsman : when the discomfited grooms lay their complaint, he tells them it served them right, and declines to pursue Wallace.

Harry's sense of character, as distinct from personality, and his feeling for the dramatic use of it, come out later, when Wallace's mistress is suborned to betray him, and then, at the last moment, thinks better of it : they show not only in the incident itself but in its repercussions later, when Wallace falls seriously in love with Marion Bradfute, and remembering the early betrayal, holds back. Marion's entry brings the light-hearted picaresque of the opening to an end. Harry makes her murder a moving thing, and does not stress the horrors, choosing rather to emphasise the change it is to work on Wallace. After,

the serious epic business of the war is less well-handled:
it does not escape a touch of the dreadful wordiness
that curses the French and English work of the time.
But Harry can always rise to a situation, when individual experience is involved. The death of Sir John
Graham, from which I have quoted, is deeply moving,
and the end is in the key of high tragedy. One *sees*
Wallace standing with the ropes on his wrists, listen-
ing to Menteith's smooth assurances, and saying
nothing. His death has the same quality of the thing
seen, and seen finely. Wallace refuses, as the historic
Wallace did, to admit himself a subject of Edward's,
and the angry king denies him a priest. The Archbishop, defying the inhumanity, shrives him, and he is
then harried by another priest, much as Montrose in
like case was by the ministers. The priest counsels
submission, and Wallace "smyled a litell at his
langage." The scene on the scaffold stresses not the
foul details of the torture, but Clifford's courtesy and
Wallace's high bearing. If Barbour is the father of
Boswell and Lockhart, one can see in Harry a forerunner of Scott . . . in spite of his Northcliffian
statistics. And it is worth noting that though the professional man of letters is much more bitter against
the enemy in general than the priest Barbour, he is
just to individuals. Percy at the beginning, the Archbishop of Canterbury at the end, are gentlemen, and
Edward's knights disapprove of his brutality to a
gallant prisoner, as Wolfe in 1746 was to disapprove
of Cumberland's. If Cressingham and some others
show a different standard, one need not accuse Harry
of bias : Hawley's exploits, for instance at Fort
Augustus Races, are tolerably recent history. And
Hawley seems to have been proud of them.

III

THE LAST OF THE MIDDLE AGES

The fifteenth and early sixteenth centuries—James I—Henryson—Dunbar—Kennedy—Douglas—the ghosts—anonymous work

HARRY marks, in a way, the end of a tradition. But in literary as in other history, " periods " are no more than a convenience of historians, an artificial mnemonic. When Harry wrote, he was already as old-fashioned as his younger English contemporary, Sir Thomas Malory. He is the end, in Scotland, of the European tradition of narrative verse that goes back to the *Song of Roland*, and links beyond that to the Teutonic epics and the sagas. During his life-time a new and brilliant school was springing up, harking back through *The Pearl* to *The Rose* (and to both its authors) and beyond them, ultimately, to those Provençals of the twelfth century from whom, through Italian, derives so much Northern work we are accustomed to think of as Renaissance. It is a school, in the main, of non-narrative poetry, lyrical, reflective, or satiric : one of definitely " literary " work, brilliant in technical accomplishment, written mainly for the Court. In the later fifteenth and early sixteenth century, in fact, Scots literature is the most vigorous in Northern Europe. There is nothing in fifteenth-century English verse to put alongside Dunbar or Henryson (23), nothing in French but Villon. And fine as Villon's great work is, it is only a part of his by no means bulky total output.

A complete account of Scottish literature is no more possible for this age than for that which precedes it. Non-narrative poetry certainly did not begin in Scotland with the fifteenth century, or even with the late fourteenth. We know for certain that a great deal of fourteenth century song, and probably some older, once existed, and is completely lost. That is to say, in the usual language of literary history, there was a fourteenth century lyric, that has vanished. Songs were perishable stuff, passed about by word of mouth or on scraps of paper, and the Reformers made eager war on them. It is no speculation, either, but definite evidence that informs us that a large body of fifteenth century Scots literature, probably as large as the amount we possess, has been lost completely. Some of it, no doubt, was inferior to what has survived : some of it may have been better. There is no evidence: it is gone as completely as what Good Lord James sang when he obliged the company after supper, or as the equivalent of *Mademoiselle from Armentières* that (decorously out of Queen Elizabeth's hearing) enlivened the Carrick camp-fires in 1306. And this is true, not only of the fifteenth century, but of definite men, of considerable note in their day, who lived little before the middle of the sixteenth.

In spite of the enormous gaps, however, we know a good deal about the fifteenth century, although many of the elements of that knowledge are ignored by most historians of our letters, who say something about the influence of Chaucer, mention Four Scottish Chaucerians, *et passent outre*. In fact, the Scottish Chaucerians are a myth, or three of them are. King James is a Chaucerian, and Blind Harry—who is not included in the official Four. Douglas, Dunbar, and even

Henryson, are probably less disciples of Chaucer than I am. To be sure, a reader whose first-hand knowledge of mediaeval literature is confined to Chaucer will see a good deal of apparent similarity if he reads *The Goldyn Targe* immediately after the Prologue to *The Legende of Goode Women.* The likeness, however, is a misleading one. Both are using a device extinct in our own time, but in theirs a favourite poetical form all over Europe. Critics whose knowledge is intensive rather than extensive are apt to see imitation of X in Y when X and Y are merely using subjects or forms that were " going about " when they wrote (24). Douglas, Dunbar, and Henryson all admired Chaucer, and being men of intelligence, no doubt admired him sincerely. That is natural. He was the greatest poet the common language of the two countries had so far produced, and remained the greatest for a century and three-quarters after his death. By both his intrinsic merit and the prestige of his royal disciple's patronage, he " took " at the Scots court. James undoubtedly was his follower : some of the lost poets may have been. It is natural to suppose he would be a stimulus : he certainly was that to Henryson. But there is no evidence of any more, and he was not the only stimulus. Scotland all through the fifteenth century was in a state of lively intellectual activity, and the strongest foreign influence is not England, but France and Flanders, especially the former. English architecture of that century, for instance, was far from sharing the decadence of English letters and had in fact developed a purely native style of uncommon beauty : but it had so little influence on Scots that Margaret Tudor's perpendicular windows at Linlithgow feel as exotic as the Italian wing at

Crichton. On the other hand the kinship of French and Scots work is so close that when, with a Scots friend, I first entered the courtyard of Langeais, we both said in a breath " This might be Scotland " : and conversely, when someone once sent me a post-card of Falkland Palace, my first thought was, " I didn't know she was in France."

Scotland, in fact, by the reign of the third Stewart, was recovering from the dismal half-century after Bruce's death. She had saved herself by a hair's-breadth, but saved she was, for a trio of generations at any rate. Her fifteenth century was scarcely quiet : it flickers from end to end with civil war. But a country that had won clear against eight-to-one odds led by soldiers like Edward I and Edward III could take the Douglas troubles in her stride.

The latter part of the fourteenth century had seen her relieved of the English menace. England, in fact, had her hands more than full in France, where Edward III was burning his fingers badly ; and after about 1370 her teeth were drawn. The unlucky accident of the Heir-apparent's capture at sea, in time of truce, was a serious blow to Scotland, killing the old King and producing the inevitable scramble for regency. But when England recovered after 1400 she turned south first, and the knock-out of France after Agincourt did not last long. Baugé (a Scots battle) comes six years after, and when St Joan rode into Orleans in 1429 (to be met, incidentally, by a Scots bishop) the tide had turned definitely, and England had a quarter-century of steady disaster abroad, followed by thirty years of civil war at home, to keep her from aggression upon her neighbours. South Scotland, the richest of the country and at the same time the most vulnerable, had a chance to do something more than fight for existence. Even with two kings too old for active rule, followed by three long minorities, she took that chance.

The period from 1369 to 1513 is comparable, as a time of progress, with the century that followed the Treaty of Canterbury in 1189. Scotland, to begin with, came back into Europe again, after ceasing for some three generations to be an effective Power. The marriages of James I's children show the extent of her foreign alliances by the end of the first third of the fifteenth century. James, his heir, married the niece of the Duke of Burgundy, the great central power, then at its zenith, that held the balance between France and the Empire. The unlucky Margaret, "with the face like starlight," was Dauphine of France, while Eleanor was wife of the Emperor's nephew, Sigismund Duke of Austria. Isobel was Duchess of Brittany, the last, save Burgundy, of the great independent French provinces, counterpoise to Burgundy across France, as Austria was on the far side of the Empire. Mary sealed the alliance with powerful Flanders, by her marriage with the heir of Campvere. James' own wife was of the English royal house, and he was on friendly terms with Scandinavia, a princess of which, Margaret of Denmark and Norway, was to marry his grandson. His two remaining daughters, Annabella and Jean the Dumb, attached —for a time—the great houses of Douglas and Gordon, the strongest in South and North Scotland, to the throne.

As a natural consequence of this network of alliances, Scots trade increased, bringing economic prosperity, though the chief export was still soldiers—not mere

E

cannon-fodder like the eighteenth-century Hessians, but men like the Seigneur d'Oizon or James' own cousin, the Connétable de Buchan, Commander-in-Chief of the French army and founder of the great fighting house of Stuart d'Aubigny. France showed her gratitude not only to leaders like the Douglases, who were seigneurs of Longueville and dukes for generations of the great royal province of Touraine (which was to have a Scots Duchess again in Queen Mary) but to the Scottish people at large, to whom were accorded the full privileges of French citizenship, without formality of nationalisation.

The constant coming and going of Scots soldiers, Scots diplomats, Scots merchants, and naturally, Scots scholars, brought a great quickening of the national life. The more peaceful condition of the country, and the less peaceful one of Paris in the Burgundian-Armagnac collisions, induced the Bishop of St Andrews to raise its old *studium generale* to a properly constituted university. The Bishops of Glasgow and Aberdeen followed his example. All three of the pre-Reformation universities were modelled directly on the University of Paris, and to this day have a closer kinship with their French colleagues than with at least the older English ones (25). They were well founded, handsomely equipped in both personnel and fabric (I wonder what came to Elphinstone's cloth-of-gold hangings ?) and organised from the first with an eye to growth. It shows the increasing interest in the sciences that Aberdeen had a chair of medicine from its beginning—the senior university medical foundation in Great Britain.

The arts, not yet divorced from scholarship, flourished along with it. It was a great age of Scottish architecture, the greatest until one comes to Gibbs, the Adams, and Gillespie Graham. In one sense, indeed, it almost had to be that, for the fourteenth century had left the country in much the case of the West Front in 1919. There was a wave of fine building, religious and secular. Very little of the former remains—mere fragments like Roslin, the choir, no more, of an unfinished collegiate church, or the magnificent Flemish oak, saved by a fighting Principal, at King's College, Aberdeen. Scotland has produced some of the finest modern glass in Europe, but of all the splendours of her pre-Reformation windows there exists a matter of some six square feet, of the mid-sixteenth century. Bare ruined choirs. . . .

The secular architecture had better fortune, although quite late buildings of considerable importance have shared the fate of the abbeys and of Mary of Gueldres' Hospital of the Trinity, which survived Hertford and the Reformation to die of a railway and the crassness of the capital's Civic Fathers. The Holyrood of James V was a ghost in his daughter's time, and nothing but one tower and part of a ruined chapel are left of hers. Linlithgow is a shell, its great hall with the triple fireplace open to the sky. Stirling has not fared very much better. Queen Marie de Guise's gorgeous little palace has nothing left but a door or two in museums. Enough survives, however, to show the castles of the time (26), still, in the main, fiercely defensible for war, but with scope within their defences, as at Borthwick or Craigmillar, for state and splendour, for the rather fantastic gorgeousness of living that is the note of that age all over the North— in Roslin, in Henry VII's chapel at Westminster, in the west front of Rouen Cathedral, above all in the

67

costume of the day. It is the age when the business-like severity of mail has hardened into the engraved magnificence of plate-armour, when the close soft wimple of the mediaeval lady sweeps aloft in horns and pinnacles and great cloudy wings of fine lawn over jewels, when the men go with one leg scarlet and one green, and wide sleeves dagged in a fluttering forest of leaves.

These things—the fantastic dress and the buildings that were made to be its setting—are all of the North. Italy had ceased already to be mediaeval. It was France and Flanders and Burgundy and the Empire, Scotland and England, that stooped their tall hennins under the incredible stone of the " flaming " Gothic or the intricate fan-vaultings of the " perpendicular." And the literature of Scotland, of that time, has the gorgeousness that goes with these externals. Its persistent note is the gorgeous. But it can carry it. It never loses a certain arrogant virility, never becomes blurred intellectually, nor, however ornate, loses hold on the actual. These are its virtues.

It has the defects of its age along with them. That magnificent time was a very brutal one—much more so, in its essential quality, than the twelfth and thirteenth centuries had been. Those did not lack either cruelty or brutality : no age has done that, since mankind began its still incomplete emergence from the ape. But they did show a tremendous soaring of both the intellect and the spirit, a high and noble humility and strength, revealed alike in the work of the great philosopher theologians and in the artists who made the sculptures of Chartres, the glory of burning light in the Sainte Chapelle. St Francis, St Thomas of Aquin, St Louis, St Catherine of Siena,

68

grew out of their age, and it venerated them all. St Joan was a living contrast to hers, and it burnt her. Not all churchmen of the true Middle Ages were St Francis or St Thomas Aquinas, of course, any more than all kings were St Louis or all merchants' daughters St Catherine of Siena. None the less, it was an age that understood them, even when it disobeyed, as it understood, even when it perverted, the great chivalric code, an institution which the modern man has ceased to be able to grasp intellectually, because he has lost an intellectual grasp of the idea of the sacramental that is its key, and can only see the fantastic abuses of either (27).

By the fifteenth century, however, the two great dominants of social conceptions, the life of the Church and the life of chivalry, were poisoned under the gorgeousness of their trappings. Both, all over Europe, had sickened after the great anti-climax of the ineffectual end of the Crusades (28), the apocalyptic terror of the Black Death, with its heavy drain, precisely, on the Church's shock-troops, on the best alike of the Orders and the secular priesthood. In Scotland also the Church had suffered, as nowhere else in Western Europe, from war. It recovered, materially, with the recovery of economic prosperity, but the loss in personnel was never made up. The bad tradition of the Columban church, the attachment of great offices to the tribe, to the family, instead of to the district, had never quite lapsed, and now it rose again. Bishoprics and abbacies became endowments for bastards of noble houses—a plentiful tribe. James IV himself, sincerely religious on one side of his fiery and complex nature, made his son Primate six years before he could be even a priest : though age apart,

Erasmus, who was the lad's tutor, bears witness that the choice might have been no bad one. One must not, of course, exaggerate. Even under that very James IV, there were men like Elphinstone, Bishop of Aberdeen, a scholar of vision, a patriotic statesman, and a man of blameless life and sincere devotion.

None the less, the last Scots churchman to be canonised died forty years before Alexander III (29). And it is certainly true that fifteenth and sixteenth century Scots literature shows, as the former century advances, the breakdown of the mediaeval moral code and the onset of that moral callousness or imperceptiveness that goes alongside the intellectual quickening of the Renaissance, the age's contentment, save at illuminated moments, with the lust of the flesh, the lust of the eye and brain, and the pride of life. Thus, Henryson apart, the literature of that age, accomplished and vigorous as it is, has little of the spiritual depth that marks the highest type of poetry. What it has is enormous vigour, very brilliant technical accomplishment—brilliant is in fact the word—and at its best, strong emotion to lift it from mere distinguished construction to real creation.

The four major names of the tradition are James I, Robert Henryson, William Dunbar, and Gavin Douglas. King James is the oldest, and, as poet, the least. It is he who is the Chaucerian among them. Henryson goes back, though very much in his own fashion, to an older tradition than Chaucer, Dunbar to that of the *Rose*, and Douglas, in his own manner, to the *Rose* and the classics. James precedes the others by a good deal, having been born in the fourteenth century, in 1394, and murdered in 1436, nearly a quarter of a century before Dunbar was born.

None of the four was a " whole-time " man of letters, and James was least so : indeed, in his short twelve years of active reign he proved himself one of the most vigorous and capable sovereigns of a country that required an efficient government. If he had lived for another twenty years, he would certainly have saved us from many of the troubles of the mid-century, and consolidated his work both at home and abroad. But he was a Stewart, and it was not to be.

An efficient King of Scots had much to do besides writing poetry. James' work, even with what is lost, does not seem to have been copious, though he was always, like his daughters and so many of his descendants, a lover of the arts. According to Hector Boece, " he was well lernit to fecht with the sword, to just, to tournay, to worsle, to sing and dance, was an expert mediciner, richt crafty in playing baith of lute and harp and sindry other instrumentis of music. He was expert in gramer, oratory, and poetry, and made sae flowand and sententious versis : he was ane natural and borne poete." He seems to have been a musician of great merit. Nearly two hundred years later an Italian, Tassoni, speaks of him as one of the pioneers of " modern " music, saying that " he invented a new kind, plaintive and melancholy, in which he was imitated by Carlo Gesualdo, Prince of Verona, who in our age has improved music with many new and admirable inventions." It is possible that the new songs were based on Highland airs : James was a noted performer upon the clarsach. He did write many songs, whether set to his own music or to Highland, but these are lost, and his only surviving writings are a rather fine ballade on *Trust in God*, much in the key of Chaucer's gnomic work, and a very modish allegoric vision-piece, *The Kingis Quhair*, written about the time of his return, in 1424, from his long imprisonment. In spite of its traditional celebrity, it came near enough joining his songs, for it exists only in one MS. of nearly the end of the century, long hidden in an English library.

The Quhair (=quire, book) has always had a sort of popular fame by reason of its romantic history, of the young captive king looking from his window on the garden beneath, and straightway " striken to the herte " by fair Joan Beaufort. It has been said by scholars that the story cannot be true, because the same thing happened to Arcyte : it is extraordinarily difficult to convince a certain type of mind that a thing which occurs in fiction can do so in fact. This may not have, but it is not an unlikely thing to happen to an ardent, imaginative, and imprisoned young man in his twenties, with the Stewart susceptibility to a fair face. In any case, if it is not a literal account of his first sight of a lady he undoubtedly did love, to the point of being one of the few Stewart kings who did not complicate Scots politics by the production of several illegitimate offspring, the prison window and the free lovely garden make a true image of their circumstances. We know that the poem was written for Queen Joan : and the parts that speak of her are very much the best of it, bringing sincerity into its graceful convention. Literary imitation is not inconsistent with that : it is a mere naivety to deny it.

The poem uses the same convention as *The Pearl*, *The Hous of Fame*, *The Goldyn Targe*, and *The Divine Comedy*, to take a varied batch of its applications : the dream-allegory made popular nearly two centuries before by Guillaume de Lorris (30). The elaborate ornament, like the pageantry of symbolical figures in the tapestry, fresco, sculpture, and illumination of the time, is a regular feature of the type, and not by any means confined to Chaucer, as discussions of the *Quhair* sometimes imply. None the less, Chaucer is clearly James's master in verse, and he uses the gracious seven-lined stanza Chaucer had devised for *The Parlement of Foules* and used so exquisitely in *Troylus* that it was popular till the seventeenth century. James writes it gracefully, but he never quite succeeds in getting Chaucer's lovely plangent note. Blind Harry (though not in that metre) beats him there. The language also shows, very strongly, Chaucerian influence. It is much less decorated than that of *The Pearl* or of Dunbar, but is a definitely " poetic diction," though possibly less artificial than it looks, for the strong southern element is only what might be expected of a man who had lived in England from twelve to thirty, at a time when the fifteenth-century change in English speech, that approximated its accidence to the Scottish, had scarcely begun.

The poem begins with the prisoner unable to sleep. He sits down to read Boethius, and recalls his capture, with a real emotion : although the imprisonment was a gilded one, the shock of its treachery, to a sensitive boy, the eighteen years of forced inaction to a youth of James' fiery disposition, must have been bitter, beside the glittering success of Henry V, his senior only by half a dozen years. Then, as he looks from the window, he sees a lady, and the graceful conventional verse fires with real passion :

> Onely throu latting of myn eyen fall. . . .
> My hert, my will, my nature, and my mynd
> War changit clene ryght in ane ithir kynd.

73

It is the old, recurrent astonishment, " l'image toujours neuve."

The vision that follows, after the lady has gone and he has fallen asleep with his head on the stone, is conventional enough, after the modish forms, though graceful in its tapestry-patterning. One has to remember, reading these many visions, the pictorial imagery of the age. One can never understand any one art, in a given period, without knowing something of what the rest were like : the best commentary on Milton is Wren's St Paul's. The sleeper finds himself at Venus' court : the goddess cheers him and sends him to Minerva, who discourses on wise and unwise love, on honesty in love, on Fortune and free-will. He passes on by a river to a meadow, then to a garden, the rich formal garden that was one of the major mediaeval delights, where Fortune is in the midst above her wheel. She pities him, and bids him mount the wheel and take his chance. . . . But he wakes, seeing nothing of the Charterhouse of Perth on a winter night, and a white dove flies to him with a wall-flower bearing a message of comfort in golden letters. Then he explains that Fortune has been kind, and he is writing as a thank-offering, and ends by praying to Venus for all lovers and for those too dull of soul to love, and commending his book humbly to those of Chaucer and Gower, in rather the spirit of Charles IX's lines to Ronsard. The classical imagery all through has the mediaeval *presentness*, that sees nothing incongruous in invoking Calliope in the name of Our Lady. That was absurd to the post-Renaissance mind. But looking back from the twentieth century one wonders at times if we have not, perhaps, lost something in losing that irrecoverable power of unity of vision—not " changeden substance into accidente " ?

James of the Fiery Face,

> —le roy scotiste,
> Qui demy face euct, dit-on,
> Vermeil comme une amathiste—

and who was killed at thirty, was less an amateur of the arts than his father, his son, his brilliant grandson, or even his sisters. His reign, with its jangle of Queen Joan's fierce vengeance, of Crichton and Livingstone, of the Douglas wars, did not make for peaceful letters, though it saw the foundation, four years before Arkinholm, of Glasgow University. His sister, the young Dauphine Margaret, one of the most tragic figures in her tragic family, was, like her father, a poet, but the little of her rather copious work that has survived is all in French, as is the very touching little lament for " la sienne suer o cuer courtois " ascribed to her sister Isobel Duchess of Brittany. Another sister, Eleanor, translated *Ponthus et Sidoine* into German for the benefit of her husband, Sigismund Duke of Austria. Nothing in vernacular letters survives from James' reign except *Wallace* and some scraps of popular song, including the ominous tag

> Edinborough Castle, tour and toun,
> Guid grant thow sink for sin,
> And that even for the blake dinner
> Erl Douglas gat therinne.

Very early in the minority of James' successor, in 1462, we first hear of Robert Henryson, matriculating at Glasgow, but already a graduate in arts and law. We know little of him but that he was schoolmaster in Dunfermline, possibly in its great Benedictine

Abbey, and apparently also practised as a notary. His life was a long one, and since his extant poems are clearly those of a man no longer young, they probably belong to the later years of James III and the reign of James IV. We know that he was dead by 1506.

Of the major poets of his century, Henryson is, superficially, most like Chaucer in temper and outlook and in the peculiar quality of his humour. The likeness, however—the more as it extends to choice of subject—throws strongly into relief his very marked individuality both as man and as poet, which shows most clearly in, precisely, the poem whose subject is avowedly suggested by Chaucer. Chaucer's *Troylus and Criseyde* had been a version of a favourite mediaeval addition to the tale of Troy—how the young prince Troilus loved a fair Greek hostage, how they were happy, and then she was exchanged and returned, and betrayed him with Diomed, so that he died despairing. Shakespeare was to take it up again, with its passion and pity turned to a sardonic anger of disillusionment. Henryson set himself to continue Chaucer's poem, in a spirit that is neither Chaucer's nor Shakespeare's : it is nearer, in fact, the temper of Shakespeare's own tragedies. Instead of the novelist's analysis of emotion in Chaucer's *Troylus*, which is in fact the first great English novel, there is a fierce condensation, a darker and sterner pity, not pathos but the swordstroke tragedy of the ballads. The poem takes its note at once. It is winter : he sees the planet Venus rise on a cold clear night of wind, the east wind of Fife, then mends the fire and " beikis him about,"

And toke ane drink, my spreitis to conforte,

and then reads *Troylus and Criseyde* and after it,
another, imaginary, tale of the end of the story, whose
substance he recounts. Cresseid is jilted in turn by
her new lover, and goes back to her father : their
brief interview has a fine sense of the dramatic.
Calchas is Venus' priest, but Cresseid is too shamed
to show herself in the temple. She prays instead in a
secret oratory, reproaching Venus who has led her to
trust in the beauty that has betrayed her. There is
the inevitable vision then, without which no large-
scale poem was complete—a gorgeous procession of
the Old Gods that recalls the pageants of the *Faerie
Queene.* Cupid charges her with blasphemy of his
mother, and the eldest and the youngest planet, the
cold star Saturn and the Moon, are bidden to judge
her. Saturn strikes her with his frosty wand, and she
is filled with the leprosy that was so insistent a mediaeval horror. She wakes from her dream, goes to the
glass to reassure herself, and learns the truth of it,
and her ruined beauty. There follows a scene of wild
misery with her father, who takes her privily to " the
hospitall at the tounis end," where her fellow-lepers
comfort her with hard-won philosophy. She who
has been fair and desired and lived daintily, must e'en
make the best of it, and live " eftir the law of lippar-
leid." Then comes the climax. As she begs with
them at the gate, Troilus rides past them from
victorious battle. She is too blind by now to recognise him, and her face so marred he cannot know her
either. Yet something about her recalls to him
Cresseid : he changes colour, and moved by the
memory, throws her his purse and rides away in
silence. From her fellows' chatter over the good
fortune she learns who he is and swoons, rousing

before she dies to send him, by a fellow-leper, the ruby ring that had been his first gift to her. He hears the story, crying " Scho was untrew, and wo is me thairfoir," and has her buried richly under marble, with the curt sufficient epitaph,

> Lo, ladyis fair, Cresseid of Troyis toun,
> Sumtyme countit the flour of womanheid,
> Undir this stane, late lippar, lyis deid.

The whole thing has a stark sense of the east wind —one of those bleak Fife days with white water on the Firth. But its stern justice has a profound and aching pity, and something also of the sense of redemption that comes at the close of a tragedy of Shakespeare's.

It is not, by any means, Henryson's only note. He can write things of the shrewdest and liveliest humour, with a homely realism instead of the stately pageant of the gods : but even under their most whimsical there is always a certain sense of the ironies—below the mirth a sense of the tragic littleness of humanity, and below that again, what is not common anywhere in that century, a grave underlying assurance of stable law. One has it beneath the whimsy of the *Fables*, delightful *remaniements* of " Esope myne autour," in the vein of the *Nonnes Preestes Tale*. It is interesting to see how Henryson's own temperament informs their lively and homely realism of humour as much as the tragic fantasy of *The Testament of Cresseid*. They have the same humanity, but it is comic, not tragic, as in the genteel *refanement* of the " burgess mouss : " yet there is a tenderness in the amusement, for the innocent terrors of the " rural mous." They show also another quality of Henryson, the sharp percep-

tion of surroundings, not merely as decoration, as in
romanticism, not merely as something to put down,
as with most realists, who remind one so often of a
small boy with a camera who must keep letting it off
at no matter what, but as an essential element of the
complex experience he is portraying. This is notably
so in his handling of natural phenomena. The
English climate is no better than the Scots,—that of
London, in fact, is more treacherous than that of any
Scottish district known to me : but for centuries
English literature ignores wet weather, storm, the
wilder aspects of the country, rather as in another
century it ignored the wilder aspects of sex so much
that when they became mentionable again it could
scarcely bring itself to talk of anything else. It liked
nature, but tidy and obliging nature : it had forgotten, or felt only as horror, the fierce sense of the
storm, of moor country, that shows again and again
in pre-Conquest poetry, West Saxon and Northum-
brian alike, as in *The Seafarer* :

> Nap nihtscua, norþan sniwde,
> hrim hrusan band : hægl feoll on eorþan,
> corna caldast, (31).

—and the next lines are not revulsion, but the stir
that moves a man to seek *elþeodigra eard*, the country
of strange folk, over the steep seas. This receptiveness
to nature in all its aspects, not merely in the kindly,
is a constant note in Scots poetry for centuries before
James Thomson carried south of the Border a fashion
that was to produce Wordsworth, and which, reduced
to a popular sentimentality, looks like burying all the
wild nature we have left under a layer of sardine-tins
and paper bags.

Less important than either *Cresseid* or the *Fables* is *A Traitie of Orpheus Kyng and how he came to yeid to Hewyn and to Hel to seik his Quene.* It is graceful enough, and more classical in feeling than the *Kyng Orfeo* of the fourteenth century, but is marred by too much learning—in this case, theory of music. The intrusion no doubt pleased the scientific fashion of the age, like Chaucer's flourishes of astrology or the 1920 novelists' of the subconscious. Nothing goes out of date so quickly as science, or makes a work of art so soon look obsolete.

Henryson's shorter poems are generally meditative and didactic rather than lyrical, their verse in the tone of recitative rather than song. The exception is his best, which has lyrical movement with the dramatic feeling of the *Testament,* though it is love's comedy now instead of tragedy, a dry ironic comedy that does not empty passion but encloses it. *Robene and Makyne* is a pastoral duologue of a type popular in mediaeval France. Its verse has a delightful impish dance, unusual in Henryson, and largely due to the fact that he has " swung " it by using a blend of metrical and alliterative form, in the manner of *The Pearl* and of much of Dunbar. The theme is conventional, but there is more than convention in the wicked humour of Robin's semi-surrender and the denouement. The indifferent Robin is wooed by his passionate fair, and submits at last : since the lady wants it so much, he will oblige—if his sheep don't happen to stray at the crucial moment. There is a certain devilment in Makyne's remark, when the tables are turned and he has become the wooer, " As thow hes done, sa sall I say."

The man who wrote *The Testament of Cresseid* was a greater *man* than William Dunbar, with a type of

imagination that in " literary " poetry—there is plenty
in the ballads—Scotland was scarcely to see again
until the closing chapters of *Waverley*. But of all the
Scots writers of his age, Dunbar is, taking him all
round, the most considerable. Mrs Annand Taylor,
in a charming if slightly exasperating book, has
scolded him severely for not being either Malory or
Rossetti. The charge, if irrelevant, is true. He was
certainly neither, but he was much himself, and no
less what was the essence of his own time. He had in
fact the makings of a great poet : that he is one in
the lesser kinds of poetry is as true of him as of
Alexander Pope, and in both because they abound so
exceedingly in the sense of their age and of their society.
He has a fine firm intellectual quality ; an intense degree of the " more than ordinary organic (=sensory)
sensibility " that Wordsworth considered the essential of
the creative temperament ; and a spectacular technical accomplishment. But he comes in an age that all
over Europe is almost devoid of spiritual intensity, and
his experience rarely brought him the intensity of
emotion that, poetically speaking, might have made up
for it. He was a priest and a courtier together, one of

> Those gay abati with the well-turned leg
> And rose i' the hat-brim, not so much St Paul
> As saints of Caesar's household—

—the type of the eighteenth century *abbé de salon*.
Now, priests have written great poems, and so have
courtiers, but the combination is a hampering one for
the highest kind of poetry. The man who is both can
never be wholly either, can never, at heart, desire
wholly what is of either, with a sense that the desire,
however far from his power, is within his right.

Dunbar thus remains below the pinnacles : he writes superb court-poetry, but though he can dance divinely he seldom soars. And partly because of that very limitation it is he of all Northern European poets who most fully expresses the spirit of his own age, its intricate, rather brutal gorgeousness, its hard intellectual quality, its intense vitality of the will and the senses and its numbness of the finer spiritual perceptions. Emotionally, he is nearer Dryden (who, by the way, was partly of Scots descent) than anyone else who writes the common language, and he would have been completely at home in the Paris of the Fronde (32). (His views on the *Carte du Tendre* might have been unacceptable in the Hôtel de Rambouillet . . . yet I don't know. He liked both allegory and a pretty woman.) Indeed, though I have compared him to Pope and Dryden, he is nearer the French seventeenth century than anything in English except, significantly, Ben Jonson. The likeness, however, is in spirit, not in literary technique. The great French writing of the *Grand Siècle* has a quality of marble, of wrought bronze. Dunbar's is like gorgeous many-coloured enamel, hard, glittering, and full of reflected lights. His greatest work would have staggered Jean Racine : and yet, perhaps, it has a good deal in common with the rooms that lead onwards from the Salon d'Hercule, the rooms through which a court passed to see *Georges Dandin*.

We have a considerable body of Dunbar's work, although its survival, as usual, was rather a near thing. Chepman and Myllar printed *The Goldyn Targe*, *The Twa Maryit Wemen, Quhen he wes Seik*, and four other pieces, in 1508. The rest of him is in the Bannatyne, Maitland, Asloan and Reidpath MSS., and there was no collected edition till 1834. His life is more distinct than those of his predecessors. He was probably born in the last years of James II, and the main associations of his maturity are with the brilliant court of James IV. His restless vigour gave him a wandering youth. He turned to the Franciscan order, and as a novice tramped all over England, preaching in Canterbury Cathedral, but he never took the vows, becoming instead, unfortunately for himself and for the Church, a secular priest—secular, in fact, in more senses than the technical. Like Chaucer before him he went into what we should call the Civil Service. We know that he went with the Scots Ambassador to France in 1491, and after James had declined the Spanish match, to England with the envoy who arranged the King's marriage to Margaret Tudor. Diplomatic business also took him to Germany, Italy, Spain, and Norway, on the coast of which country he claims to have been wrecked. Although he never held any important post, he was a personal favourite with both King and Queen—little as their tastes, for the most part, agreed—and although James steadily refused him the benefice for which he clamoured, he was pensioned in 1500. In his later years he was a sort of official court-poet, turning out a good deal of brilliant " occasional " verse for official functions, the official compliments of a royal or ambassadorial visit. A good deal of his unofficial work is also more or less occasional, and between that and his laureate pieces he gives a shrewd, witty, vigorously coloured picture of the Scots court life of the time, on its less serious side. There was a serious side. James was the true Renaissance prince, avid of beauty as his father had been, an impassioned scholar (Ayala says he spoke six languages besides the two that were native to his country), and as interested in science as his descendants Prince Rupert and Charles II—a religious man, too, in strange passionate alternations between the love-affairs that (save perhaps for Margaret Drummond's) suggest vivid energy and a heart too twisted in youth to find any peace : he never, to his last day, forgot that at fifteen he had helped, however unwittingly, to kill his father. Something fated about the man, more than in most of his line, suggests the White King, who was also Scot crossed with Dane. It is in Holbein's strangely haunting portrait. But James had far the finer brain of the two, and that intense power of vitality that was coming to be applauded under the misconception of it called *virtù*. The Renaissance and Middle Ages fuse in him, in one of those personalities who suggest that a reason why Scotland has little great poetry or drama is that she has never needed to create it as enlargement of experience. Her passions found outlet in immediate action, and the impulses that elsewhere made epic and tragedy, in her made the naked fact of her history.

But in spite of its brilliance, and of the King's personality, the splendour of that court was of its age, and soulless. It was gorgeous, but corrupt. Margaret of Denmark was dead, and the women who led it were the King's fleeting mistresses, or Margaret of England, who had the Tudor vulgarity without the Tudor brains : Holbein reveals her with disastrous completeness. (Cross *that* with Douglas arrogance, not too intelligent, in Angus, and the shrillness of Lennox, and you may well breed Darnley.) Dunbar had plenty of material for the satire that is the note of his greatest work, and plenty of cause for the weariness under his laughter. And the reckless magnificence of his style was in the picture. Scots architecture, between the climate and the hard native stone, was severer than French or English, but its builders took out the difference in gorgeousness of person. Grafton Herald remarks with patriotic annoyance that at the handing over of Queen Margaret the Scots outshone his countrymen in " apparell and riche jewels and massy Chaynes "—and Henry's court did not go Quakerish (33).

All these things show in the greatest, and grimmest, satire in our literature, *The Twa Maryit Wemen and the Wedo*. The subject is one that has occupied writers from the Prophet Isaiah to Mr Noel Coward. To use a phrase that is now become old-fashioned, it deals with the expensive Bright Young Person, and one could wish that our own contemporaries, who are so fond of writing of similar types, could do so with Dunbar's force and concision. It is one of the most flaying things in literature, and of uncommon technical interest, not merely because it is the last important piece in unrhymed alliterative verse, but because of the way in which its many-coloured brilliance of decoration is made an integral part of the satire itself, made to be " burning instead of beauty," though it is beauty and recognised for that.

It begins with the splendour of midsummer night in a palace garden, all green and coloured flowers and glittering lights, and three lovely delicate ladies as gay as the flowers, and as exquisite :

I saw thre gay ladeis sit in ane grene arbeir,
All graithit in to garlandis of fresche gudelie flouris.

85

So glitterand as the gold wer thair glorius gilt tressis,
Quhill all the gressis did gleme of thair glaid hewis.
Kemmit wes thair cleir hair, and curiouslie sched,
Attour thair schuldres doun schyne, schyning full brycht,
With curches, cassin thame aboue, of kirsp cleir and thin.
Thair mantillis grein war as the gress that grew in May
    sesoun,
Fetrit with thair quhyt fingaris about thair fair sydes.
Of ferlifull fyne favour war thair faceis meik,
All full of flurist fairheid, as flouris in June,
Quhyt, seimlie, and soft, as the sweit lilies,
New vpspred vpon spray, or new spynist rose,
Arrayit ryally about with mony rich vardour,
That nature, full nobillie, annamallit fine with flouris
Of alkin hewis under hewin, that ony heynd knew,
Fragrant, all full of fresch odours, fynest of smell.
    Ane marbre tabile coverit was befoir thai thre ladeis
With ryall coupis upon rawis, full of ryche wynys.

They solace themselves with the wines until their tongues are loosened, and they chatter of the subject in which they take most interest. There are no men about : it is strictly *inter augures*. They are of the type for whom harlotry is a hobby rather than a profession, but skilled amateurs who make a good thing out of it. And they discuss their methods as they might their service at tennis, completely satisfied with their own outlook as a natural and adequate view of life.

Then, when they have said enough to strip themselves naked, without a word of comment we are made to visualise them again, their delicate loveliness in the rich setting.

The morow myld wes and meik, the mavis did sing,
And all remuffit the myst, and the meid smellit.
Siluer schouris doun schake, as the schene cristall,
And berdis schoutit in schaw, with thair shrill notis.

The golden glitterand gleme so gladit thair hertis
Thai made a glorius gle amang the grene bewis.
The soft souch of the swyr, and soune of the stremis,
The sweit savour of the sward and singing of foulis,
Myght confort any creature of the kyn of Adam,
And kindill agane his curage, thocht it was cald slokynt.
Then rais thir ryall wivis, in thair riche wedis,
And rakit hame to thair rest, through the rise blosmyt.

There is not a word of condemnation. We simply
see both the inside and the out, *together*. And that is
devastating. The thing is ghastly, but superb in its
kind. It makes most modern work on the subject
extraordinarily thin, diffuse, and flat.

It is the greatest of his satires. There is a pair to it,
a companion-piece " forty years on," in *Rycht early on
Ash Wednesday*, where two old cummers whose sensual
delights are reduced to food and drink hold forth
on the unwholesomeness of fasting. It has the same
grim detachment, but naturally cannot achieve the
superb horror of the contrasts in the other, using
instead a hard-bitten black and white, like certain
woodcuts. Satire dominates the greater part of his
work. Although Dunbar was a man of family, there
is a certain bourgeois strain in him : it is one of his
seventeenth-century qualities, and perhaps one of the
reasons why he got on better with Margaret Tudor
than with her husband, who tolerated and probably
liked him, but steadily refused the advancement for
which he clamoured. And the favourite bourgeois
emotion is disapproval, which is not at all the same
thing as contempt. Contempt is sure of itself, and its
note, in art, is " Non ragionam di lor, ma guarda, e
passa." You find that, magnificently, in *The Twa
Maryit Wemen*, where he does look and pass, without a

word, but the look sees everything, and assesses it.
There are times, however, when he does *ragionare*, in
a grumble not without envy of what he dislikes. To
be fair, one must distinguish this from the mere joyful virtuosity of invective for its own sake, in which he
is a master. But the element shows its head in him
now and then, as it was to do increasingly in Scots
society in the next generation, until some century
later it swamped Scots art and drowned it : one has
glimpses at times of its authentic differentia, the
hatred with an envy of the thing hated, a self-conscious self-assertion in the hater, that leads—though
not as yet, and not in Dunbar—to the rancorous
loathing of all things that are gracious and assured,
from fine manners to the carved work of the sanctuary.

As yet it is only here and there, however, that one
catches this unpleasing quality, unless there is perhaps
a little of it in the very predominance of satire in
Dunbar's work. His subjects are the customary ones,
the Church, the law, the court, and of course women.
After the dispassionate venom and the sheer decorative quality of the *Twa Maryit Wemen*, the best,
artistically, are the very dissimilar *Feinzit Freir of
Tungland*, where satire, or rather lampoon, caracoles
in exultant vehemence of the grotesque, and *The Dans
of the Sevin Deidly Sinnis*, which has the Cellini exuber-
ance of decoration that marks his pageant-poetry, to
which this, in fact, is a sort of anti-masque.

The *Freir* is a topical caricature, of one of the King's
scientific protégés, an Italian physician who made
unsuccessful experiments in both alchemy and aviation, damaging himself badly in an attempt to
" glide " from the Rock of Stirling. Dunbar, who
had not the type of mind that is sympathetic to

attempt at the unachieved—as I say, he has a touch of the smug Lallan bailie—gives a lively if libellous account of his medical and clerical past, and a really joyful gallopade of his adventures among the fowls of the air, who are astonished at this strange creature in feathered wings :

> Sum held he had bene Daedalus,
> Sum the Minotaur mervalus,
> Sum the Martis smith Wlcanus,
>   And sum Saturnus kuke.
> And evir the cushattis at him tuggit,
> The rukes him rent, the ravynis him ruggit,
> The hudit crawis his hair furth druggit,
>   The hevyn he micht nat bruik.
>
> The myttane, and Sanct Martynis fowle
> Wend he had been the horned owle :
> They set apone him with a yowle,
>   And gaif him dynt for dynt.
> The golk, the gormaw, and the gled
> Beft him with buffettis quhill he bled,
> The sparhawk to the spring him sped
>   Als fers as fyre of flynt.
>
> Thik was the clud of kayis and crawis,
> Of marleyonis, mittanis, and of mawis,
> That bikkrit at his berd with blawis,
>   In battaill him abowt.
> They nibblit him with noyis and cry,
> The rerd of them raiss to the sky,
> And evir he cryit on Fortune, Fy.
>   His lyfe wes into dout.

It has the headlong grotesquerie that is a recurrent note in Scots literature, from *Colkelbie's Sow* to Outram's *Annuity*, and since, to *Juan in America* : one finds it again, and with more sympathy, in *Kynd Kittok*, which is not so much satire as grotesquerie for its own sake, like *Tam o' Shanter*. The lady is an ale-wife who dies of drouth, and sets out for Heaven : she meets a newt riding on a snail, who gives her a lift, and dodging St Peter, contrives to get through the gate. The Deity is so amused at the way she jouked the saint that He lets her be, and she lives soberly for seven years as Our Lady's henwife. Then, looking out, she is homesick for her own ale—" the aill of Hevin wes sour." She slips out for a drink, and this time St Peter is more on the alert, so she is keeping a pub to this day between earth and Heaven, and Dunbar begs his friends to stop there as they go by, and have a drink for the good of the house.

The Sevin Deidly Sinnis is, as I have said, an anti-masque to such things as *The Thrissil and the Rois* and *The Goldyn Targe*. Its allegorical pageant-procession goes back to Lorris, or rather to Jehan de Meung, and the Seven Sins themselves were a favourite medi-aeval subject in all the arts. There is no greater test of an artist's originality than the way in which he deals with such stock material. Dunbar's handling of this has splendid vigour, with the same glittering solidity, in a strong and rather angular design, that one finds in contemporary Flemish painting. But this is not painting : it is a dance, and it moves, with a sort of violent ballet-wheel, the rapid couplets, mostly on double rhymes, caught back hard against the four-times-repeated rhyme of the short lines, that gives its verse the strange harmonised movement of concurrent rhythms of which few men are masters but Dunbar a great one :

> Nixt him in dans cum Covatyce,
> Rut of all evill and grund of vyce,
> That nevir cowd be content.

Caityvis, wreches, and okkeraris,
Hud-pykis, hurdaris, and gadderaris,
    All with that warlo went.
Out of thair throtis they schot on oder
Het moltin gold, me thocht a fudder,
    As fireflawcht maist fervent.
Ay as they tomit them of schot,
Feyndis filld them new up to the throt,
    With gold of alkyn prent.

His other pageant-work is very unlike this, being
courtly decorative stuff, the equivalent in verse of the
masque and ballet that all through the fifteenth and
sixteenth and (out of Scotland) the seventeenth centuries, till the Roi Soleil grew too old to dance, were
a regular part of any festival, whether civic, courtly,
or academic. *The Thrissil and the Rois* was written for
the King's wedding. It is completely traditional stuff
in the same convention as Chaucer's wedding-masque,
The Parlement of Foules, and beautifully done, with a
lovely opening of landscape, " anamcllit richly with
new azure lycht," just touched with dry realism in a
hint at the contrast between the May of poetry and
the May of East Coast fact. After the crowning by
Nature of the Lion and the Eagle as Kings of Beasts
and of Fowls, the " awful Thrissil," " kepit with a
busche of speiris " is given " a radius crown of
rubeis " and wedded to " the fresche Rois, of cullour
reid and quhyt," and the close is an enchanting
chorus of bird-song whose rhyme-royal takes on a
strange chiming harmony, not Chaucer's plangent
note, but individual and beautiful, the suggestion of
the choiring of many voices that is one of Dunbar's
greatest gifts. One has something of it again in the
little song sung after dinner on the wedding-day, with

the refrain, " Welcome of Scotland to be Queen."
There is nothing in it, but the enchanting pattern of
sound, unresolved until its close, has grace enough to
make it a fitter offering for Margaret's grand-
daughter.

Dunbar's greatest thing in this masque-type, however, is the magnificent *Goldyn Targe*, the finest thing
of its kind in the language, above even Chaucer's
work in this type of poem. It is not an " occasional "
piece, but a love-allegory, and in fact an odd production for a priest, though to be sure he does seem to
have resembled the Abbé d'Herblay, better known as
Aramis, and his relations with pretty ladies like Mrs
Musgrave may not all have been on the spiritual
plane. But it may have been written for the King or
some other patron. There is a sort of rueful sincerity
under the convention, but it need not mean that
Dunbar was, on that occasion, speaking for himself—
at any rate in more than the expression of his habitual
delight in certain forms of beauty. There is no doubt
about that. From its lovely opening in a May dawn
it is full of the jewelled glittering colour, the *net*
enamelled luminescence, that he loved.

> Full angelike thir birdis sang thair houris
> Within thair courtyns grene into thair bouris,
>   Apparalit quhyte and reid wyth blumis suete.
> Anamellit was the felde with all colouris,
> The perly droppis shuke in siluer schouris,
>   Quhill all in balm did branch and levis flete.
>   Depairt fra Phebus, did Aurora grete :
> Her cristall teris I saw hing on the flouris,
>   Quhilk he for lufe all drank vp with his hete.

Above all there is his joy in clear water and the clear
lights of Northern sun under a washed sky.

Doun throw the ryss ane ryuir ran with stremys
Sa lustily agayn thae likand lemys,
   That all the lake as lamp did leme of licht,
Quhilk schadovit all about with twynkling glemis
That bewis bathit wer in secund bemis,
   Throw the reflex of Phebus visage brycht.
   On every syde the hegis raise on hicht,
The bank wes grene, the bruke was full of bremys,
   The stanneris clere as stern in frosty nycht.

His eye for it shows in the play of *reflected* light in

   The roch agayn the ryuir resplendent
   As low enlumynit all the levis schene.

The patterning of the sense of colours is notable :
they are not merely chance bright splashes, but parts
of a visualised design, built up before the mind's eye
like architecture. These glinting reflections of water
succeed a perfect rainbow of jewel-names and
heraldic tinctures, and then, out of the richness,

   I saw approach agayn the orient sky
   Ane saill als quhyte as blossum vpon spray

is climax and resolution of the symphony of colour as
much as close to the action of this iridescent prelude.
The ship bears " all the chois of Venus cheualry," and
Jean Fouquet made no more decorative design in
those lovely miniatures of the castled Loire country.
The transparent quality Dunbar gives all his lights
may seem faintly unnatural to an English reader, if
he has any : but Dunbar was a man of East Scotland,
where light does give that sense of being seen through
crystal. Chaucer's " Al the Orient laugheth of the
lighte " is deservedly famous. But it can be paralleled,
and surpassed, a hundred times in Dunbar, from what

is obviously his own direct observation, not a remembrance of

Lo bel pianeta . . .
Faceva rider tutto l'oriente.

In praising *The Goldyn Targe* above Chaucer, I do not mean to call Dunbar the greater poet. He was not. He has a much lesser range, nothing of Chaucer's great narrative gift, his pity, and consequently his humanity. But in this pure decorative verse, the equivalent, in letters, of the Cellini tradition of goldsmith's work, Dunbar's only equal, at his best, is Spenser, whose set-pieces rival him in the softer, more flowing and ample Italian manner, as against Dunbar's French and Flemish *netteté*. It is not the greatest kind of poetry : but Dunbar is on the pinnacle of the kind.

It is in some of the shorter pieces that his note is deepest. They are not all deep : some of them are occasional compliment, like the description of the elaborate pageants that graced a royal visit to Aberdeen, or the stately praise of London : one observes, by the way, that he has *seen* the city—seen it, no doubt, in highly complimentary terms and without any reference to the local stenches, but seen it undoubtedly. There are the sufficiently numerous begging-pieces : Dunbar was as impecunious as most poets. Not all are either begging or compliment. Things like the famous *Flyting of Dunbar and Kennedy* are the precise reverse of any aureation of praise. These cursing-matches in verse were a literary game that goes back to the *tenso* of the Troubadours, and Dunbar's immense vocabulary and swinging verve of metre made him a formidable antagonist. His metrical skill seldom left him. Some of the finest examples of it are in the graceless and probably tactless *Dregie*, a parody, sufficiently profane, of a requiem, addressed to the King, who had gone into retreat at Stirling. Listen to the peal of the bells in the *responsiones*. (The *-ioun* termination is in two syllables.)

> Tak consolatioun in zour pane.
> In tribulatioun tak consolatioun,
> Out of vexatioun come hame agane.
> Tak consolatioun in zour pane.

The serious lyrics are sometimes very lovely. Some of these are occasional pieces also, like the lament for Bernard Stuart d'Aubigny, Commander of the Garde écossaise, Marshal of France, and one of the great captains of his day, who came to his own country as French Ambassador, and died there of fever in 1508. (It was he once, captured in Spain, who made terms for his command, that they should go free with the honours of war, but " fier comme un Écossais," refused them for himself, and " sharply rebuked two young lords his kinsmen, for that more faintly than was fit for men, namely for their being Scotsmen and of the blood royal, they did bewail the unfortunate success of the war.") " Laureate " work as it is, it has genuine feeling. Indeed, it is usually in the darker moods that his lyrics are best, though there are exceptions like the lovely Hymn to Our Lady that begins *Rorate coeli desuper*, happily using the introit for the Annunciation to open a Nativity Carol like a tall painted window in winter sunlight—a Strachan window with silver lights in it.

> Rorate celi desuper !
> Hevinis distill zour balmy schouris,
> For now is rissin the bricht day ster
> Fro the rois Mary, flour of flouris.

> The cleir Sone, quhome no clud devouris
> Surmounting Phebus in the est,
>   Is cumin of his hevinly touris,
>   *Et nobis Puer natus est.*

The companion *Ballat of Our Lady* is perhaps less lovely, though it is a marvellous tour de force as metre. It has not the organ-roll of

> Dame du ciel, régente terrienne,
> Emperière des infernaux palus (34) :

it is in fact the equivalent of the crazy richness of decoration in Roslin Chapel, but like Roslin it is not " pretty : " there is an arrogant vigour under the wild intricacy.

> Haile, qwene serene, haile, maist amene,
>   Haile, hevinlie hie empryss.
> Haile, schene, vnseyne with carnale eyne,
>   Haile, rois of paradys.
> Haile, clene, bedene, ay till conteyne,
>   Haile, fair fresche flour-de-lyce.
> Haile, grene daseyne, haile, fro the splene,
>   Of Jhesu genetrice.
>   *Ave Maria, gratia plena,*
>   Thow bair the Prince of pryss,
> Our teyne to meyne, and ga betweyne,
>   Ane hevinlie oratrice.

These are not his only " divine " poems, though they are the best known, and *Rorate coeli* is perhaps the most beautiful. In his older years, perhaps when the shock of Flodden had sobered him and turned his mind towards the *Summa rerum*, he made a *Ballat of the Passioun of Christ*, a fine thing, nowise conventional, that marches through stark steady detail of vision, like a Flemish painting, with a deep sense in it of pity and of contrition, rising to a grave hope in the Resurrection, to be ratified in the Communion of Easter.

> With greiting glaid be than come Grace,
>   With wourdis sweit saying to me,
> Ordane for Him ane resting place,
>   That is so werie wrocht for the.
> The Lord within this dayis thrie
>   Sall law undir thy lyntell bou,
> And in thy hous sall herbrit be
>   *The blissit Salvator Jesu.*

Among the more serious of the " lay " lyrics, there is a bitter grace in the song to a lady who has no rue in the garden of her beauties, but as far as love-poetry goes, Dunbar's best outside the *Targe* is the *débat* of *The Merle and the Nichtingale*, who hold the poetic equivalent of the formal academic disputes the flytings parodied (35), this time between sacred and profane love. The matter is conventional, though it does not sound insincere. The form has nothing second-hand about its use of the familiar octave, and the conclusion, where the two sing together, has something of the harmonic quality of the bird-song in *The Thrissil and the Rois*. One hears it again in the piece that has some of his sincerest feeling in it, the Ash Wednesday bird-song with the famous

> Come nevir yet May sa fresche and grene
> But Januar come als wode and kene.
> Wes nevir sic drowth but anes cam rain.
> All erdly joy returnis in pane.

He revolts at times, worldling though he is, against " the wavering of this wrechit warld of sorrow." Sometimes there is a reconciliation, as in the famous *Meditatioun in Wyntir*. But it is never a very deep or

G

lasting reconciliation. He was a man of his age, intensely conscious of the black gulf of nothing that stretched around its violent opulence and with little hold on the ultimate Sense of the Cross to bridge its dark night. He knows, as the rest know—the remembrance of it is passionate and recurrent—that " thy pomp shall go down to the grave, and the noise of thy viols, the worm be spread under thee, and the worm cover thee." They could not but see the skull behind the beauty, yet could not sit easily enough to mortality to accept it, as the true Middle Age had done, and reach out beyond. There is a grim and profound sense of evanescence in the sombre procession of the dead that is perhaps his most famous piece of work, where all his jewellery of rhythm and colour subdue themselves to a stark grey onward movement, like the vaulting of a crypt. It is not the defiant fantasy of the *danse macabre*, but a march of hooded shadows that have been men.

The dirge of dead poets that is its epilogue was grim enough for Dunbar, " quhen he wes seik." Our history has made it grimmer still, for out of twenty-five poets that he mentions, how many mean anything to a modern Scot ? Of five, indeed—and he speaks of them with praise—not a single letter of their work is left, and more than half the rest are only shadows.

In that world of ghosts, the two others that are clearest in that generation are Walter Kennedy of the *Flyting* with Dunbar, and Gavin Douglas, Bishop of Dunkeld. And one of these is as much a *memento mori* as the lost men, Heriot and Traill and Ross and Stobo. Kennedy was a man of family, and a scholar, Master of Arts of Glasgow, where he served as examiner in

1481. He was a figure at the brilliant court of a king still Invictissimus : Douglas—no mean judge—puts him above Dunbar, as " the greit Kennedie." But scarcely a line is left of him but his share in the *Flyting* —and what would Dunbar's be as sample of Dunbar ? We know that he could write with vigour, and his *Prais of Age*, a sober acquiescent elegiac, shows that flyting was not his only mood. But whether he may have written a *Goldyn Targe* . . . *Autant en emporte ly vens*. He may have lived to see Chepman and Myllar print, but even much later it was the common habit of court-poets, in all countries, to circulate their works in MS. and print only when their friends took to mangling what they copied. " Literary " literature, at any time, appeals to only a small proportion of a nation. In a country whose total population was just about that of the modern City of London in working hours—that is, a million—that proportion, even if relatively high, is numerically small. And the court of the Stewarts was very much, by the time the monasteries were degenerate, the cultural centre of Scotland. Even the Highland gentry came about it : one of my forebears, whose habitat was a far cry beyond Lochow, was on James's Privy Council. The war on the arts that was so soon to follow had a very vulnerable enemy.

Gavin Douglas is much less shadowy. In fact, we know more of him, as a man, than we do of Dunbar, and we have at least the greater part of his work, which places him among the traditional major Four of the middle Stewarts. He was an important person, a Red Douglas—a son of Archibald Bell-the-Cat, no less, so that it is scarcely surprising that Erasmus comments on his regal dignity of bearing. He was born under James III, about 1475, graduated at St Andrews, became a priest, held charges in the North-east and in the Lothians, became Provost of St Giles and a freeman of Edinburgh, and seems to have had a peaceful and honourably successful career in the Church and in letters, until middle age, when Flodden threw him into the storms of James V's minority. As a Lord of the Council of Regency he helped the Queen Dowager's marriage with Angus his nephew. It made him Bishop of Dunkeld, with a promise, never kept, of the Primacy : but Albany's return from France couped the Douglas creel, and sent Douglas, with Angus and the Queen, into exile. He died of plague in 1522, at the court of his niece-in-law's brother, and was buried in the Royal Chapel of the Savoy, as became a grand-uncle of the Margaret Douglas who was more than once proclaimed heir to the English throne (36), to which her grandson in fact was to succeed. His epitaph is *Patria sua exul*.

The only work we know definitely for his consists of two poems in the pageant-allegory tradition, *King Hart* and *The Palice of Honour*, and his remarkable translation of Vergil, the first in verse in either form of English. He translated also the *Remedium Amoris*, but this is lost : he is also said, on rather doubtful authority, to have written certain *Comoediae Sacrae*, but if he ever did, they have disappeared.

The Palice is a dream of the difficult path to true glory, and the less elaborate *King Hart* sees the Heart of Man as a king in his castle, with a suggestion of the tumultuous Stewart minorities in the courtiers, Strength, Wantonness, Disport, and so forth, who attempt to control him. They are court-pieces in the aureate tradition, but although their morality sounds sincere enough, they have not the glittering beauty of Dunbar. None the less, there are strokes of fine imaginative quality in things like the picture of King Hart's castle, the contrast of the feasting within and the salt sour water circling it about. There is considerable dramatic sense, too, in the handling of the narrative, and its figures are given a certain concreteness of personality. In his method of handling allegory he recalls Spenser so strongly that it seems probable the latter was his pupil : the *Palice* was printed in London in 1553, and Douglas's reputation in England was considerable, so that the younger poet must have known him . . . must have liked him, too, for there is real poetry in Douglas, of a kind and quality by no means common in the English poets in the century-and-three-quarters between Spenser and his greatest master, Chaucer. Sackville, in fact, is the only Englishman of the period one can put beside him, and Sackville is admittedly one of Spenser's models. But the general artistic method of the *Faerie Queene* is closer to *King Hart* than to *The Mirror for Magistrates*.

The deeper poetic qualities of Douglas's work show to more advantage, in his *Eneidos*. His version of the famous passage in Book VI will serve as example :

Thay walkit furth so derk oneath thay wist
Quhidder thay went amyddis dim schadowis thare,
Quhare evir is nicht, and nevir licht dois repair,
Throwout the waste dungeoun of Pluto king,
Thay roid boundis and the gousty ring,
Siklyke as quha wald throw thik woodis wend,
In obscure licht quhare none may nat be kend,
As Jupiter the king etherial
With erdis skug hidis the hevynnys al,
And the mirk nicht with her vysage grey
From every thing has reft the hew away.

The translation itself is notable enough : perhaps it northernises Vergil to some extent, gives him a certain colour of something like *Beowulf*. (But Vergil, after all, was not a Latin.) He does not achieve the Vergilian music, however. His couplets are competent, but they have no more chant than Pope's—much less indeed, than his own rhyme-royal in *King Hart* : his visual imagination is stronger than his auditory. It appears, very notably, in the famous interludes between the books, which are the best of his original work, and show him not only a poet but a pioneer, in more than the great group of Renaissance translators. He is the first poet in our language to take landscape in itself and for itself as a subject—not merely a setting for a subject—of poetic emotion. The quality and the reality of the emotion—his own, with no tradition to guide or arouse it—show in the famous summer nightpiece of the Thirteenth Prologue :

> Yondir doun dwinis the evin sky away,
> And vpspringis the brycht dawing of the day,
> Intill ane other place nocht far in sondir,
> Quhilk to behald was pleasans and half wondir.

The late W. P. Ker, that teacher *valde deflendus*, says of it : " He sees a new thing in the history of the world ... and in naming it he gives the interpretation, also, the spirit of poetry : pleasance and half wonder." The Seventh Prologue, of Winter, is perhaps more famous, and as description more original.

> Bewtie wes lost, and barrand schew the landis.
> With frostis haire ourfret the feildis standis.
> Soure bitter bubbis, and the schowris snell
> Semyt on the sward ane similitude of hell,
> Reducyng to our mynd, in every steid,
> Goustly schadowis of eild and grisly deid.

Thik drumly scuggis derknit so the hevyne,
Dim skyis oft furth-warpit ferful levyne,
Flaggis of fyir, and mony felloun flaw,
Scharp soppis of sleit, and of the snipand snaw.
The dowy diches war all donk and wait,
The law vaillé flodderit al with spait. . . .
Broun muris kithit thair wysnit mossy hewe. . . .
The wynd maid wayfe the reid weyd on the dyke. . . .
The grund stude barrand, widderit, dosk, and grey.
    Wide-quhair with fors so Eolus schouttis schyll
In this congealit sessoune scharp and chyll,
The callour air, penetrative and pure,
Dasyng the bluide in every creature,
Made seik warm stovis, and beyn fyris hot,
In double garment clad and wylycoat,
With mychty drink, and meytis confortive,
Agayn the storme wyntre for to strive.

This is not new to us. But it *was* quite new. Douglas
is the first poet in any form of the language deliberately to paint wild weather—indeed to paint landscape
on any considerable scale—for its own sake, to find
the aesthetic pleasure in it as such, not merely as the
appropriate setting for some thrill of adventure among
wildness. He is thus a figure of cardinal importance
in the development of all nature-poetry, not only in
English. (And after the Gulf, it was a Scotsman,
James Thomson, the forerunner of the eighteenth-
century Risorgimento, who recovered that note and
brought it into England, making it one of the main
elements in the great Romantic movement that was
to colour the literature of Europe.) Once, too, as I,
or rather Ker, have just said, he states in a line the
very core of that movement. And he brought Vergil
into our language, not as a remote enchanter or a
distant quarry for tales, but as a piece of literature.

It is not an inconsiderable achievement for a bishop-diplomat of an age in the main fundamentally un-poetic. None the less, although he is the dawn of that Renaissance we were never to possess, he is, as artist, less considerable than Dunbar. His verse is rougher, less finished, less professional, and his mass of observation, as close and true as it is, does sometimes over-load and blur his design.

There is, by the way, an interesting point about his language. Perhaps because he was an exile, he calls it " Scottis." He is the first to use the word in that sense. Dunbar and Henryson—Barbour for that matter—do not write the same language as Chaucer, and presumably were aware of the fact, as Mr Herges-heimer is aware that a Scot or an Englishman takes his luggage by railway while he takes his baggage by railroad, and (quite rightly) considers both idioms correct for the country of their respective use. So Dunbar considers Chaucer's speech and his own both forms of " Inglis "—and Lindsay, writing a generation later, but before the anglicising movement begun by Knox, calls Douglas himself " of our *Inglis* rhetorike the rose." In practice, of course, the patriotic poet tries no tariff measures of vocabulary. Like his brethren, he took his wealth where he found it. If no native word was to hand, he imported one—French, Latin, English, or Scandinavian, " as the Romans did Greek " (37). The analogy happens to be Douglas' own, when he had to apologise to his purist con-science. The language in fact was in the later fif-teenth century passing into the almost violent stage of growth that English in England was to know a little later, in preparation for the great Elizabethans. But Scotland had Knox and Melville for Marlowe and

Spenser, and they tickled her muses othergates than the latter.

Douglas outlived Dunbar, and is not in that ghost-procession of dead makaris, who drift, *da morte disfatti . . . come d'autunno le foglie*, in the rear of Dunbar's lament, pitiful echoes of the court of a king who so loved music and the gracious arts. They were, for the opening sixteenth century, the conspicuous names of the last century and a quarter, the men who, to a chief poet of his day, were the memorable figures of that time in Scottish letters, or at any rate enough to conjure up these, for the list is not necessarily a librarian's catalogue : we know it is incomplete, for one of the most conspicuous of all, the poet great-grandfather of Dunbar's chief patron, is omitted, although earlier names are there.

Three of the twenty-five are distinguished foreigners. " The noble Chaucer, of makaris flour," has the pre-eminence that was his due, and the English Gower and Lydgate, fashionable and successful men of letters in their day, and the former a writer of considerable talent, go with him. Then come twenty-two of his own fellow countrymen,

> Throwout the waste dungeoun of Pluto king.

Barbour and Blind Harry, Henryson and Wyntoun and (if hc is Hucheon) Sir Hew of Eglinton, are less " bereavit " than the rest, though we know for a fact that about half of Barbour's work is lost. But as for the others . . . these ghosts are all but voiceless. Ettrick and Heriot, Lockhart, Ross, and " gude gentill Stobo " have been sunk without trace. They may have been responsible for some of the anonymous verse that survives, and is often of beauty. Some of the rest are scarcely less unsubstantial. James Affleck *may* be the author of one poem in the Selden MS. John Clerk, who like him practised " ballat-making and tragedie," is a shade more fortunate. He *may* have been the gentleman to whom Dunbar describes Andro Kennedy as leaving " Guid's braid malison and mine," and he *may* also be the author of five pieces in the Bannatyne MS.—varied, for the five include religious, amorous, and satiric-humorous. One of them is the pleasant *Wowyng of Jok and Jinny*, a lively rustic affair with a burlesque description of the tocher, in a tradition that comes down through Burns to Violet Jacob and Charles Murray. Clerk of Tranent I have spoken of already as among the last romancers. Holland was a priest, exiled to England with the Douglases. We have a political allegory of his, *The Boke of the Howlat*, but its allusions are so intricately up-to-the-minute it is difficult to follow. Hay, a knight, a graduate in arts and law, and Chamberlain to Charles VII of France, wrote poems, and is one of the claimants for *Alexander*, but his known work survives only in prose, which is described elsewhere. Johnstone has one religious piece in the Bannatyne MS., and he acted plays before James IV : we know no more of him. Mersar is highly praised as a poet of love, and was still famous a generation later, but all that is left of him appears to be one grim recension, in the Maitland MS., of the old " Earth upon earth " poem, on the text

> Eird gois apone eird glitterand in gold,
> ȝit sall eird go to eird sonar nor he wold,

and three pieces in Bannatyne, one a warning to women against lightness, in a curious hitched metre,

one another warning against the wiles of inconstant
men, and the third a sermon in verse on the Whole
Duty of Lovers : it is pleasantly sententious, but none
of the four suggest a technique on the level of Dunbar's. Of the two Rules all that we know is where
they lived, that they were good fellows, that one of
them is presumably the author of a religious satire in
the Bannatyne and Maitland MSS., and that he, or
the other one, wrote a rather endearing piece of invective, *The Cursing of Schir John Ruill apone the Stelaris of
his Foulis* : the two are not much as the total " remains " of a brace of poets. Brown is so vague that
there has been serious argument as to whether he was
a man or merely a misprint : Bannatyne reads " tane
Broun " where Maitland has " done roun." But one
religious poem in the former's collection is attributed
to him. Shaw, the last to die, has at least an identity,
as the son of James III's Ambassador to Denmark—in
fact, a person of some social standing : but all that
remains of his writings is one shrewd satire, on the
text " Knaw courtis, and wynd, has oftsys vareit."
And as for Dunbar himself, it is true that we have
what may be most of his work. But if four manu-
scripts had chanced to be lost before 1834, in three
centuries of assorted (and Scottish) history, he would
be almost as ghostly as most of his neighbours. And
he was the laureate of a brilliant court, at one of the
pinnacles of our history, very little more than four
centuries ago.

To these ghosts may be added Prior Henry of
Kelso, who *floruit* about 1500 and is said to have made
a translation of Rutilius' *De Re Rustica*, and a Greek
poem on Our Lady for Lorenzo de' Medici ; and one
or two other names which appear in Bannatyne, and

may belong more or less to this time. A patriotic poem, *the Ring* (règne) *of the Roy Robert*, describes the pointed retort of Robert III to a claim for homage made by Henry IV of England, who is forcibly reminded both of past treaties and of that habit of his own country, of being perpetually under foreign rulers, that in fact is one of the curiosities of its history. It is ascribed to one Dean David Steill, but we know no more of him, nor even whether his deanery was ecclesiastical or municipal : one may guess the latter, as two love-poems are ascribed to *Steil* in the Bannatyne MS. As Queen Caroline said, however, " Cela n'empêche pas," at that period : but there may have been another man of the same name, and in any case, no one is born in orders. Lichtoun, a monk, has a couple of poems in Bannatyne, one with the stately opening, " O mortal man, remember nicht and day," not ill followed up, the other a rather tedious non-sense-piece, remarkably like some ultra-modern poetry of the nineteen-twenties. The printer's adver-tisement of *The Thrie Talis of the Thrie Prestis of Peblis*, three " moral stories " resembling in manner the more decent ones in the *Decameron*, and printed in 1603, though written, apparently, before 1491, mentions a " delectabill discourse," *Biblo*, which is lost. No reference to it has been traced anywhere else.

On the assumptions of an age that believed more fully in the trousered god Progress than in the Trinity, the fact that these men and their works are lost shows that they could not have mattered. But the exquisite work of Alexander Scott survived precariously for centuries in one MS. copy, that might have vanished in any siege or spring-cleaning or fit of religious fervour that happened to come to one of its various owners. And if all but one of my works were to be lost I think I should like to choose which was to survive. One wonders how blindly the poppy has been scattered.

IV

WHAT SHOULD HAVE BEEN OUR RENAISSANCE

Flodden and after—Lindsay—more ghosts—the Reformation—Queen Mary—Scott—The Bannatyne and Maitland MSS.—anonymous work—Montgomerie—Boyd—Hume—James VI—Drummond—Ayton—Stirling—Ancrum—Hannay—Mure—Charles I—Montrose—the end o' the sang

THE earlier sixteenth century continued the literary traditions of the late fifteenth, though as a rule with less of " aureation," and although there is no single figure as notable as Dunbar, for some time yet the marked superiority of Scots literature over the contemporary English work still obtains. The best things of Alexander Scott compare very favourably with the best of Wyatt or Surrey. The Englishmen show the coming of the new, Italianate, inspiration, that was scarcely to touch Scotland, though it lit France and England so gloriously, but their attempts at the new have little merit except as pioneering, and their really accomplished work, things like Wyatt's beautiful *Forget not yet* and *My Lute*, do not show the new fashion : and lovely as they are, they are not above Scott's best. The Scottish poets have the advantage, of course, of writing with a fuller and richer native literature immediately behind them. England had less of that even than appears to us, for the fifteenth century changes in the language, which brought it much nearer the Scottish than Chaucer's had been, had made Chaucer's obsolete, and so blinded readers to his exquisite craftsmanship : he became merely a good-natured barbarian who told pleasant stories in a broken-backed metre—a specimen, in fact, of " l'art confus de nos vieux romanciers," who was to require, even at the end of the seventeenth century, to be *débrouillé* for polite consumption. Since Chaucer—and he was over a hundred years dead—there had only been Malory, Berners' translation, a handful of songs, and Skelton's lively rattle, while Scotland during the same period had a flourishing literature with a high standard of craftsmanship.

But in 1513 came the beginning of the end. James, *Rex Pacificator* by his papal title, found that his efforts to keep the peace were useless, and moved to help his ally Louis XII. He and his father had created a useful navy, that included the largest warship of her time ; and captains like the Woods and Sir Andrew Barton had shown its efficiency against English pirates. He led a fine army, finely trained and equipped, and so far as is known without the common disunion of command that wrecked most Scots military enterprises involving the handling of large masses of troops. But its arms were old-fashioned : it relied on the long straight pike, with the long cutting sword as second weapon, that in Swiss and Flemish and Scottish hands had made the schiltrom formidable since Courtrai. The Englishmen were armed with the " brown bill."

It was like Sadowa and the needle-gun. The axe-head of the bill shore off the pike-point, leaving it a mere clumsy wooden stave : the cutting sword was useless against the bill with its six-foot ironed shaft. The King and his officers, leading on foot with pikes, went down at the first onset : their men, with no one left to bring them off, died where they stood. Surrey testifies to their courage, but it was less a battle than a massacre. The bloody business of slaughter went on till dark. The King was killed, two bishops, two mitred abbots, twelve earls, thirteen lords, five eldest sons of peers, gentlemen from every family of name in Scotland, and ten thousand at least, it was computed at the time, of their troops. Scotland was left to the old men and the women, a King of two years old, a wanton fool of a Queen Dowager.

The sheer magnitude and completeness of the disaster, and something in it like the endings of the sagas, have made it stand out in Scots national remembrance, by Bannockburn itself. But although it caught the imagination like the Mohacs of the succeeding generation, reverberating across Europe till there were ballads on it in Italy, it was not a Mohacs—directly. Scotland stiffened to a tearless resolution : the proclamation of the Edinburgh Town Council sends one's head up yet. In fact, the immediate political and military consequences were less serious than those of some lesser defeats. But the day before Flodden is the crest of the wave. In 1500 Scotland was a European power, important out of any proportion to her size, with a lively national culture. In 1600 she was still politically important, her alliance sought as far as Italy, but her civilisation was rapidly going to pieces. In 1700 she was negligible, both culturally and politically, and although by the end of the century her culture had made a brilliant recovery and her intellectual influence in Europe was very much greater than most historians care to recognise, Cromwell had ended her as a political force. Popular tradition, in fact, has not been wrong in seeing in Flodden something like Ragnarok.

If the King had been older, things might have been better. But there were years of turmoil when no man was master and many strove for mastery. Ten years after Flodden, Surrey could so ravage the Border that Wolsey boasted, in a phrase that might be Attila's, " there is left neither house, fortress, village, tree, cattle, corn, nor other succour of man." *Cet animal, en effet, était bien méchant* to object to annexation by the Lord's chosen. James struggled to manhood, to a torn kingdom, a wrecked palace, a treasury plundered by a regent who stole his father's plate and jewels. If he had lived to be more than thirty-one, he might have pulled matters round : he lacked neither courage nor intelligence—we owe him, for instance, such things as the first Coastal Survey—and he was luckier in his wife. If gallant level-headed Marie de Guise, one of the bravest figures in Scots history, and one of the most ungratefully vilified, had been in Margaret Tudor's place after Flodden, or perhaps still more, before Flodden, the course of Scots history might have been different.

Inter arma—especially *inter bella civilia*—*silent musae*. But the partial recovery of James' too short personal reign, the influence, after, of a brilliant Queen-Dowager bred at the court of François Ier, postponed for a while the *Götterdämmerung* of Scots letters. The tradition, the temper that made them possible, was still there, and until well past the middle of the century Scotland had still a literature of distinction.

The early part of the reign has not much to show, except the work of David Lindsay, a voluminous and successful writer, of considerable merit, whose posthumous fate, however, is rather disproportionate, merit considered, to that of some of his fellows. Later on, there is still some beautiful work from Mont-gomerie, Alexander Scott, and a number of more ghostly figures, and even after the establishment of the Reformation had staved off a Scots Renaissance to the far side of 1750, the tradition of Scots literary poetry survived in a thin trickle, in the work of a half-dozen or so of Royalist gentlemen, into the first half of the seventeenth century, though all its practitioners except Montrose (who as a poet is the least of them) were born in the sixteenth, and most of them grew up in it.

The oldest of the post-Flodden men is

Sir David Lindsay of the Mount, Lord Lyon King at Arms,

who was a courtier of James V's through that monarch's life-time, and lived well into Queen Marie's regency, dying in 1555. He had been a member of James IV's household : we know that he acted in a play at Holyrood in 1511, and was attached to the infant Prince of Scotland, that he had much to do with the many dramatic entertainments of the Court, and that like Dunbar he went on embassies—one to Germany to inspect some proposed Queens of Scots and another to Antwerp, renewing treaties of commerce—and, again like Dunbar, that he was a sort of semi-official King's Poet (38), writing a *Deploration of the Death of Queen Magdalene* and a little later superintending the " fearsis and plays " at the reception of her successor. He had the King's personal favour until James' death, and was Lyon King at Arms from 1529. Like Dunbar he was habitually a satirist, and as such did not lack matter. But he is not in the same intellectual class : he has nothing that so combines power, vision, and venomous subtlety as *The Twa Maryit Wemen*. His satire is largely of the prevailing looseness of morals, but itself shows a considerable gusto in sculduddery, found frequently, but seldom with such frankness, in the tastes of professed reformers of public morals. It is not impossibly his combination of this element with a pungent anti-clericalism that caused his popularity to survive the Reformation. He was read and praised for a couple of centuries by men who would certainly have agreed with those who were scandalised by Charles I's affection for Shakespeare ; he was praised, if not read, for most of a couple more : only this morning, in fact, I saw him called " a Founder of the Scottish Reformation " by a reverend gentleman who, if he happened to have read *Squyer Meldrum* or the Induction to the second *Thrie Estatis*, might possibly have thought the claim, though true, was not altogether tactful.

From the purely literary point of view his work, though it never reaches the level of Douglas or Dunbar, shows both vigour and considerable talent. Though not of Dunbar's quality, it descends in the main from his school, with nothing that anticipates the *dolce stil nuovo* of Alexander Scott. His satiric allegory, *The Dreme* (1528), is rather in the key of Douglas's work of the kind, and tolerably dull, though there is some excellently vigorous winter landscape in its induction, where he walks on the sands in January. He wanders through Hell, Purgatory, the Stars, Heaven, Earth, Paradise, and Scotland, the last two of which do not greatly resemble each other. It ends with some sensible advice to the King, a recurrent note of Lindsay's, a shrewd and rather commonplace man of the world, but genuinely attached to a master who never forgot how he had played with an harassed and humiliated small boy who had even more than his share of the trials of a normal Stewart minority, that do so much, as in the parallel case of Louis XIV, to explain the Stewart tendency to absolutism. *The Dreme* sets the principal key for Lindsay's work : his long *Monarchie*, written in 1553, two years before his death, and dedicated to " James our Prince and Protectour and his brother Our Spirituall Gouernour and Prince of Preists in this Natioun" (The Regent, James Hamilton, Earl of Arran and Duke of Châtellerault—grandson of Princess Mary —and his half-brother John, Archbishop of St Andrews) is in the same vein, as are some intermediate works—a fact which coupled with Lindsay's known favour at court, suggests that both James V and his widow Queen Marie were considerably more tolerant than popular tradition admits. *The Monarchie*, which to his own day, and probably to Lindsay himself, was his principal work, is a very long dialogue, between Experience and a Courtier, on the unhappy state of the world, with a long account of the human race, from Creation to Judgment. I find that I have twice used *long* in describing it, and indeed the modern reader may well be forgiven if he finds himself bogged, for its 6000 lines need some heroism to tackle. Heavy as it was, it hit the taste of its day and the next generation : it was reprinted at Paris in 1558, with a delightful woodcut of Lindsay in his herald's tabard over what, from the combination of contemporary bonnet with buskins *à la grecque*, may be either a classical tunic or a kilt. An English version was printed in London in 1566, and frequently reissued, and a Danish one appeared in 1591. It is just possible that it may have affected the unfortunate Fifth Book of the *Faerie Queene*, where politics threaten to drown the poetry.

Between *The Dreme* and *The Monarchie* there are several other works, more or less in the same vein. The chief early piece—early relatively, for Lindsay's literary career does not seem to have begun till his late thirties, though as usual we do not know what is lost—is of 1530, *The Complaynt of the Kingis Papyngo* (parrot), an outspoken satire of Kirk and State, from the King downwards and inclusive, but directed especially against the religious orders. Its prologue, in praise of his brother Scottish poets, recalls the ghostly procession in Dunbar. There is a more personal venom in the piece that in his later work plays the same part to *The Monarchie* as the *Papyngo* to *The Dreme*, *The Tragedie of the umquhyle Maister Reuerende Fader David be the mercy of God Cardinal and Archbisshope of Sanctandrois*. It appeared in 1547, and is a professed imitation of *Bochas' tragedies* (Boccaccio's *De Casibus*) and a rather clever piece of sarcastic, rather than satiric, mock-heroic—a pseudo-tragic monologue in the mouth of the Cardinal's own ghost, who is made to confess his sins in the way of gambling and extravagance and, especially, of stopping the proposed visit of the King to England and refusing to make peace with the latter country unless on terms satisfactory to France : Lindsay, like most of his party, was strongly pro-English, and in spite of his affection for his master, he edges rather lightly round Solway Moss, an affair whose blame was not with the Cardinal's party.

There is a considerable bulk of minor satire, one of the liveliest and best known being one on fashion, *Anent Syde Taillis*, the enormous sweeping skirts of the early century. Outside satire, the sincerity of Lindsay's moral indignations may be gauged from *The Historie of Squyer Meldrum*, a sort of novel in the key of the *Heptameron*, but with the Scots preference for verse : it is in a rapid competent octosyllabic couplet. Meldrum was a real person, though Lindsay's portrait is said to be rather synthetic : it is certainly very typical of its age. He is drawn as—in contemporary phrase—*grand tueur de dames* and a tall man of his hands. He serves with the Scots Navy at the sack of Carrickfergus, where he behaves with commendable restraint in a rather embarrassing *bonne fortune*, and goes on to Picardy, where he dresses down a boastful Englishman, comes home again, via a really excellent sea-fight with a big English galleon, travels, receives *bon souper, bon gîte, et le reste* from a charming widow with rich lands in Strathearn, who is eventually married off while her protector lies wounded, and eventually dies in the odour of sanctity as the respectable Sheriff-depute of Fife. It was popular till late in the seventeenth century, an edition of which time has an engaging frontispiece of the Squire in the smartest garments of 1620, puffing most doggishly at a long pipe. It is in fact quite a lively piece of narrative : there is no personality, but the action moves, and with one exception, it is the most forward-looking of Lindsay's work, anticipating the *Heptameron* of eight years later rather than looking back to the romance.

The other exception is what, from a modern point of view, must be considered as his principal work. This is a play, of merit in itself and of great historical interest as almost all that survives of early Scottish vernacular drama. *Ane Plesand Satire of the Thrie Estaitis in Commendatioun of Vertew and Vituperatioun of Vyce* appears from a contemporary description to have been played in the great banqueting-hall at Linlithgow, before James and Marie de Guise, as part of the

Twelfth Night revels of 1540. The copy of it in the Bannatyne MS. says it was played in 1552, on the Castle Hill at Cupar, and the earliest printed text, Charteris's, gives it as represented two years later, on the Playfield at Greenside, before Queen Marie again, so that it appears to have been popular. As it antedates Bale's *Kyng Johan* by some seven years, it would seem that the secular development of the drama had moved more quickly than in England, probably through the close relation with France, where the secular use of the form had been current ever since Adam de la Halle in the mid-thirteenth century. Lindsay's English contemporary, Heywood, was in fact writing secular interludes, but *The Thrie Estaitis* is a much more elaborate business, and, seven years before Bale, who is usually described as the first dramatist in English to introduce individuals, it shows the development among its characters of not only personifications of qualities or type-figures (the Poor Man, the Cobbler, the Cobbler's Wife) like those of the modern expressionist drama, but individualised representatives of a type, of a kind common in Elizabethan drama and later, down even to the present day, though modern usage, in the last half-century, has generally dropped such label-names as Lindsay's Sandy Solace, Shakespeare's Slender, Sheridan's Joseph Surface, Trollope's Mr Nearthcwinde, and even Mr Shaw's Flawner Bannal. *The Thrie Estaitis* shows side by side such abstract figures as Dissait and Chastitie and such almost-abstract types as the Cobbler and the Prioress ; the intermediate figures John Commonweill and Sandy Solace, who is one of the group of characters to which the first two belong ; and fully concrete individuals, like Fynlaw of the

Fute-band, Bessy the Old Man's wife, the Tailor's daughter Jenny, Robene Rome-raker the pardoner, and Wilkin his boy.

Perhaps for this reason, he escapes the general dullness of the morality, a form which as a rule is so much heavier than its predecessor the miracle-play. *The Thrie Estaitis* is as coarse as you please, but it is also a very lively caricaturist's presentation of the weaknesses of contemporary Scottish life, in all classes. It is a long affair, in two parts, with an interval for refreshments, announced as such—rather needed, as it took nine hours to play. The first, in two acts, " tickles the catastrophes " of the Court. After a decidedly unedifying farcical prologue on the perennial humours of cuckoldry, the King Humanitas is tempted by the Lady Sensualitie, and falls, accepting the lady, who is sponsored by Wantounness, Placebo, and Solace, as *maîtresse en titre*. (And one would like to know what Lady Douglas of Lochleven thought of it.) Flatterie, Falset, and Dissait arrive disguised as Devotioun, Sapience, and Discretioun, and are made welcome. Gude Counsell attempts to win a footing, but is headed off, and Veritie and Chastitie fare no better. The second act, however, shows the downfall of the false courtiers, the King having been enlightened by Correctioun. Between the two acts, like the subplot of an Elizabethan play, is an interlude of broad—rather more than broad—farce in an alehouse, between a Soutar, a Tinker, and their wives. (Lindsay, at least, is no inverted-snob : he tackles all classes with an impartial bombardment.) It is linked to the main plot by the appearance of Chastitie, and the poor girl has a very thin time of it. A similar interlude ends the first part, of the Poor Man and the

Pardoner, the latter, like his brother in Chaucer, being one of the pedlars of indulgences, with a side-line in fake relics, who did much, in the decadence of the late Middle Ages, to discredit the Church, and naturally were peculiarly obnoxious to the business-like middle class of Northern Europe. His patter is worthy of his Chaucerian colleague :

> My patent pardonis, ye may se,
> Come fra the Cane of Tartarie,
>   Weill seald with oster-schellis.
> Thoucht ye haif na contritioun
> Ye sall have full remissioun
>   With help of buikis and bellis.
> Heir is ane relict, lang and braid,
> Of Fine Macoull the right chaft-blaid,
>   With teith and al togidder.
> Of Colling's cow heir is ane horn,
> For eating-of Makconnel's corn
>   Was slain into Baquidder.
> Heir is ane cord, baith grete and lang,
> That hangit Johne the Arnistrang,
>   Of gude hemp soft and sound.
> Gude halie pepill, I stand for'd
> Quha evir bein hangit with this cord,
>   He nevir sall be dround.

Soutar and Soutar's wife reappear to sue for a divorce —an extremely unedifying episode—and the scene ends with a fight, in which the Pardoner is very properly thrashed by Pauper.

Part II is connected only by the satiric purpose, and by the reappearance of some of the characters. The Court having had their turn in the pillory, Kirk and State get theirs : it begins with the Three Estates of the Realm walking backward in procession, led by their appropriate vices. Correctioun, John Commonweill, and Gude Counsel apply the appropriate remedies, and it ends with the hanging of Falset and Dissait, with for after-piece another interlude, the highly topical Sermon of Folly, which is kin to the French *sotie*. There is genuine humour and vigour under the coarseness, and a considerable feeling for both dramatic construction and " sense of the stage."

Apparently it was not Lindsay's only work of the kind, for the Bannatyne MS. gives two fragments from other plays, one acted at the Playfield in 1515, and the other at Greenside—presumably the same place : but they are no more than fragments.

Lindsay, like Dunbar, has his train of ghosts. Of the seven dead poets in the *Papyngo* prologue, Henryson and Douglas are still tolerably substantial in spite of losses. Holland survives, in the rather corpse-like mode of the defunct ultra-fashionable. Hay—as a poet at least—Quyntin, who is presumably Quentin Shaw, Kennedy, Rule, and Mersar are among the shadows in Dunbar's procession. Of the seven living, Inglis was soon to join them, at all events if he is the Inglis who was the King's Chaplain, Abbot of Culross, and in 1527 the King's master of works for the new buildings in the royal castle of Stirling, for the ink was hardly dry on Lindsay's praise of his " ballattis, farses, and plesant plays " when he was murdered, and every line of his work, so far as is known, has vanished. Of Kyd, Galbraith, and Kinloch, nothing whatever is known but this reference here, though apparently they were about the court. The two Stewarts are apparently, between them, the writers of some dozen pious or amatory pieces in Bannatyne, of no outstanding quality, good or bad. Bellenden was Archdeacon of Moray, and by his translations of Livy

and Hector Boece, one of the founders of our prose :
Lindsay's description sounds that of a promising
young court-poet with a career ahead of him, but his
only surviving verse is the competent but not very
distinguished accessory matter to his translations.
Other ghosts, who may possibly belong to this time,
are Laider, Moffat, Fethy, Balnaves, Flemyng,
Blyth, and Watson, who have a poem apiece in Bannatyne : Blyth's is a lively dance of metre in the key of
Gaudeamus, Watson's a good drinking-song in praise of
Allan-a-Maut, and Moffat is credited (though in a
later hand than Bannatyne's,) with the authorship of
the delightful *Wyf of Auchtermuchty*, which tells in a
wicked dance of verse how a farmer thought his wife
had a soft job, and the lady thereupon offered to swap
for his. He takes over cheerfully, and fairly makes a
day of it, having a terrible time with byre and poultry,
and when he has them redded at long last, at the loss
of a day's milk and all the goslings

> Than to the kirn that he did stoure
>   And jumlit at it quhill he swat.
> Quhan he had jumlit a full lang hour,
>   The sorrow crap of butter he gat.
> Albeit na butter could he get,
>   Yit was he cummerit with the kirn,
> And syne he het the milk ower het,
>   And sorrow spark of it wald yirn. . . .
>
> Than he bure kindling to the kiln,
>   But scho stert up all in a lowe.
> Whatever he heard, whatever he saw,
>   That day he had na will to mow.
> Than he yede to tak up the barnis,
>   Thocht to haif fund thame fair and clene.
> The first that he gat in his armis,
>   It wes all dirt up to the een.

One Clapperton also has a cheerfully graceless piece in Maitland, about a lady who has a husband and wishes she hadn't : she has views that were " modern " in the nineteen-twenties, in favour of " free association " :

> I suld lufe them that wald lufe me.
> Thair harts for me suld nevir be sair,
> Bot ay unweddit suld I be.
> *Wo worth maryage for evirmair.*

One may just mention the classicist Florence Wilson, of King's College, Aberdeen, for though all his original writing was in Latin, he had perhaps the widest literary fame of any Scot of his day, except David Lindsay, since his work, published at Lyons in 1543, was reprinted until as late as 1751, editions appearing at Paris, London, and the Hague, and in his comparatively short lifetime he was famous in both Italy and France, as Florentius Volusenus. Some of the anonyms may come hereabouts, work, perhaps, of the forlorn ghosts I have mentioned, but it will be more convenient to treat them together later on.

The storms of James's minority, the economic disaster of Surrey's invasion of 1523, might be expected to have an effect on the arts in general. In his active reign, however—roughly the fifteen-thirties—there were signs of revival, and a good deal, especially, of both spiritual and intellectual redding-up in the Church, including an elaborate scheme for sending certain selected monks to the universities, in much the fashion of many orders, of both men and women, to-day. Low as the Scots Church had sunk in the fifteenth century there had always been men like Elphinstone of Aberdeen to keep up the tradition of St Gilbert. They were beginning to make their influence felt on the mass of the Church, and reform might have come, as so often in the past when an institution half-human, half-divine, had, being half-human, grown corrupt, from within. But neither she nor Scotland had known in time those things which belonged unto their peace. The riches of the Church, in countries of poor, greedy, and active nobles, the decay of the sacramental idea of chivalry, the enormous growth of a powerful burgess class to whom, narrowly pragmatic, untrained in manners or imagination, the practices of the Church were tiresome nonsense, and their beauty, like all beauty, distrustworthy—to whom further, uneasy socially, despised by *noblesse d'épée* they could have bought hoof and hide with a week's income, the doctrine of Election, with its offer of supreme (and unchallengeable) aristocracy, was an evangelium beyond all price . . . these, all through the North, and in the South of France, had left the wealthy and many of the nobles against the Church, and ready to accept with eagerness doctrines enunciated by men whose fevered enthusiasm for Hebrew and Greek antiquity had made them lose sight of the growth of fifteen centuries—not quite unpardonably, for there was no doubt that much of the great mediaeval culture was dead. And many of the poorer—not the poorest, but the lower middle-class of the towns—found the sorning of the degenerate friars and the exactions of worldly and lazy parish priests a very real and legitimate grievance, that made them willing soil for any new doctrine that dealt these a buffet. There were now not only reformers within the Church, like Benedict, Bernard, or Thomas, Francis or Catherine of Siena or Teresa : there were also those desirous of abolishing not abuses or accretions but the Church itself, from its smallest practices, even kneeling at prayer, to the Nicene Creed that stated its foundations, and substituting for it a new religion based on the Jewish Church of the Pentateuch (omitting such things as the command to build the Tabernacle with its Altar of Incense, but retaining that to put a witch to death) and inferences from various sayings of St Paul, detached from relationship to context or to the circumstances of their writing. The final test for holiness soon came to be not " Is it good ? " but " Do Catholics do it ? " : the representation of Our Lord dying for mankind became " the emblem of Satan " : they spoke of His Mother as they would have allowed no man to do of their own : Christian burial of any kind was abolished, and even the *Our Father* was forbidden, in spite of the categorical injunction of its Composer. In practice, their devotion to the literal letter of Scripture was queerly patchy : those methods of worship enjoined by Moses or approved by St John were, somehow, shocking, though a number of things not mentioned by Biblical writers (who had no occasion to do so) were therefore banned. More seriously, the very core of St John's teaching and his Master's, that God is Love, is in the flattest contradiction to the eagerly accepted doctrine of Predestinate Damnation. And under this mixture of greed, snobbery, and unbalanced scholarship (a mixture for whose existence the Church herself was largely to blame, for if she had done her duty it could not have happened) was that element of good and of nobility without which no evil thing can have any power—a number of men and women narrow indeed but of a sincere and genuine fervour, a desire for cleanliness, for purgation of evil, that cannot but command our reverence, even if the spiritual arrogance, the ὕβρις that is part of the Renaissance, made them seek strange new creeds as men sought strange new countries.

The flamboyant and disloyal fifteenth century, an age of civil war, of complex treacheries all over Europe, gave birth to the most arrogant age in history —an arrogance of individuals, of every man as an infallible Pope on all subjects, that had never been seen in the ancient world it copied, and that led inevitably to a regimentation based on negatives that had never been guessed at by the positive logic of mediaeval conceptions. And Scotland, in the matter of arrogance, is not very near the bottom of the list, whether in good pride or, alas, in evil. These clashing arrogances made fiercer hatreds than any that have been seen in history.

The new movement took Scotland, with her complex Continental relations, pretty early, though the so-called Lollards of Kyle are scarcely part of it. There had always been these little heretical bodies, often well meaning, very often half crazy, and frequently with tenets that would have startled their Victorian admirers as much as (if they had happened to know about it) would Luther's declaration that polygamy was not inconsistent with Scripture (which of course it is not, if you choose the Scripture), or Milton's warm defence of the same institution, in his posthumous *De Doctrina Christiana*. But George Wishart was executed in 1546, and since they had not yet the power which they afterwards so freely exercised, of burning people themselves, his death probably did more to popularise his party than his life would have done, to judge by the fine contemporary portrait, which shows a neurotic young man with a sensual mouth. But he had been eloquent, and the Scots town populace is fiery tinder for rhetoric, as Clydeside (a great Reforming district) showed in our own day (39). His death, too, was very ably used, by men whose major political desire was to embarrass the party whose active leader was the Chancellor, Cardinal Beaton : it was, in fact, a godsend to the nobles who opposed the French alliance with which Beaton and Queen Marie had secured the stability of the Crown in the most dangerous of the Stewart minorities. And apart from Arran's ambition for a crown blocked from him by a baby girl, the Douglas blood-feud against the wife and daughter of the King of the Commons, the Douglas alliance with the England whose King's sister had married their head, men poor by constant war—not all their own seeking—saw the rich Church, saw Englishmen and Germans looting theirs, and had a good popular excuse to do likewise. The honest Reformers in Scotland, the men who really cared for the new religion as religion, nearly all died poor men : the nobles who won them their establishment reveal an ethical practice that suggests an enthusiasm scarcely doctrinal, though possibly the freedom from moral responsibility afforded by predestination may have appealed to the more imaginative. Charles I's attempt to reform a Reformation that had managed to empty the baby out with the bath was wrecked hardly so much by the lack of tact of a Scotsman brought up in England, and therefore understanding neither country, as by his naive attempt at recovering Church property from secular use, that united against him all the southern gentry. One of the things, in fact, that did most to make his father's Bishops unpopular was Spottiswoode's attempt in 1616 to give being to Knox's dream of parish schools, by establishing a school-rate to endow them. Even Knox and Mary Tudor had known better !

The Regent Arran, next heir to the crown, and willing, to gain it, to be another Baliol, found the pro-English Reformers, the needy nobles, the wealthy middle-class, the fierce Edinburgh mob, invaluable allies : Henry VIII, and later, Edward VI's ministers, made the most of the situation. The natural head of the Crown party, the nationalists, was a baby in France : but she had, luckily for Scotland, a very active and courageous mother. Queen Marie and her Chancellor, Cardinal Beaton, put up a superb fight to hold Henry off, and the Auld Alliance, that had once saved France, was invoked now again to be the safety of Scotland—not too dangerous a safety, as has been averred, since France was too far off to " swallow " Scotland even had a child of Mary and François II succeeded, in course of time, to the double throne. Marie and Beaton, who though his personal morals were negligible was a loyal Scot, a loyal servant of the Crown, and a man of political wisdom and high courage, saved Scotland from becoming another Ireland. Their reward has been consistent vilification, and the acceptance as gospel of the spinsterly scandalmongering of that Knox whom Queen Marie begged off from his sentence as art and part in a very ugly murder, concluded by the deliberate pollution of the victim's body in a manner not to be decently described (40).

When Queen Marie died, worn out in her forties by eighteen years of heroic struggle to preserve her daughter's kingdom—which, incidentally, refused her Christian burial—Scotland was still an independent

I

state, and in touch with the stirring life of the Continent. After the middle of the century the old literary tradition, quickened, perhaps, by the influence of the Pléïade, of the Ronsard who was the guest of James V and his daughter's friend, revives for a little in the work of Scott, Montgomerie, and some others, who belong to Mary's brief personal reign and the long minority and the early reign of her son. Mary herself, of course, loved letters, and wrote verse in French, Latin, and Italian, though not, apparently, in Scots, except for one sad couplet on a window at Fotheringay. The French includes some lines to Ronsard, a lament for François II, and a very pitiful sonnet written in prison, but the famous *Adieux* are said not to be hers, and the best known of the others attributed to her is a most moving little Latin invocation, said to have been written in her *Hours of the Blessed Virgin* at Fotheringay.

> O Domine Deus, speravi in te,
> O care mi Jesu, nunc libera me.
> In dura catena, in misera poena, desidero te.
> Languendo, gemendo, et genu flectendo,
> Adoro, imploro, ut liberes me.

George Bannatyne, by the way, gives a very charming love-song ascribed to Darnley, though it sounds not at all unlike Alexander Scott, who is the chief poet of the middle century. Scott was probably some fifteen years the Queen's senior, born about 1525 and dying some time in the fifteen-eighties, during the regency of the younger Arran. The bulk of his surviving work is not great : we have only some three dozen pieces, none of them long, of assorted kinds and rather various merit, but in the main of an uncommon beauty. He is the most musical of all Scots poets, with the lyric

" cry " in his verse that one rarely finds in Dunbar. We know little of him beyond that he was an Edinburgh man and a courtier. It is not even clear to which party he belonged, though he was one of the many men, not all of the new religion by any means, who desired reformation : his *New Yeiris Gift* to the young Queen in 1562 mixes floreated compliment with a very vigorous handling of both parties, begging her to act against both the frankly catalogued abuses of the old faith and such shortcomings of the new as scriptural dispute by the unlearned, the backbiting and rancour of the pious, and the new idol of covetousness that is tempting those to whom " kirkmennis cursit substance semis sweit." He does not, however—in his extant works at least—concern himself greatly with politics or religion. He does try his hand at comic manners-painting in the vein of *Peblis to the Play*, in *The Justing and Debait up at the Drum*—quite a good thing of its kind—and at satire. But much the greater part of his work, in both senses of greater, is pure lyric, which is mainly—all the best of it—lovelyric. Even Burns yields to him there. He shows that the aureate tradition is past, for there is no rich embroidery of images or diction. He concentrates on the pure emotion, and generally relies, in presenting that, less on the words than on the sheer sound and cadence of metrical pattern, though he does occasionally play with language in the way the English Elizabethans were to do later, as in the *Heart* poem, where the word *hairt* appears twice or more in every line :

Haif hairt in hairt, ye hairt of hairtis haill :
Trewly, sweit hairt, your hairt my hairt sall haif. . . .

The effect ought to be absurd, but in fact it comes off.

This is in rhyme-royal, but he works usually in a shorter line, as in *The Lament of the Master of Erskine.*

> Adew, my awin sweit thing,
> My joy and conforting,
> My mirth and sollesing
>   Of erdly gloir.
> Fairweill, my lady bricht,
> And my remembrance rycht.
> Fairweill, and haif gud nycht.
>   I say no moir.

or in

> Oppressit hairt, indure
> In dolor and distress,
> Wappit without recure
> In wo remediless.
> Sen scho is merciless
> And causis all thy smert
>   Quhilk suld thy dolor dress,
> Indure, oppressit hairt.

Both poems illustrate his gift for the *poised* measure, its tune unresolved to the fall of the last line. The Erskine piece is ostensibly vicarious emotion, a dramatic lyric. But it was an emotion Scott understood. We have it again in two other parting songs, the lovely *Hence hairt*, whose combination of *concetti* with gripped passion is an anticipation of Donne, and the more bitter piece, the defiance of a lover who has been betrayed, *To Luve Unluvit*. I have spoken elsewhere of the fine anonym, " My hairt is heich abufe," with its combination of exultant passion, tenderness, and laughter : its metre—

> My hairt is heich abufe,
>   My body is full of bliss,
> For I am set in lufe
>   As weill as I wald wiss.

> I lufe my lady pure,
> And scho luvis me again.
> I am her serviture,
> Scho is my soverane—

suggests *aut Scott aut diabolus*. Perhaps his best-known poem, and among his best, is " Lo, quhat it is to lufe."

> Lufe is ane fervent fire
> Kendillit without desire.
> Short plesour, lang displesour :
> Repentance is the hire.
> Ane pure tressour without mesour,
> Lufe is ane fervent fire.
>
> To lufe and to be wyse,
> To rege with gud advyce.
> Now thus, now than, so gois the game.
> Incertain is the dys :
> Thair is no man, I say, that can
> Baith lufe and to be wyse.

Scott's measures take a queer grip of the memory.

With Scott one may just mention one or two lesser figures, such as Sempill, writer of violent and sometimes effective polemic verse, who died in 1595 ; Norval, whose *Mirror of a Christian* was published by Lekprevik in 1561 and who has a poem in Bannatyne ; and Arbuthnot, whose few surviving pieces, also in Bannatyne, include a rather charming reply to the stock accusations against women, a dancing little epigram on true love, and a heartfelt complaint on *The Miseries of a Pure Scolar*, which reflects the instability of the age in its sense of not knowing whither to turn in either politics or religion, and the instability of the writer's trade in his bitter sense of its humiliations. It has a genuine and stinging feeling, and its every line would fit the present year.

The three Maitlands represent two generations, but though Sir Richard was born as early as 1496, his long life lasted until 1586, and he did not commence poet until he was sixty : so he may be placed here with his son and daughter. Scholar, patriot, statesman, Keeper of the Privy Seal to the Regent Marie, in later life, in spite of his blindness, a Lord of Session and Lord Privy Seal to Queen Mary, he was a man of wisdom and high character, respected by everyone except John Knox, who in his customary light-hearted fashion accuses him of taking a bribe for which there is no evidence except to the contrary. His greatest literary distinction is the substantial one of a share with Bannatyne in the preservation of much that otherwise would have perished, through the compiling of the famous MS. collection of one hundred and eighty-two pieces of verse—a collection given by his great-grandson Lauderdale to Pepys, who to judge from the binding he gave it, respected it more than Maitland's own country, at that time, would have done. It is still in Pepys's collection at Cambridge.

Some forty of Maitland's own appear in it. For the most part they are shrewd sententious reflections on current affairs, marked less by poetic imagination than by wisdom, patriotic feeling, and a neat, vigorous, and well-bred turn of phrase : their literary atmosphere, in fact, is less that of their own century than of the age of Dryden and Bossuet, La Roche-foucauld and Molière. This applies, however, rather to their temper and aesthetic method than to their content, for they are nearly all more or less topical, many of them, indeed, being written for specific occasions : he seems to have played at Queen Marie's court and at her daughter's the part of semi-official laureate filled formerly by Lindsay and Dunbar. They throw valuable light on the state of affairs in contemporary Scotland, as viewed by a wise and honest man of affairs, sincerely devoted to his country's welfare—the note of passion in that is unmistakable— and old enough to recall the days before Flodden. His most characteristic work is in such things as the *New Yeir* pieces of 1557 and 1560, or in the stately compliment on the Queen's marriage to the Dauphin, which gives an interesting picture of the festivities of all classes, who are bidden to rejoice in the manner of " our eldars Dayis." There is a congratulatory address to Henri II on the recapture of Calais—the last piece of unrecovered France—by the brother of the Queen Regent, and a poem of advice to his son at court, that shows no mean conception of the duties owed by a servant of the Crown to his honour, his sovereign, and the commonweal : one regrets that the son in question should have been Mary's " Michael Wylie," " the Chamæleon," as accomplished a traitor as has cursed our history. Indeed, it is sufficiently ironic that one point in his father's address on the Queen's return to her " auld fre land " should be a prayer that she might choose faithful servants. There is profound sadness in the verses during the troubles of 1559, that call on Scotland to unite, and in others like *Agane Oppressioun of the Commonis*, which bewails the affliction of the former Kirk tenants at the hands of their new and greedy masters, and bids these be merciful for the sake of the commonweal, and " Help the comouns bayth Lord and Laird." Another on the miseries of the time deals roundly with both

135

religious parties, and yet another in the same key contrasts the dismal present with " the blythness that hes bein "—there are

> No gysars all this yeir
> But kirkmen cled like men of weir.

In a lighter mood there are pieces like the joyful and complicated curse on the Thieves of Liddesdale, and the lively satire on the luxurious burgess wives who lift their skirts to show their tasselled garters and silk stockings, and in another key there is the gallant and pitiful retort by the blind man of seventy-three to the spoiling of his lands, in time of truce, by the English. Maitland, in short, is a personality, and one that, apart from our debt to him, one cannot help liking.

His son John, Lord Thirlestane (1537-95), was a famous lawyer, who succeeded his father as Mary's Lord Privy Seal, to lose the office for his loyalty to the Queen, though her son later made him Secretary of State and Lord Chancellor. He wrote verse in Latin and Scots, but very little of the latter remains, nothing beyond an admonition to the Regent Mar and a satire against slander, a subject on which no doubt he could speak with authority. His sister, Mary Maitland or Lauder, apparently assisted her father after his blindness in the compilation of his collection of poems, and also made another of her own, of ninety-five pieces, some half of which appear also in her father's. An anonymous poem in her own collection, addressed to herself, calls her a third to Sappho and " Olimpia," but the only known poem that can be attributed to her—and very doubtfully—is one in her MS., a prayer to Diana that she may " end this worthelie."

The Maitland collections, and the smaller Reidpath MS., which appears to be derived from them, are our only sources for some twenty pieces other than Maitland's own. Many of these are Dunbar's, and they include the superb prologue to *The Twa Maryeit Wemen*. The Maitland MSS. are also our only sources for several anonymous pieces, including *Peblis to the Play* and *The Murning Maiden*.

With the Maitland MSS. one may mention the Asloan, which is what is left of a similar but earlier collection, of about 1515. It contains both verse and prose. A list of contents shows that it once included *Rauf Coilʒear*, *Golagros and Gawaine*, *Colkelbie Sow*, and Henryson's *Fables*. The chief of these collections, however, is that of the invaluable George Bannatyne (1545-c.1608), an Angus man who was later an Edinburgh merchant. He was not much of a poet himself, though he did write verse, but he has more than earned " a place in the story," for the sake of the MS. that bears his name. It is a folio volume of some eight hundred pages, *Ane most godlie mirrie and lustie Rapsody made be sundrie learned Scots poets and written be George Bannatyne in the tyme of his youth*—to be precise, in the last months of 1568. It is not uncharacteristic of our history that we owe the survival of so much of our older poetry to a man diverting himself in time of plague : he is, for instance, our only source for Alexander Scott and for much of Dunbar, and his three hundred and thirty-four poems include not only work by forty-five named authors (of whom six are English, there being nine pieces of Chaucer's and three of John Heywood's), but also the best part of two hundred anonymous poems, many of them of great beauty, of which only eleven make their appearance also in one of the other collections I have mentioned. The manuscript is no haphazard common-place book, but a carefully edited anthology, grouped and indexed and set forth with some flourish of penmanship : the grouping has its curiosities, for Dunbar's *Timor Mortis* poem comes among those described as " ballattis and solacious consaittis," next door to a very lively drinking-song. They range in length from little epigrams of a few lines to the full text of Henryson's *Fables* and the greater part of Lindsay's *Thrie Estaitis*, and the whole is rounded off with a prologue and epilogue of the compiler's own, and opens with a well-meant if rather wooden ascription of praise to the Deity.

Bannatyne appears to have been a Catholic in the religious sense, for his opening section, which consists of religious verse, includes a piece in praise of the benefits of confession, and some Hymns to Our Lady, whom the Protestant Reformers considered a person it was really shocking to mention. His tastes were also catholic in the other sense, for his anthology varies from serious " literary " poems, sacred and profane, in the decorative and aureate tradition of fifteenth and sixteenth century courtly verse, to others —not at all necessarily by different writers—in the tradition of comic manners-painting that runs from *Colkelbie Sow* to Sir Harry Lauder, and, outside verse, begat one notable element in the Waverlies, most of Galt, and (going to bed maudlin) the Kailyard School, with its inverted form the Green-shutterites (41).

The anonymous pieces, work, perhaps, of the forlorn ghosts I have mentioned, before they passed " to bear the red rose company," are as varied as the rest. A large number, naturally, are love-poems, many of them well worthy to stand by Scott's. A long and very moving piece on the sorrows of an unhappy lover, " Sen that the eyne," has been claimed as the lost love-song by James I beginning " Yas, sen—." This, however, is an impossible attribution. It is good enough to be his work, with the note in it of a sharp and weary passion :

> Evin as men may the turtil trew persaif
> Once having lost hir feir,
> On the dry brainche, ay faithful to the graif,
> Bewayling perseveir,
> So my desyre,
> Kindlit in fyre,
> Dois soir lament,
> My luif absent.
> O God, gif amour be ane paine to beir.

The handling of the verse, with its delayed last rhyme, is notable, but whoever wrote it, he was not James I : instead of his anglicism it is unusually gallicised, a number of French words being borrowed directly, as in the last line of the stanza quoted, and used, it would seem, quite naturally and without affectation, as by a writer more or less bilingual.

These anonyms, in Ballantyne and elsewhere, are very difficult to date with any precision, but they would seem to cover about a century and a quarter at the outside—from Dunbar's generation, more or less, to Scott's. One of the oldest, probably, is a sort of ballad, *The Murning Maiden*—ballad in the sense that it is half lyric, half story, but not of the kind of *Sir Patrick Spens* : it is nearer the Renaissance pastoral, though the lady is less like a shepherdess, even the shepherdess of court masquerade, than a nymph in a Florentine picture. It is in an intricate metre, gracefully handled, but the whole thing feels somehow more mediaeval than the time of Dunbar. I should put it quite early in the fifteenth century, somewhere about the age of Charles d'Orléans :

> This greit disese for lufe I drie.
> Ther is no tong can tell the wo.
> I lufe the lufe that lufis not me.
> I may not mend, but murning mo,
>> Quhill God sen some remeid
>> Throw destinie or deid.
> I am his freind and he my fo :
> My sweit, allas, quhy dois he so ?
> I wrocht him nevir na feid.

Tayis Bank is a delicately wrought piece in the same fashion, but frigid in its grace : the fair lady whose portrait it paints in a setting of spring landscape appears to have been lovely Margaret Drummond, James IV's mistress or possibly morganatic wife, who was poisoned in 1501, In spite of the colours of its landscape and the delicate pattern of alliteration laid like a fret or descant upon its metre, it scarcely rivals some others, more of the song type, such as the *Welcome to May*, where " the gressis gleme of licht " in a manner very characteristic of the time, or another even more charming piece, again full of " Preluciand bemis before the day," whose refrain is " Throw gladnes of this lusty May." The harmonised pattern of verse, the descant of alliteration or internal rhyme laid over the main form of the stanza, in a manner that goes back to the *Pearl*, shows in several, as in *Tayis Bank*, or the elaborate inlay of rhymes in the octave of

> The tyme hes bene and zit may cum agane
> We ma convene to talk in gudliness.
> Tho in distress ze leif me in grit pane,
>> I may complane zit to zour lawliness,

Vnto zour pes to tak my sympilness :
    It wald incres zour honour evir mair.
Na bissiness to lufe sall gar me sess,
    Tho auld kyndness *ze haif forzetten clair.*

An equally mournful lover—ostensibly—has a pretty
song, *Quhair luve is kindlit confortles* : he professes to be
very sorry for himself, but the twinkle of his metre
gives him away, and one hopes for the sake of dis-
cipline the lady gave him his paiks before relenting.
Some of the simpler ones are probably later, but no
less charming : there is an enchanting lute-and-bird-
music in a song published in 1682, in the Aberdeen
Cantus, but probably of the sixteenth century or earlier.

In a garden so green, of a May morning,
Herd I my lady plene, of paramouris.
Quod she, My love so sweit, come ye not yet, not yet ?
Hecht ye not me to meet, among the flouris ?
    Eloré, eloré, eloré, eloré,
    I love my lovely love, eloré, lo.

There is another in the same collection, an eerie thing
where all the bright pattern of flowers ends in

The new faen snaw to be your smock,
    It becomes your bodie best.
Your heid sall be wrapped in the eastern wind,
    And the cauld rain on your breist.

. . . though that, perhaps, belongs rather with the
ballads.

Perhaps the best of the group are *Baith gude and fair
and womanlie*, which has a point of view not very usual
in either literature or life, of the lover who is unloved
and yet glad that he loves, and *My hert is heich abufe*,
a delicious thing, with an exultant tenderness touched
with laughter. It may, as I have said, be Alexander

141

Scott's. These two, by the way, are not aureate, but of straightforward simplicity, that depends for effect on the grace and music of the metre.

Besides the love-poems, there are a number of religious and meditative pieces, like that whose refrain is *Welcum eild, for youth is gane,* and the piece in Mary Maitland's collection about the reeds in the loch. There are complimentary verses, like the rather charming ones in praise of that same lady's home, Lethington—

> Sua everie poet hes sum place
> To prayse, and to commend,
> For some excelland gift and grace
> That God hes to it send.

There is topical work of one kind or another, like the vigorous piece of honest manly anger over the Douglas betrayal of the unlucky Northumberland, which the author very properly resents as a national disgrace ; and closely allied with that, there is satire of Kirk, Court, and State, some of it of admirable point and vigour, if not always remarkable for decency. This shades easily into the humorous manners-painting of a type whose spirit links with the fabliau. The same tradition made the " low life " stories in the *Canterbury Tales* and a considerable element in the Elizabethan drama : but though Chaucer and some of the dramatists and pamphleteers handled it with considerable verve, it has always been stronger and more widespread in Scotland and France than in England : there is more than a touch of it in Maupassant. (It is perhaps worth remark that Mr Kipling, whose early poems give in places a modern English analogy to a form that, south of the Border, had become

extinct, was not only Maupassant's disciple, but half
Scots by blood and—especially in his earlier, harder,
work—with many of the qualities, as an artist, of
Dunbar (42).) As is usual in the fabliau, satire,
broadly humorous rather than bitter, is prominent—
a good-tempered raillery rather than hatred, in the
vein, more or less, of the already quoted *Wyf of
Auchtermuchty*, though venom is not altogether absent
in some, as in *The Freirs of Berwik*, a typical fabliau,
resembling the bluer stories of the *Decameron* : it is
excellently done, and might possibly be Dunbar's.

The most considerable of this group—and both are
excellent—are the famous *Christis Kirk on the Green* and
Peblis to the Play. They have been attributed to
James I, which for several reasons is very unlikely,
and to James V, which is not unlikely in the least, for
we know that, like his father before him, the Goodman
of Ballengeich had, or took, facilities for first-hand
research into proletarian conditions—let us be modern
now and then, for a change—and the Stewarts had
almost all too much natural inborn dignity not to be
able to lark with the common man : of the four
exceptions, James VI had no dignity but had the
homeliness, James VII and his son had eaten the
bitter bread of exile in youth too much for their
dignity not to be self-conscious, and Charles I was
brought up in England, where they are nervous about
that kind of thing—especially, one observes, among
well-to-do Socialists.

The James who could share a *Flyting* with Davie
Lindsay was as capable of enjoying a row at a fair as
of dazzling the court of François Ier, being adored
by three French princesses, or playing host to Ronsard.
Why not ? I will not affirm that he did write the

two : there is no evidence at all that he could not or would not, except the shocked emotions of professors, but the evidence that he did is mere popular tradition : and the popular tradition of our country has made the Covenanters defenders of freedom.

Both pieces are country merrymaking, like the kermesses of contemporary or rather later Flemish painting. The language is certainly after the mid-fifteenth century, and looks to me to be after 1500, but the complicated stanza with its bob-and-wheel close (the rhymes are more complex in *Christis Kirk*, but the shape is the same) is an oldish one : this may mean that our version has been modernised, but it is quite as likely that they were written to an old tune and followed its form, in a way of which Burns' songs are the great, though very far from the only, example. *Peblis* seems older : the other appears to refer to it. Both are cheerfully full of rough country gaiety, *Peblis* with a row as interlude but an ending of hearty kisses audible in the lanes where " the sun is strikand shaftis," *Christis Kirk* concluding with a really gorgeous free fight, that sends the giggling lasses flying—

> With forkis and flailis they lait greit flappis,
>   And flang togidder like freikis.
> With bowgaris of barnis they beft blue cappis,
>   Quhill they of bernis made briggis.
> The reird raise rudly with the rappis
>   Quhen rungis wes laid on riggis.
> The wyfis come furth with cryis and clappis,
>   " Lo quhair my lyking liggis,"
>   Quo thay,
>   At Chrystis Kirk of the Grene.

But for all its stour and noise the row does no real harm, ending cheerfully when the village boaster, his jeering women-folk behind him, comes out to brag what he would have done if he hadn't been too late to take a hand.

Returning from this company of ghosts, we find beginning the last verse of the song, that comes with the reigns of Mary's son and grandson. Alexander Montgomerie, the chief poet of James VI's earlier reign, shows both the end of the old tradition and the first seed of the new, that was to bear such pitifully little fruit. He is not the last " courtly makar," but he is about the last of importance to use a definitely and characteristically Scottish language for verse of what may be called the " literary " type. After his day the Lowland gentry and men of learning were bilingual, and the " royal " tongue, in writing at all events, assimilates rapidly to that of England. The assimilation in idiom, vocabulary, and pronunciation is even yet not absolutely complete, and so long as the two are mutually intelligible it is scarcely desirable that it should be so. But from about the Union of the Crowns the standard speech of the two countries differs no more than either differs from that of modern America.

Montgomerie, like most of the makaris, was a man of family, a cadet of the house of Eglinton. His birth-year is anywhere between 1540 and 1556, he seems to have been born in Germany, and he lived until after the Union of the Crowns. He was an officer in the body-guard of the Regent Morton, had and lost the favour of James VI, and was banished from court for a share in Barclay of Ladyland's conspiracy in 1597. Poetically he follows Scott and Ronsard, but with a vocabulary inclining to the older, more ornate tradition, though metrically he is an innovator, for—

K

so far as we know—he is the first Scots poet to practise the sonnet. He does so to a considerable extent : we have some seventy of his, in various forms, some of them direct translations from Ronsard. He is the first poet in either form of the language to use the original Italian form, of octave and sestet. His work, like that of most of the others, is of assorted kinds, varying from a flyting with Hume of Polwarth to a number of translations of Psalms. His major pieces, *The Bankis of Helicon* and *The Cherry and the Slae,* are both of the allegorical semi-pageant type, descended from the *Rose* through *The Goldyn Targe* and its kind. Both are in a very elaborate " broken and cuttit " stanza, a favourite form of Montgomerie's, but used, though deftly, without too much discrimination, for its pace, the dance of rhymes into which it breaks at the close, is wrong for the slow allegorical pageant-procession of images. It fits better with the shorter *Adieu to his Mistress.*

> Albeit my body is absent,
> My faithful heart is vigilent
>   To do you service true.
> But when I hant unto the place
> Where I wes wont to sie that face,
>   My dolour does renew.
> Then all my plesur is but pain,
>   My cairis they do incres :
> Until I sie your face again,
>   I live in heavynes.
>   Sair weeping, but sleeping,
>   The nichtis I ouerdryve,
>   Whylis murning, whylis turning,
>   With thochtis pensityve.

Some of the sonnets are beautiful things, but what is, and probably deserves to be, his best-known poem is a very vigorous and delightful description of morning, where his dance of metre has justification.

> Hay, now the day dawis,
> The jolie cok crauis,
> Now shroudis the shawis
>   Throu Nature anone.
> The thrissil-cok cryis
> On lovers wha lyis,
> Now skaillis the skyis,
>   The nicht is neir gone.

It is a court-piece, a morning of tournament : one can see it from the country palace of Linlithgow, high and square over its lake with the swans, in the open Lothian plain and clear early light. The threefold repetition of the double rhymes, caught back on the single one that carries the refrain, gives admirably the intoxication of the movement of bright armour and gleaming horses in the bright green country.

Along with Montgomerie go his fellow-conspirators Barclay of Ladyland, also a sonneteer, Rolland, whose translation in Scots verse of the collection of tales called *The Seven Sages* was published in 1592, and Mark Alexander Boyd, traveller, soldier, scholar, physician to Henri IV, and author of excellent Latin verse and one fine Scots sonnet—in the Italian form again, by the way, which thus seems naturalised in Scotland a generation before it appears in England, for Boyd was a year older than Shakespeare, and died in 1601.

Alexander Hume, Boyd's contemporary or nearly —he died in 1609—wrote a collection of *Hymnes or Sacred Songs where the richt use of Poetry may be Espied*, but where one does not espy very much poetic feeling ; a paean on the defeat of the Spanish Armada, which is a very wooden specimen of the pageant-tradition ; and one landscape-piece, *Of the Day Estivall*, which has the clear stiff coloured beauty of Dutch painting, its apprehension of minute detail within a whole. It is long, the whole procession of the day from dawn to sunset, with all the joy of Scots poets in clear light and in reflection in still water.

> The misty rouke, the clouds of raine,
> From tops of mountains skails.
> Cleare are the highest hills and plaine,
> The vapour takes the vales.

> Begaried is the saphire pend
> With spraings of scarlet hue,
> And presciously from end to end
> Damaskid white and blue.

> The ample heaven of fabric sure
> In cleannes does surpas
> The crystal and the silver pure,
> Or clearest poleist glass.

> The time so tranquil is and still
> The na where sall ye find,
> Saif on ane high and barren hill,
> Ane aire of piping wind.

> All trees and simples great and small
> That balmy leaf do bear,
> Nor they were painted on a wall,
> Na mair they more or steir.

The whole landscape is full of loving detail like

> The corbies and the kekling kais
> May scarce the heat abide.
> Hawks prunyeis on the sunnie braes,
> And wedders back and side.

By 1600 the stream of Scots letters is visibly drying up, as the new influences were gaining power. It is significant that the love-songs of Alexander Craig, in 1606, were published in London, and Patrick Gordon's *History of the Valiant Bruce* (1615), in heroic couplet, appeared at Dort. Between the ministers and the sheer poverty that followed the three ghastly invasions of the fifteen-forties, the other arts were pretty well dead already. Even architecture lapsed for over a century. In the secular there is hardly anything to put alongside the unfulfilled promise of new developments in the Italianate wing at Crichton, and one has to wait till the end of the seventeenth century before French influence returns to quicken Scots domestic architecture to the charm of Caroline Park and Auchendinny and the riches of Dalkeith, while it was not till the eighteenth that Gibbs and the Adams brothers were to adapt the classic of the Grand Siècle to an austere new graciousness. As for ecclesiastical work, between Roslin and Gibbs' churches (built for England) the best we can show is the amateurish spire of the Tron Kirk, and the worst is like a deliberate insult to Deity. It was not till the late eighteenth century that there was anything in Scotland itself : and in 1829 Montrose's tomb was still a coal cellar. Outside building there is nothing to matter but a tomb or two, like the very fine one in Dunbar Parish Kirk, spared, since its imagery is wholly pagan, in the breaking down of the carved work of the sanctuary.

Even in literature, the stream, as I say, is drying, and in " literary " literature, though not yet in " folk-poetry," it grows thin and shallow. Already in the England of the 'eighties, Spenser and Sidney and Marlowe were heading nearly forty years of one of the greatest poetic outbursts in the history of the world, with Shakespeare for moon among lesser stars that were worthy to deck his heaven. In Scotland, in the last twenty years of the century, Montgomerie is the greatest name we can show, and there are few beside him. The Muses were in disgrace for Popish hussies.

It was not the King's fault. James was a considerable scholar, and loved letters more than he did the ministers. He wrote a very interesting treatise (*q.v.p.*) on the principles of formal Scots versifying ; and he practised the art himself, his work, like Montgomerie's, including a considerable number of sonnets, besides a translation of the famous *Uranie* of his friend Du Bartas, whom his own day considered the Huguenot rival to Ronsard, though later ages, in spite of Goethe's enthusiasm, are more inclined to group him with the weaker followers of Remy Belleau. Both these and his work on prosody have merit for the work of a boy not out of his teens, but one can scarcely say more. The most interesting is a longish piece in rhyme-royal, *The Phoenix*, called *Ane Metaphoricall Invention of a Tragedie* : and its interest is historical rather than literary, for the Phoenix is kingship. It throws a good deal of light, coming when it does, on the manner in which in James as in Louis XIV the scrambling humiliations of his minority produced as reaction a fervent faith in absolute monarchy, that James was to transmit to his son Charles, and that in all three kings was to have evil results to their dynasties.

A certain new Italian note shows elsewhere. One William Fowler translated Petrarch's *Trionfi*, and Stewart of Baldinnes did *Orlando Furioso* into Scots verse, The major poetical output, however, was in Latin : there was a good deal of that, esteemed by better classicists than myself as of very high merit. Buchanan, classical tutor to both Mary and James, is said to be the finest Latin poet since Imperial Rome, and Charles I's physician, Arthur Johnstone, laureated in Paris in his early twenties and like Wilson a graduate of King's, Aberdeen, runs him a close second in the next generation.

By Johnstone's day, however—he died in 1641— Scots literary poetry was in its final stage before the long sleep between Montrose and James Thomson, and the use of a definitely Scots speech for serious literary work other than dialogue was practically over till this side of the Great War. The very few poets who come after the Union use much the same language as seventeenth-century England, and their work, though one sees traces of the old tradition, is strongly coloured by the influence of their English contemporaries, and in the case of the greatest of them, by Italian. Drummond of Hawthornden, Ayton, and Lord Stirling are accomplished, sincere, and genuine poets. But they are voices crying in a wilderness.

The chief of this forlorn generation, and the only one who is so to speak a professed poet, is Drummond, who from the purely literary point of view is the most considerable Scots writer of the seventeenth century, except Urquhart and Ben Jonson (43). He was born in 1585 and died in 1649, the year before Montrose, leaving a gap of three-quarters of a century until Thomson. He was fortunate enough to be able to live for the most part abroad or in retirement : he was a gentle soul, who in spite of his sympathy with the King's cause, took little share in the troubles of the sad 'forties. His work is of a stately classicism, coloured with Horace and the Italians, and has the same sort of clear-cut grace of versifying, marmoreal even at its most exquisitely fragile, that one finds in the non-dramatic work of his friend Jonson, or, when it is less airy, reminding one of that of the young Milton—or more than anything, perhaps, of the Franco-Italian decorative sculpture that adorns the châteaux of the early Renaissance. His best work, as one might expect from that description, is in the sonnet and the short ode, or the madrigal, where he can be enchanting, though *The River of Forth Feasting*, the last piece of the pageant-tradition, is notable : it was complimentary work for James' visit of 1617, and its couplets, by the way, are of a firm closed type that anticipates the age of Dryden.

The madrigals can be like the cut gems that age loved. " Like the Idalian queen," and " This life that seems so fair," are so universally known that I will quote :

> My thoughts hold mortal strife.
> I do detest my life,
>> And with lamenting cries
>>> Peace to my soul to bring
> Oft call that prince which here doth monarchise.
>> But he, grim-grinning King,
> Who caitiffs scorns, and doth the blest surprise,
> Late having decked with beauty's rose his tomb,
> Disdains to crop a weed, and will not come.

and

> New doth the sun appear,
>> The mountains' snows decay,
> Crowned with frail flowers comes forth the baby year.
>> My soul, time posts away,
>>> And thou yet in that frost
>>> Which flower and fruit hath lost,
>> As if all here immortal were, dost stay.

> For shame ! thy powers awake,
> Look to that heaven which never night makes black,
> And there, at that immortal sun's bright rays,
> Deck thee with flowers that fear not rage of days.

The sonnets have the same lucid grace, and are full of lines like " The sad memorials only of my pain." Perhaps the greatest, though not the most characteristic, is the magnificent one on St John Baptist, which towers superbly upwards to its conclusion (44). But Drummond is most himself in the elegiac.

Sir David Murray of Gorthy wrote a *Tragicall Death of Sophonisba* and a collection of sometimes rather charming sonnets, *Coelia*, published in London in 1611. The traveller, William Lithgow (1582-1645 ?) was a better traveller than poet : the narrative of his *Rare Adventures and Painful Peregrinations* (1632) was reprinted into the nineteenth century, but his poetry has only a scarcity value, and the same may be said of his brother voyager, Simeon Graham (1570 ?- 1614), whose best claim to a place on the roll is that his prose *Academie of Humours* may have given a suggestion to Richard Burton. Patrick Hannay, a Galloway man who died about the end of the sixteentwenties, published a volume of poems in 1622 : it includes some rather undistinguished lyric, an heroic poem, *Sheretine and Mariana*, on a subject from Hungarian history, and a *Philomel* in Montgomerie's favourite stanza, which suggests that Galloway lungs must have been efficient, for though there are 1700 lines of it the printed text gives it a musical setting. Hannay's work is competent, but no more : its main point of interest is the language, which though definitely English is a definitely Scottish English, both in pronunciation, as seen in the rhymes, and in the frank use of specifically Scottish words. A younger man, Sir William Mure of Rowallan (1594-1657), shows in his own person the change that came upon the times. In his youth he was proud of being Montgomerie's nephew, and claimed an hereditary right to Helicon. As a very young man he did in fact produce a *Dido and Æneas* (not printed till 1898) of reasonable merit, and some love-songs which include the really pretty

> Must I unpittied still remain,
> But regaird
> Or rewaird,
> Nothing cared,
> But by my sueitest slain ?

Later, however, he abandoned " profane poetry " for a not very impressive discourse on *Doomsday*, some political and theological polemic in metre, and a version of the Psalms, of which some parts are incorporated in the present *Metrical Psalter*.

The best of the generation, after Drummond, is Sir Robert Ayton, secretary to two Queens, who was born in 1570 and died in 1638. He wrote verse in Greek, French, and Latin, and in English has some exquisite and individual pieces of courtly song, " few, but roses." Like Drummond he looks forward rather than back : indeed, both his verse and his temper suggest the best English lyric of the Restoration. The two best-known are both to an inconstant lady, and their grace and dignity and quiet courteous irony set them among the best things of their kind. They should be quoted whole, for they are as unified as sonnets, but space presses, and I can only give a verse that suggests their colour.

Nothing could have my love o'erthrown,
　If thou hadst still continued mine ;
Nay, if thou hadst remained thine own,
　I might perchance have yet been thine.
　　But thou thy freedom didst recall
　　That it thou might elsewhere enthrall,
　　And then how could I but disdain
　　A captive's captive to remain ?

William Alexander, Viscount Canada and Earl of
Stirling, attached successively to the households of
the two young princes, was born in 1580 and died in
1640. He is a more voluminous writer than Ayton,
his work including a *Doomsday*, and a number of plays
in verse, *Monarchick Tragedies*. They are " Falls of
Princes "—*Darius*, *Croesus*, *Alexander*, and *Julius Caesar*.
He has a stately grace, both there and in his sonnets.
A speech from *Darius* may serve as example.

Let greatness of her glassy sceptres vaunt,
　Not sceptres, no, but reeds, soon bruis'd, soon broken ;
And let this worldly pomp our wits enchaunt,
　All fades and scarcely leaves behind a token.

Those golden palaces, those gorgeous halls,
　With furniture superfluously fair,
Those stately courts, those sky-encountering walls,
　Evanish all, like vapours in the air.

Our painted pleasures but apparel pain :
　We spend our days in dread, our lives in dangers,
Balls to the stars, and thralls to Fortune's reign,
　Known unto all, yet to ourselves but strangers.

Even this late age has its ghosts. Robert Ker, Earl
of Ancrum, is indeed the last of the school, outliving
by a little his juniors, King Charles and " the great
Marquis," and dying in 1654, at the age of seventy-
six, an exile in Holland. His length of days was not

gained by playing for safety, for he was a loyal follower of his king through all the troubles of the 'Forties, and earlier was the hero of a famous duel, in which he, a sick man barely able to stand, defeated a gigantic adversary. All that is left of his work, of note in its day, is one fine sonnet, in praise of a solitary life of quiet, and a verse translation of eleven psalms.

King Charles I was like most Stewarts a lover of the arts : his collection of pictures, sold by his enemies for a contemptuous song, included many of what are now the treasures of the Louvre. He may not have written the *Eikon Basilike*, but he certainly wrote verse from time to time. It varies in merit, but includes one lovely and little-known madrigal, written, perhaps, for the children to whom he was devoted.

> Close thine eyes, and sleep secure :
> Thy soul is safe, thy body sure.
> He that guards thee, He that keeps,
> Never slumbers, never sleeps.
> A quiet conscience in the breast
> Has only peace, has only rest.
> The music and the mirth of kings
> Are out of tune until she sings.
> Then close thine eyes in peace and sleep secure,
> No sleep so sweet as thine, no rest so sure.

There is a touch in it of the Elizabethans that he loved, of Dekker, or of the dirge for the dead Fidele. The most powerful faction of his Scottish subjects considered it not least of his Popish shortcomings that he read Shakespeare and loved him—at a time, by the way, when Shakespeare was out of fashion. And almost the last serious verse of our literature, for two full generations, is the lament for him of his great servant Montrose, a strange fierce thing, only too passionate to be grotesque in its image, a cry from the soul of a man who had strength to storm Corryarrick in deep winter, will to fire a dead-beat army in the retreat from Dundee, but swooned headlong at the news of his master's death. The best known of the few poems of his that remain has for all its grace and charm a background of *concetti* from the already threatening storms of the time, and the last, our epilogue before the Gulf, is the fierce and sombre defiance written in prison on the eve of the day when

> in ghastly state,
> His head proclaimed how holiness could hate.

Montrose swung from the gallows his enemies had made to shame him, and shamed them, and the very mob they had hired to stone him. There is still the stone balcony over the Canongate, beside the stark twin spires of Moray House, where Argyle came out from the festival of a wedding, to gloat on his enemy going to a thief's death, and when Montrose had looked up at him once in silence, shrank to kennel like a whipped hound, biting his hand. And Argyle was the master of Scotland in that day. If any second of Scots history holds a country's soul in the crystal of a moment, it is that.

V

FOLK-LITERATURE

The popular tradition—lost work—the Gude and Godlie Ballatis—*songs—ballads*

THE "literary" poetic tradition of Scotland had ended in blood by the middle century, not to revive again for a long life-time : and for the last hundred years it had run thin enough, though the stream is "Helicon the clere well." Parallel with it, however, for its last century and a half, and outliving it, is another, growing stronger as that weakens, since on it the Reformation had slower effect. This is the tradition of "popular" or "folk" verse, which after it first shows is never quite cut off, surviving underground through the Valley of Dry Bones, to emerge again in the fulness of time and inspire some of the greatest things of the eighteenth-century Risorgimento —to be the seed of Burns, and transmuted, of some of the finest things in Scott.

This folk-verse is among the greatest of its kind. Incidentally, it disposes very completely of any theory that the Scottish nation is constitutionally unpoetic and has no sense of the drama endemic throughout the acts of its history, or that a condition of literary sterility is any more native to Scotland than to any other reasonably intelligent nation. It is not natural, but an acquired, or enforced, disease. The nation that made the ballads has no business to have the blind gaps in the course of its art that ours has had.

158

It is difficult to know the age of this tradition. Probably as early as any form of what is now English was spoken in what is now Scotland, there were songs in it. Caedmon's Northumbria of the seventh century, of which our Lothian was part, was a singing country. But there is almost nothing left of mediaeval popular song. I have cited the oldest scraps, and the tantalising list in *Colkelbie Sow*. There is another such list in the sixteenth-century *Complaint of Scotland*, which is nearly all the information we have for the fifteenth and early sixteenth centuries. The line between popular and courtly verse is not, of course, always an easy one to draw, and all the less easy when one knows Scotland. Some of the satiric anonyms of about 1500, like *The Freiris of Berwyk*, may be folk-literature, and they may not, at all events in the sense of literature made by " the people." *Peblis to the Play* looks as " folk " as *Uncle Tom Cobley* or *Gentils galants de France* : but it is attributed to a king, and we know that more than one scholarly courtier-poet turned out work of its kind. In a country that lays large stress on pedigree, as in Scotland and Spain, social practice can afford to be democratic. Indeed, in this division of our literature, the very ballads that are most certainly real " people's work " are precisely those that are most aristocratic in essential feeling. Again this is not surprising. The Scots peasant for at least six hundred years has commonly shown the aristocratic virtues, of courage, dignity, loyalty to a chief, and respect for those women he thinks worthy of it . . . as well as the aristocratic vices of sexual laxity and the devil's own arrogance. He is apt to lose all but one of these qualities in the Gorbals, but ballads are older than the blessings of Progress.

159

There is not much surviving, as far as one can guess, that belongs before the time of James V. These songs depended upon oral transmission, and though in England as the power to read grew more common, their equivalent appeared as broadsides, in Scotland the Kirk controlled the press, and when a man could be stripped, whipped, and his ears nailed to the gallows for drinking his sovereign's health in the hearing of those who disliked that monarch's religion, it was unwise to be heard singing anything but the metrical psalms. A certain amount of rather ghostly evidence comes from a very curious compilation of the later sixteenth century, *Ane compendious Book of Godlie Psalms and Spirituall Songs collected out of sundrie partes of the Scriptures with sundrie of other ballads changed out of prophane sangis for avoyding of sinne and harlotrie with the augmentatioun of sundrie gude and godle Ballatis not contend in the first editioun*—known for short as *The Gude and Godlie Ballatis.* It is the work of three brothers Wedderburn of Dundee, ministers of the New Kirk : the second edition is dated 1567, but no copy of the previous one is extant, and its date is unknown. About a third of it is translation from the German : there are also some psalms, but the rest shows an attempt to adapt what were evidently popular songs to pious or at any rate Protestant uses. Sometimes new words have been set to a popular tune, but in others the adaptor was economical, and one can trace a secular shadow behind the pious reconstruction, or even recognise the ghosts of songs mentioned in the *Complaynt.* One well-known example is quoted (in its more quotable verses) (45) by Scott in *The Monastery* :

> The Paip, that pagan full of pride,
> Hes blindit us owerlang,

which has the old refrain,

> Hey trix, trim go trix,
> Undir the grenewode tree.

Perhaps the nicest of all the adaptations takes the old song

> John come kiss me now,
> John come kiss me now,
> John come kiss me by and by,
> And mak no mair adow,

and proceeds after that to troll piously

> The Lord thy God I am
> That John dois thee call.
> John representis man,
> By grace celestiall.

No, the adaptor need not have had his tongue in his cheek. The average Scot has a pretty keen sense of humour, but when he is without it the vacuum is more absolute than in any other nation, except America. And precious Master Kettledrummle could have sung all that through a wholly sanctified nose, and never seen there was anything odd in it.

One or two of the adaptations, however, where the transfer from profane to sacred love has been more discreet, have real beauty and passion, as in

> All my lufe, leif me not,
> Leif me not, leif me not,
> All my lufe, leif me not,
> Leif me nat alane,

which is a haunting thing, or "Who is at my window?" which has been made into a variant of " Behold I stand at the door and knock."

Of actually surviving songs, we begin to have a fair number from the later sixteenth century onwards. Some of them, especially the tragic ones, are superb, and their range of emotion is very wide. On the one hand we have the dry shrewd humour of *The Gaberlunzie Man*, a graceless but lively affair, which may, however, be older than this time if a vague but not improbable attribution to James V is correct—an attribution which shows again the difficulty of being sure what is really of " folk " origin. With it are things like *Tak your auld cloak about ye*, or *Get up and bar the door*, the bacchanalian zest of

> Todlen hame and todlen hame,
> Wow but my luve were todlen hame,

or the wicked joy of *The Soutar of Fife*, whose tune has devilment enough for a dozen. It, by the way, is pretty certainly the genuine article, for it is a working chantey, a weaver's song with the thump of the loom treddles in its refrain.

On the other hand are things like *The Twa Corbies*, probably one of the earliest, whose last lines (which, by the way, are probably James Hogg's) are about the coldest thing in literature, with the very chill of desolate mortality. *O waly, waly* belongs here, and is one of the consummate things in all lyric. Even *Ye banks and braes* and " Had we never lo'ed sae kindly " do not overpass it.

These are only two among many. Some of them are versions of situations as old as history—the betrayed girl here with her splendour turned to shame, the cold chasm that faces a man after the fierce and sudden stroke in hot blood, in *Edward, Edward*. The lonely death of *The Twa Corbies* has its pendant in *The Border Widow*, with the lock of yellow hair binding her heart. All these are ower true tales, stories true time and again in the world's course. What is

Edward but Orestes before the Furies ? Some of them, though—and among them two of the greatest—belong not to the general pattern of human fate, but to specific particular events. *Helen of Kirkconnel* does that. It owes something to Scott, as it stands : the creator of Lady Glenallan, of Lady Ashton, could work on it. But the man who devised its stanza could make verse : the threefold rhyme drives a slow sword through the heart. It is one of the later ones, of the seventeenth century. The other is of the last decade of the sixteenth, the story of the young earl of whom King James was jealous. Huntly, his enemy, sent to apprehend him, fired the house of Donibristle at midnight, and the Earl tried to cut his way out through Huntly's Gordons. The tassels of his helmet caught fire at a spark and showed him, and he was taken. Huntly slashed him across the face, and he cried as he fell, " Ye have spoiled a better face than your ain ! " He was the handsomest man of his day in Scotland, and he was young when he died.

The piece that tells his end is essentially *song*. The words and the magnificent wild music are, as so often in this division of our letters, an inseparable unity. On paper it is like the photograph of a Cézanne. Paper, indeed, gives commonly less than that, for the anthologies all murder it, spoiling the superb alternation of grim recitative and passionate grief for perished arrogant beauty. Spoil the order, and you miss the ringing lift of the tune on the dead man's name, the cumulative dramatic force of the subtle changes in the refrain. This is the proper shape of it.

> Ye Hielands and ye Lawlands,
>   O where hae ye been ?
> They hae slain the Earl o' Moray
>   And hae laid him on the green.

> He was a braw gallant,
>   And he played at the ba'.
> O the bonny Earl o' Moray
>   Was the flower amang them a'.
>
> O wae be to ye, Huntly,
>   And wherefore did ye sae ?
> I bade ye bring him to me,
>   But forbade ye him to slay.
> He was a braw gallant,
>   And he played at the ring.
> O the bonny Earl o' Moray,
>   He micht hae been a king.
>
> O lang may his leddy
>   Look o'er the Castle Doune,
> Ere she see the Earl o' Moray
>   Come sounding through the toun.
> He was a braw gallant,
>   And he played at the glove.
> O the bonny Earl o' Moray,
>   He was the Queen's love.

The last two songs I have cited come to the edge of the ballad, in the narrower sense of the word. They have both a story implicit, and the ballad is a story shaped by its flame into a song, in country like the great smooth hills of the Borders, the deep river-glens, the stark and lonely towers beside streams of water. To illiterate and therefore uneducated peasants things like *Chevy Chase* and *The Bonny Earl o' Moray* took the place of such things as the diary of an unpleasing specimen of the gigolo, lately killed in a squalid row with his protectress, which the newspaper with the largest sale in England is advertising as a star attraction on the day on which this sentence is written. But compulsory education is, of course, a blessing. . . .

This is no place to theorise about ballads. There

are, of course, mountains of theories, mostly by men who have never written a poem. We do know all that matters—that the ballads are the work of unnamed writers, and passed on not by print as a rule, but by the astonishing memory of the unlettered : Grieg, collecting in the north-east, got three hundred and eighty-three from one old lady. " Collective authorship " has certainly some truth in it, but the collaboration is not simultaneous but successive (46). Their age is not easy to fix. Some cannot be older than a given date : *Kinmont Willie* must be after 1596, *Edom o' Gordon* after 1571, *The Laird o' Logie* after 1592. It is safer to put a late date rather than an early. Argyle burnt Airlie House in 1640, and *The Bonny Hoose o' Airlie* is true ballad. It is likely, however, to be one of the latest. *The Baron of Brackley*, which comes after 1666, is ballad stuff and in the ballad mood, though not at its noblest, but the handling is not like those we know come before the Civil War. It is not typical ballad. We may put the date of the ballad in the current sense from about Flodden to the Civil War.

They take up whatever stories were in the popular imagination, and had burnt in it till the fire kindled and the song came. Sometimes they are on the old folk-tale themes, that recur all over the world—the deserted bride coming again to her own, in *Gospatric* and *Fair Annet*, the faithless or cruel lover who is sometimes not of this world or has strange foreign spells born where

> The lilies grow
> On the banks of Italie.

Or lovers go through strange ordeals and come to triumph, like Tam Lin's fair Janet or the lady in *The*

Gay Goshawk, or to disaster like Lord William and Lady Margaret in *The Douglas Tragedy*, which is the same ower true tale that made *Romeo and Juliet*. Or the dead walk again as in *The Wife of Usher's Well* and *Clerk Saunders*, or it is the living like True Thomas who wander through strange worlds where

> It was mirk, mirk nicht, there was nae starlicht,
> And they wanderit through reid bluid tae the knee.
> For a' the bluid that's shed o' man
> Rins i' the streams o' yon countrie.

Or there is strength and beauty going down at the sweep of the steel, in *The Bonny Earl o' Moray*, which is ballad as much as song, or *Johnie Armstrong* : or fantastic cruelties of man or fate, like *Edom o' Gordon* or *Gil Morice*. And always there is war, whether the knightly combat of *Chevy Chase*, where the dead man wins a fight (as many years later was to happen in sober truth above the Garry, when the silver bullet put an end to King James's hope), or the hard-bitten humours—yet these also not unchivalrous—of *Jamie Telfer* and the rescue of Kinmont Willie, a thing I have never yet been able to read without shedding tears of sheer rejoicing excitement.

Some of them are old universal folk-themes, dreams, one could say, of the collective mind of humanity, that have their parallels in the South Seas. Others are of things that happened to given men in a given place and time—*Kinmont Willie* again and *The Laird of Logie*, whose heroine is one of Queen Anne's Danish ladies, and *Edom o' Gordon* (47) and *The Bonny Hoose o' Airlie*, and *The Baron o' Brackley*, and possibly *Bonny George Campbell*—a haunting thing, true a million times in our history. Others are fantastic versions of a true story, coloured and enriched, like *Marie Hamilton*, where the Queen's serving-woman and one of her fellows become one of the Four Maries and King Henry himself. But there is always one thing in them, the human soul confronting gallantly the brittleness of its glory. They ride under the mools with their heads high. It is the essential stuff of great tragedy—that splendour is a mark for the winds of Fate, and that none the less it is good that there should be splendour.

The ballads carry on across the Gulf. The common people might be dragooned, under penalty, into signing the Covenant, (48) and no doubt there were many who did so voluntarily : but outside Edinburgh and the south-west the excesses of the presbyterocracy had less purchase on their life than they had on that of the gentry and the universities. It was the other side of the tradition, however, that came up again first after the Restoration, with *Maggie Lauder* and *Habbie Simpson*—both, by the way, by gentlemen, the two Sempills of Beltrees, father and son. These lead the way to Ferguson and one side of Burns, and the element in Scott represented by Meg Dods and Edie Ochiltree, and to most of Galt. The ballad side of the tradition reappears in the Jacobite songs, which, though "popular" song, are rather rarely popular by origin : it goes on to our own time in such things as Violet Jacob's *The End o't*, and the elf-light in some songs of Marion Angus, though its effect on our novel has so far been confined pretty well to Scott, in such things as *The Bride of Lammermoor* or the ghastly trick that (in the unmangled *St Ronan's*) is played on Clara Mowbray ; or to one or two passages in Stevenson, like the duel in *The Master of Ballantrae*. These have as much of history as of ballad, but it is history seen with the ballad vision. Their effect on English and French has perhaps been wider, but in English verse at least it is apt to have a suspicious touch of pastiche : in *Wuthering Heights*, however, and in the greatest of Hardy and of Conrad the imaginative vision, though it expresses itself in other terms, is much that of the ballad in its quality. One notices, however, that two of these three instances belong to the work of writers who are not English. In French what one thinks of as being kin to ballad proceeds more often, probably, from a common inheritance of emotion and memory. Scotland and North France feel in the same fashion (though it is your Gascon who is said to be " l'Écossais de la France ") and their folk-verse is often remarkably alike (49) : even as late as the eighteenth century *Malbrouck* belongs to the imaginative world of *Bonny George Campbell* and *The Bonny Hoose o' Airlie*.

VI

DRAMA

Lost work—ghosts—the Thrie Estatis—*Latin work—the Reformation—Sydserf —Crawfurd—Mrs Cockburn*

ANOTHER division of our older literature, and apparently a lively one in its day, that was killed more effectively, was that of drama. It was killed so effectively, in fact, that the phrase " Scots drama " sounds a little absurd, as if one should write of Bantu aviation. Yet in the fifteenth and even quite late in the sixteenth century, drama in Scotland appears to have flourished as one of the most popular of the arts.

We know very little of it, however, beyond that it did exist and was popular. It may have been slow in developing : the earliest actual reference is as late as 1445, when *Haliblude* was performed in Aberdeen, on the Windmill Brae. This, however, does not prove very much as to lateness : few people realise how scanty war, the Reformation, the shipwreck of Cromwell's eighty-five hogsheads of stolen documents, and the economies of an English-manned Treasury have left our records : the provosts of Edinburgh itself, for instance, cannot be traced before 1307 (50). (Even a Queen of Scots of no further back than the eleventh century is nameless, though we know her parentage.) The constant association of the Scots court with France and Flanders, from the early thirteenth century at least to Mary, the constant coming and going of Scots soldiers, scholars, and merchants, at a time when

French mediaeval drama was very active, the inter-national culture and outlook which the Scots medi-aeval Church, like the French, succeeded in combining with very national politics, would all, one imagines, lead to Scots interest in drama. Certainly by the second half of the fifteenth century, there was plenty of Scots drama, both of the sacred that was partly popular instruction and partly a sort of votive offering, a representation in action instead of stained glass or sculpture, and of the festival pageantry that grew into the masque and ballet.

We have scraps and patches of information, de-scriptions of such things as the homecoming of royal brides, the names of playwrights and actors here and there. " Master John Clerk and James Affleck " are in Dunbar's lament, and seem to have been drama-tists : under James V there was James Wedderburn (1495 ?-1553), who made " divers comedies and tragedies," which include a *Tragedie of St John the Baptist* and a *Historie of Dionysus the Tyrant*, acted in Dundee about 1539. His elder contemporary, Abbot Inglis, seems to have been a voluminous dramatist. It is worth noting that when Queen Margaret went to Aberdeen in 1511 the *padyanis* included Scots history as well as scriptural.

Of actual texts, however, we have hardly anything. *The Droichis Part of the Play* is a fantastic prologue-monologue which may be Dunbar's—a very lively piece with a hint of Maître François Rabelais in its giant who burlesques old Gaelic story :

> My foir grantschir hecht Fyn Mackcowll,
> That dang the Devill and gart him yowll,
> The skyis ranyd quhen he wald scowle,
>   And trublit all the air :

He gat my grantschir Gog Magog :
Ay quhen he dansit the warld wad schog :
Five thousand ellis ʒeid in his frog
    Of Hieland pladdis of hair.
ʒit he was bot of tendir ʒouth :
Bot eftir he grew mekle at fouth,
Ellevyne ell wyde met was his mouth,
    His teith was ten myle sqwair.
He wald apon his tais stand,
And tak the sternis doune with his hand,
And set tham in a gold garland
    Aboue his wifis hair.

There is Lindsay's *Thrie Estaitis*, already described, which though apparently a court-piece is not in the pageant tradition, but moral allegory already transforming into regular drama, with suggestions of some contemporary French work. There is one very curious anonymous piece, *Philotus*, extant in a fine black-letter edition of 1603, whose printing is in remarkable contrast to that of the contemporary English playbooks. From internal evidence, it would seem to be little later than the *Thrie Estaitis* : that the comic conjuration of a ghost includes a whole string of invocations of saints is perhaps not evidential, for the scene is farce and the saints are mixed with elves and fairies : but a lady carries a missal when she goes out, and a " sympathetic " character in a serious scene swears by St Mary, neither of which details would be safe in a popular play of the late century, obviously written for actual presentation. If it is earlier than 1560, it is also earlier than 1542, for the last stanza prays for the King, and *king* is one of a triple set of rhymes. It has been said that it must be after 1583, because its plot is that of a tale in Barnabe Rich's *Farewell*. But it is just as possible that Barnabe, who like most Elizabethans, Shakespeare included, took his plots where he found them, may have borrowed from the play, or both Barnabe and the play from some lost source. If it were as late as the mid fifteen-eighties, let alone after 1600, one would expect it, in view of the known importation of English plays by James VI's court, to show some influence in its form of the blank verse which the Wits in that decade were establishing as the regular medium. But its form is as unlike the English work of the late century as its content is unlike that of anything English before Greene. The form is elaborate stanza—

> O lustie luifsome lamp of licht,
> Your bonynes, your bewtie bricht,
> Your staitly stature trym and ticht,
>   With gestures grave and gude,
> Your countenance, your culleir,
> Your lauching lips, your smyling cheir,
> Your properties dois all appeir
>   My senses to illude.

—varied in places with decasyllabic octaves and rhyme royal. The matter is romantic comedy in the vein of Robert Greene, who was to be Shakespeare's master : one may trace in it a hint of both Terence and the novelle, and touches of what was to grow into Molière. The wealthy elderly Philotus woos fourteen-year-old Emily, who in spite of the Macrell's (go-between's) enticing descriptions of a life of luxury (a lively piece of manners-painting, not without humour) refuses him and elopes in boy's clothes with her lover Flavius, her place being taken by her brother Philerno, newly returned from abroad, who submits to the paternal will, is espoused to Philotus, and handed over to the chaperonage of his pretty daughter

Brisilla. Flavius, meanwhile, has seen the mock espousals, and there are elaborate complications ending happily for everyone but poor Philotus, who is told that his misfortunes serve him right. It is not farce, but genuine romantic comedy : the young lovers are drawn sympathetically and given honourable intentions, and the main action is free from the sculduddery traditional in farce : Philerno, when as the mock bride he is handed over to Brisilla, does not behave as does Beaumont and Fletcher's Welford (*The Scornful Lady*) in like case. Farce is present, however, as it always is, even in the full Shakespearian development of the type. It appears, as almost everywhere outside Shakespeare, in a frankly pinned-on fashion, being supplied here by the part of The Plesant, a figure obviously descended, like the Ateukin of Greene's *James IV King of Scots*, from the Vice of the Moralities : unlike Ateukin, however, he has no part in the action, but comments on it to the audience, often dirtily enough. An equally extraneous Messenger speaks the epilogue.

The play is of great interest from the historical point of view : from the purely dramatic it has, except as pioneer work, not much merit. There is a certain sense of situation, but the characters are mere outlines and the situations themselves are handled with less eye to the stage than in Lindsay : one wonders if the text is complete, for Flavius in one speech is promising to procure Emily her boy's clothes, and Emily in the next is escaping in them, no provision of any sort being made, as the text stands, for the interval.

After *Philotus*, very little survives. There are Lord Stirling's *Monarchick Tragedies* in 1607, which in many ways anticipate the Heroick Drama of the Restoration. There is Ben Jonson, writing like him in England (curiously enough his two plays on Scottish subjects, *The Scottish Tragedy* and *Robert II King of Scots* are lost) and one of the great figures in his age's drama. And that is all until we come to the Restoration, when Scottish drama reappears—in England— in the work of three dramatists whose work, if scarcely great, all has merit in its kind.

Since none of them have been reprinted, it is perhaps worth while to describe them. The senior of the three is Thomas St Serf or Sydserf, son of that learned Bishop of Galloway who suffered severely in the Civil War, the terrible charge being brought against him of having said that he found the sight of the Crucifix an aid to devotion. Thomas was, naturally, a Cavalier, and fought under Montrose : apart from his solitary comedy, he is worth mention here as the founder of Scottish journalism by his *Mercurius Caledonius* (51), established in 1660, to lapse in a short time through lack of support. *Tarugo's Wiles, or The Coffee-house*, printed in 1668 with a dedication to Huntly, is a lively if rather rambling comedy of intrigue—considerably more decent, by the way, than the average Restoration work of the kind. It strongly suggests early work of Molière's, not only because it follows the same Italian models—the resourceful Don Tarugo, though not a serving-man, plays much the same part as Schiappino-Scapin—but because its theme, though not its plot, is very much that of *L'École des maris*. Patricio imprisons his sister Liviana, for the same reason that Sganarelle does Isabelle— because he considers it the only way to keep her out of mischief. The commentary is supplied by her

174

friend Sophronia, who stands for both Ariste and Léonor : Patricio loves her and she him, but she will very properly have nothing to do with him until he shows more faith in her sex, so she throws him over, and helps Liviana's lover, Horatio, to get her out, with the assistance of the resourceful Tarugo. The piece is as loosely hung together as are most of its kind, but it is not unamusing. Though English-women evidently bored him (Tarugo has just returned from England, and not been very greatly impressed by it) Sydserf had no liking for the Puritan contempt for women. The keynote of the more serious part of the play is Liviana's retort to her brother, " Fear not the ease of your mind, if it depend on the preservation of my honour, for 'tis within my breast can do that better than all your restraints," which is quite in the vein of Molière, but not at all in that of Wycherly or even Congreve. The casual interludary stuffing— " farce " in the literal sense—that had come down from the Elizabethans, includes a coffee-house scene of varied and argumentative guests who hit off types of the day, including the old soldier, the scientist (with rejuvenation-scheme), and the art critic, and show, as in all manners-painting that is done with an eye on the object, how very little society really changes.

The comedies of David Crawfurd (1665-1726) have again a certain echo of Molière. He was a son of Crawfurd of Drumsoy, a graduate of Glasgow, and an advocate, and became Queen Anne's Historio-grapher Royal. His work in that capacity consists of *Memoirs of the Affairs of Scotland from 1567*, whose main intention is a vindication of Queen Mary from Buchanan's scandal-mongering. Crawfurd's chosen muse, however, was not Clio, for besides his one history he wrote three novels and a couple of comedies, both of considerable merit. *Courtship à la Mode* appeared in 1700 with a prologue by Farquhar. It is comedy of intrigue of the usual Restoration type : its crowded bustle of action, set spinning by the professional match-maker Mrs Decoy, shows a sense of the stage and is carried on in natural and amusing dialogue, with some genuine humour. The characters are the usual Restoration figures, Winmore, Bellair, Alderman Cholerick, and so forth, with a comic Scots serving-man, Willie Beetlehead, who talks an idiomatic and racy Doric. The printed version, with a cheerful cheek, has two epilogues, to be used according as the piece is applauded or hissed.

Love at First Sight (1704) is of much the same kind. It opens with Courtly's speech, " Heaven defend us ! Of all Plagues that attend us mortals, this Love, this Damned Vertuous Love, is sure the worst ! " In spite of the gentleman's objection, the moral tone is that of Steele rather than of Congreve, and he has in the end to dwindle into a contented husband, after a complicated but not ill-constructed plot, with a Tartuffian sub-plot. There is a real sense of social comedy in it, especially in the scene where Lovewell and the boorish Sir John Single court Fidelia in duet, and Single, who represents the typical English attitude to women (" Pray Sir, ask the young lady's opinion." " Opinion ! Women shou'd have no Opinion.") thinks Lovewell, who carries his arguments to their logical conclusions, is backing them instead of exploding them. Crawfurd, like Sydserf, was something of a feminist, or, being a Scot, appears so among his English contemporaries, for the Scots attitude to women, like the French, has always differed—outside one section of Scotland—from that underlying the quaint English custom of refusing a surname to " Mary, wife of John Smith."

The third of these waifs is the rather interesting personality whom the contemporary Queen of Prussia describes in a letter as " la Sappho escossoise." Catherine Trotter or Cockburn was the daughter of a naval officer of some distinction in the service and of good family, related to the Maitlands of Lauderdale and the Drummonds of Perth. Born in 1679, she was an Episcopalian convert from the Roman Church, and married an Episcopal minister in Aberdeen. She lived to see both Risings, dying in 1749. Mrs Cockburn was considerably a personage both in London and in Episcopalian Scotland, for—though her portrait suggests that her reputation as such came from charm rather than features—she was both a noted beauty and a distinguished scholar. Philosophy and theology were her main subjects : she was a friend of Leibnitz, and at twenty-two was one of the first to defend Locke in print, producing, in 1701, an essay which greatly pleased him. Her other philosophical works include a treatise on logic and an apologia for her conversion. In pure literature, she has some songs with a touch of the Restoration grace, that include a translation of St Francis Xavier's *O Deus, ego amo Te*, familiar nowadays in Faber's version, and a number of plays highly esteemed in their time. She was precocious as a dramatist, for her first tragedy, *Agnes de Castro*, which is based on a French novel, was acted with much applause when she was sixteen, and *The Fatal Friendship* comes only three years later. It was followed by a comedy called *Love at a Loss* (1701), and two tragedies, *The Unhappy Penitent* of 1701, whose preface

M   177 shows excellent dramatic criticism, and *The Revolution of Sweden* in 1706. Her tragedies are in the Heroick manner, and in their sufficiently artificial kind have real dramatic quality and some vigour of dialogue, though, as one might expect in plays all written before the author's middle twenties, they do not show any depth of character-drawing.

After her, there is a gap of half a century, till we reach *Douglas* in 1756, played in Edinburgh and written by a Whig and a minister, which shows a very significant change in outlook, although the poor man had to resign his charge. But these ten plays and Bannatyne's two or three fragments are all that is left of a Scottish drama before George III.

We do know a little about what is lost. It goes on, in Scotland, for longer than is usually assumed, for the Reformers' objection to it did not become active immediately. The Latin plays written by George Buchanan at the Collège de Guyenne, and performed there by his students, had no influence in his own country, but a very considerable one in France, where, through Jodelle and Garnier, they helped to determine the form of the great French classic drama of the Grand Siècle. As late as 1568 a play by one Robert Sempill was acted before the Regent Moray, the last man to do publicly anything disapproved by the pious : Moray indeed in private had no vices, except those of avarice and treachery, which are not of sufficient importance to forbid his appearance as saint and martyr in one of the stained glass windows in St Giles. Even John Knox went to see a play representing the taking of Edinburgh Castle and the hanging of the Queen's Governor and his officers, captured by the English auxiliaries of the Regent

Morton, who had succeeded Moray as Commander of the Faithful.

The Reformers were at pains, however, to see that their drama was of the right complexion. In 1575 they prohibited plays based on Scripture, and set up a rigid censorship of the rest. None the less, when Anne of Denmark and Norway arrived as a bride in 1590, there were still pageants arranged by the City Fathers ; and after the native drama had been strangled, English companies occasionally came north : " the Inglis Comedianis "—probably the Queen's Men—were in Scotland in 1594, perhaps for Prince Henry's baptism. In 1599, however, when an English touring company took a house in Edinburgh, the Kirk Session were specially convened to protest, though the Privy Council, under Court influence, protected the players : Queen Anne loved masques, as she showed when she came to Whitehall. There was a similar company in Aberdeen in 1601, with the style of His Majesty's Servants, and the Town Council of that never very Presbyterian city stood them a civic supper. The King, in fact, had a court company of English actors, headed by Laurence Fletcher, who later was one of the King's Men in London ; but apparently their corporate existence did not survive 1601, and after King James had entered his new capital, with William Shakespeare walking in his train in new scarlet cloth, the system of an infallible pope in every parish, backed by the civil arm and a company of appointed delators, had nothing that could be an effectual check, and except for the work of a few exiles, a Scottish drama became impossible.

The ruin is very much to be regretted. The two Scots plays that survive from the early sixteenth century suggest that our drama was making a lively start. Looking at the state of affairs in 1540, we might expect to see, later, something corresponding to the superb English outburst of the period from 1580 to 1620. The Scottish people have always had a strong sense of the dramatic in life, a sense of gesture, of the vivid representative action. The Douglas Dinner may possibly be legend, but if so it is all the better as illustration : the dramatic sense in the ballads is undeniable. That of the later sixteenth and early seventeenth centuries, however, seems to find its expression, for the most part, in very actual violent death. Scots murders are apt to show a sense of style, and so, no less, does the business of being murdered, whether judicially or by private enterprise. Indeed, in that age, one could almost say that there *is* a Scottish drama, a tragic drama relieved by fierce comedy, that reminds one often of Middleton or Webster. But its dead men do not rise and go home to supper, though some of their murderers may " fall to prayer with great composure of spirit and enlargement of heart more than ordinary," as one of Archbishop Sharpe's remarks in his journal, after helping to kill an old man in front of his daughter. No one who knows the history of the three countries is likely to be very much surprised when critics bred in the cosy English tradition find French and Scottish fiction melodramatic, or cry out on Walter Scott for impossible plots that happen to be authentic history.

VII

PROSE

So far, in this survey of three centuries, I have spoken only of verse. Prose, in fact—English or Scots prose at any rate—was very late in developing in our country. It comes everywhere, as a literary medium, later than verse, but in Scotland the lateness is especially marked. The prose of France dates from early in the thirteenth century, with Villehardouin and *Le Faux Turpin* : the first French translation of the whole Bible is in 1255. In England, *The Ancren Riwle* is not much later, though it is only literature by chance, being directions for a little group of women recluses, not regular nuns, who presumably knew no Latin. But we can fairly date English prose literature from at least as early as the mid fourteenth century, while if there was any Scots prose before the fifteenth, and fairly late in it at that, it is lost.

A difference of over two hundred years from the country intellectually, of a hundred from that geographically, nearest to us, is more than a little surprising, especially as that period, at any rate in its later part, shows some excellent work in " the other harmony." There would be, of course, the usual reasons for lateness that are found everywhere, the mediaeval habit of taking for granted the use of verse for what seem to us odd purposes, for theology, history, the sciences ; the persistent feeling that prose was scarcely a worthy medium for literature—a feeling likely to be specially strong in a country whose taste in verse was for the elaborately gorgeous. Again, prose naturally begins as the vehicle for works of learning : and learned men wrote for the international republic of letters, and if they wanted an audience of any size, in the international language, Latin (52). The earliest prose historians of Scotland, Fordun, Boece, and John Major, all used Latin. The vernacular, especially in a small country, was more likely to be used for popular exposition, for such things as were equivalent to the newspaper articles of Sir Arthur Thomson or Sir James Jeans, or for political or religious propaganda. That there should, until the sixteenth century, be practically nothing of this in a country with a vigorous and distinguished literature and a traditional respect for learning suggests a considerable diffusion of at least sufficient scholarship to read Latin. James IV's Education Act made a schooling in " perfyte Latin " compulsory on the eldest sons of all freeholders : but learning had long been the *younger* son's gate to a career. The mediaeval Scot, of all classes, was for obvious reasons something of a linguist, and while the mediaeval methods of teaching Latin were no doubt less scientific than ours, they do seem to have taught far more people its free use. With all allowances, however, the extreme lateness of Scots prose remains surprising. One cannot help wondering if among the reasons for it is the simple one that certain work has vanished : we know that so much verse has disappeared—nearly a score of known authors are sunk without trace : but there is less evidence for such loss in prose.

The earliest known piece of Scots prose, outside legal documents, is a little treatise on *The Craft of Deyng*, a grave and not ungracious moral discourse, which apparently belongs to some time in the mid-fifteenth century. The Gilbert Hay of Dunbar's lament has three translations or adaptations from the French, extant in a MS. of 1456 : these are *Le Gouvernance des princes*, *L'Arbre de batailles* of the warlike Prior of Saluces, Honoré Bonet, the standard treatise on the law of arms, and *L'Ordene de chevalerie*, done into English a little later by Caxton, with an amusing difference : the English bourgeois is careful to stress the distinction between the knight and his inferiors, while the Scots knight, chamberlain to a King of France and as blue-blooded a person as you please, says he exists to defend the Faith, his natural lord, and " the pepill in thair richtis." He writes a pleasant straightforward prose, but, of course, he is no more than a translator, and (until we reach the middle of the sixteenth century) the same is true of all other early prose-writers except for the social-philosophy sermon of John of Ireland. Nisbet's New Testament, based on Wyclif's, appears about the late fifteen-twenties. John Gau's *Richt Vay to the Kingdom of Heuine*, published in Sweden in 1533, and the earliest Protestant treatise in Scots, is a translation two deep, being a version of a Danish translation from the German. The principal figure, in prose, under James V, is John Bellenden, Archdeacon of Moray (1495-after 1550), with very competent versions of Livy (1532) and of Boece's Latin History of Scotland (1536). The famous *Complaynt of Scotland* is translation in part, but translation freely adapted to a fresh purpose, and mixed with much that is original. It survives in four copies, of which two are in the Harleian collection. It has been attributed to Lindsay, presumably by somebody who had not read it : there are surface parallels, but only in literary devices that were more or less common form, while apart from differences of language, Lindsay is consistently pro-English, while the author of the *Complaynt* is a friend of France and by no means affectionate to the country that was just then (1549) doing her best to abolish his own. Abbot Inglis of Culross, another claimant, was killed some time before the book appeared. The most probable attribution is one made in the Harleian Catalogue of 1743, apparently on the strength of a title-page which has disappeared, though Pinkerton, in his edition of the Maitland MSS., says he had seen it. (Some leaves of the Harleian copies are known to have vanished between 1801 and 1872.) The Harleian entry is *Vedderburn's Complaynte of Scotlande vyth ane Exhortatione to the thre Estaits to be vigilante in the Deffens of their Public Veil.* Who Wedderburn is, however, is unknown, for since he was a Queen's man and anti-English, and though a Reformer, an obviously Catholic one, he can hardly have been one of the three Dundee brothers of the *Gude and Godlie Ballatis.* Whoever he was, he was a patriotic and clear-sighted Scot, with an eye in his head, and a good deal of classical learning, courage, and zest in life. Requiescat.

The book was published, apparently, in Paris, and part of it is adapted from *Le Quadrilogue invectif* of the fifteenth-century Senecan, Alain Chartier (1394-1439), the ugly poet whose mouth that spoke beauty was kissed by a Scots Dauphine—or so says a story that unluckily has no historic warrant. The author's claim that it springs from " my gude intenione that procedis fra ane affectiue ardent fauoir that I hef euyr borne touart this affligit realme quhilke is my natiue cuntrie," is not necessarily less sincere for that : the orthodox critics of it appear to forget that Scotland in the fifteen-forties was in almost the same case and precisely in the same dangers as Chartier's France, and that the *cri du cœur* of a patriot from the one can express the real emotions aroused by the other.

The book is a very curious affair. It begins with an elaborate dedication to Queen Marie, in stately aureate terms full of scriptural and classical allusions. The writer surveys the desperate state of the Scottish nation, which in fact since Bruce had never been in a worse, and discourses on government and on the apparently approaching end of the world. Then, to vary his discourse, comes a long interlude, the famous *Monolog Recreatif*, and after it he returns to the state of Scotland, adapting pretty freely from Chartier in his vision of Dame Scotia as a lady " of excellent extractione and of anciant genolygie," but with her rich robes all ragged. There is a genuine passion in her address to her three sons, which is the author's own, though the discourses of the sons (the Three Estates) are from Chartier. It includes some uncommonly plain speaking to all three : the Spirituality are told roundly, by the way, that persecution is worse than useless, in much the vein of St Simon's denunciation, as a loyal Catholic, of the Revocation of the Edict of Nantes. If they want to keep men from falling into heresy, the remedy is not persecution, but their own piety and learning.

Between these two passionate discourses the picture-gallery of the famous *Monolog* comes at first sight rather oddly. None the less, it is rather crude criticism to dismiss it as an irrelevant interpolation. It may conceivably have been added later, but it has a definite artistic purpose, besides being the most original part of the book. Into the author's passionate concern for Scotland comes a sort of vision of an old and kindly land, where men work and play and are themselves and happy. The technique of the picture is not that of the nineteenth century, though in fact there are places where it resembles more modern work ; and if one is willing to take it at its own pace, it is effective and genuinely moving, even in itself, much more as background for Dame Scotia's suffering. The author walks in the country on a summer evening : there is sunset and sunrise, rather heavily handled, though he has an eye for nature in such touches as that of the wind scattering the fruit-tree blossom among the grass, and in the curious catalogue of the country sounds at morning and the crying of the birds. These catalogues were, of course, a regular mediaeval device that lasted through the Renaissance —Spenser's are famous—and up to Milton, and have revived in our own time : and this one has both precise observation and an enormous and precise vocabulary to convey it.

He comes to the seaside then and sees a galliass getting under way at sight of a strange sail, and there is another little symphony of sounds : it is noisy with sea-orders, some of them still in use : the helmsman is told to " keep her full and bye," and there are snatches of chanties, both capstan and hauling. The men go to action stations as their ship gets way on her, the enemy is engaged, and there is a spirited fight, done again almost all in terms of sound. He leaves the two ships grappled in a cloud of smoke, and walks on till he meets a company of shepherds, one of whom holds forth at length on the advantages of a pastoral life, the discourse unfortunately gliding into a lecture on astronomy and physics, which the lecturer's wife describes, not unjustly, as " a tideous melancolic orison." They fall to play then, with tales and songs and dances, and the ghostly catalogue of these is one of our most valuable clues to the limbo of our lost mediaeval letters (53). He passes then to a meadow filled with flowers, where he falls asleep, and has the bitter vision of what is to come to that ancient and kindly world. I have described him at some length, for the book is genuinely important for both social and literary history, and, from the critical point of view, in itself, as the work of a man of considerable literary having and a good deal of artistic initiative, who is attempting to do in his own language what he has seen and admired in others.

It is not, however, till a decade later, at the time when the stream of verse is running thin, that prose becomes anything like common. Lindsay of Pitscottie's well-known *Chronicle* comes in 1575, continuing Boece, and itself continued to 1604 by another hand : the full title is *The Historie and Cronicles of Scotland From the Slauchter of King James the First to the Ane thousande fyve hundrieth thrie scoir fyftein zeir*. It is lively journalism rather than history proper : he has no sense of perspective, and is too violently partisan to be trustworthy : not for nothing was he a cousin of Mary's fierce opponent, Lindsay of the Byres. But it certainly is lively, not to say lurid : he gives a story with uncommon raciness and an eye for telling detail, and his information comes very often from the sons or grandsons of the men concerned, or from themselves. He has the tale of James V's death, for instance, from a man who was there and heard the pitiful cry, " Adew, fairweill, it come witht ane lase, it will pase witht ane lase " : and so with such matters as Admiral Wood's capture of the English pirate Stephen Bull, or the warning ghost in St Michael's Kirk at Linlithgow.

I have already referred to George Buchanan's Latin work, and his odd position as one of the founders of French classical drama—a forerunner of the creator of Tartuffe. These Latin writings made him a towering figure in the European literary society of an age of classicists, and are still, according to good judges, supreme in their kind. His work in Scots is less notable as literature, but its effect on the Scots politics of the time, and on historical tradition, at home and abroad, to this day, has been so enormous that it demands some consideration. He was born in 1506 and died in 1582. He spent much of his middle life abroad, mainly at the Collège de Guyenne, and part of it as the tutor of Montaigne—some of it also, which explains his emotions if hardly his methods, as prisoner of the Inquisition, who do not, however, seem to have done him any damage. He came to Scotland in Mary's active reign, and the Queen showed him great favour, appointing him her classical tutor and employing him in a sort of Universities Commission, besides giving him a considerable pension and the temporalities of Crossraguel Abbey. His part in vernacular letters is the writing of pamphlets in her vilification. Some of them belong to the time when he also was writing Latin odes in her praise. His *Detectio Mariae Reginae*, published in 1570, when he had just become tutor to Mary's son, is a very interesting piece of work. A Scots version of it in 1572, at a time when the memory of her brief six years was still vivid but the popular knowledge of it blurred and distorted, did infinite harm to her cause.

One may take as a sample of Buchanan's controversial methods the famous account of Queen Mary's visit to Bothwell at Hermitage in 1566. It is one of the best-known episodes in her career : what is perhaps the most generally reliable of short histories of Scotland repeats it in detail, and as for the novelists ... ! No wonder : what could be more convincing than this, from a sober scholar of European fame, Principal of a St Andrews college and lay Moderator of the General Assembly ? Could the evening papers now print a more luscious and delightful story against a young, beautiful, and royal woman, of exasperating intelligence and charm ?

She heard of Bothwells wound, whereupon she flingeth away in hast like a mad woman, by great iourneyes in poste, in the sharpe time of winter, first to Melrose and than to Jedworth. Thare, though she heard sure newes of his life, yet hcr affectioun, impatient of delay, cauld not temper itself, but neids shc must bewray her outragious lust, and in an inconuenient time of the year, despising all discommodities of the way and wether, and all dangers of thieffis, she betook herself hedlong to hir iourney, with sic a company as na man of any honest degree wald haif aduentured his life and his gudes amang tham.

A hundred and twenty-five words, and even if we accept Buchanan's estimate of the Queen's escort, which included his master Moray, there are ten categorical lies in it, all which Buchanan quite certainly knew were lies, for he was Moray's intimate hanger-on, and Moray was there. Unfortunately for Buchanan's posthumous reputation, the actual truth is much less picturesque—which is unfortunate also for Queen Mary's, for the story is so juicy that nobody wanted it to be disproved. Royal movements go down on things like Assize Registers : people about a Queen often write letters and occasionally date them : and even in Scotland these things sometimes survive . . . although, as Buchanan well knew, they are unlikely, in an age of no newspapers, to be accessible to the public five years later.

This is Buchanan's material in fact. Mary received news of Bothwell's wound on the 9th of October, hardly " the sharp time of winter." She made no fantastic journey by Melrose and Jedburgh, because she was *at* Jedburgh when the news reached her, having come there for nothing more romantic than Jeddart Assizes. She may have been upset at the news, but her behaviour was hardly indiscreet, for instead of " flinging away " she put in a week's work at legal business. Then, making a very natural decision for a hard-riding young queen who had had a boring week and was by habit kind and friendly towards her servants, she set out to visit, not merely a high official wounded in the execution of his duty —Bothwell was Warden of the Middle Marches, and had been hurt in the course of some police-work—but a faithful servant of her beloved mother's and very nearly the only man about her who had not, to her knowledge (and she was twenty-five and sensitive), betrayed her to serve his own interests. Hermitage was twenty miles off : there and back in a day is a fair ride, but not " great journeys by post." I can remember my father riding seventy-six in one day, in an emergency, over Highland roads, and his horse had spunk enough left to shy at the gate as he came in. And Scott, a heavy man, once rode a hundred in twenty-four hours, from Cumberland to Dalkeith—though he, presumably, was riding post. Disregarding " the incommodity of way and weather," which was no worse than a constantly moving Scottish sovereign was accustomed to take the chance of in any autumn—and early October, as a rule, is as far from being the most " inconvenient time of the year " on the Borders as it is from " the sharp time of winter "—she rode out on the 15th October, with her brother, Buchanan's owner, and Huntly for chaperons, and the customary royal escort, which ought to have disposed of any " peril of thieves." She spent two hours at Hermitage, entertained by Lady Bothwell, and discreetly rode back to Jedburgh. The weather did turn " inconvenient," and she got drenched, and went down, not with emotion (since Bothwell, even by Buchanan's account, was in no danger) but with what appears to have been rheumatic fever . . . not very surprising in a fragile girl three months from a childbed complicated by being held, three months earlier, by her child's father, to watch the extremely messy murder of her confidential servant, or by the desperate flight to Dunbar that followed, and her husband's craven callousness on the road.

Buchanan does not miss the opportunity. He adds, with unction,

Quhen (Bothwell) was ones brought thether (to Jedburgh), thair company and familiar haunt togither was sic as was smally agreing with baith thair honours. Thare,

191

whether it were by reason of thair nightly and daily trauailes, dishonourable to tham selfis and infamous amang the pepill, or by some secrit prouidence of God, the Quene fell into sic a sore and dangerous sicknesse, that scarcely thare remained any hoip of hir life.

We happen to know, from a contemporary letter of the Bishop of Ross, who was there, and deeply concerned, that Mary was very ill on the 16th October. On the 25th, she was given up for dead, and Moray, as Buchanan does not say, was demanding her jewels. *On that same day*, Bothwell arrived in Jedburgh, in a litter, and still unable to put his foot to the ground. One could give further instances, in at least one of which the evidence that proves Buchanan a liar comes from a source so bitterly hostile to Mary as a confidential despatch of Bedford's. But the subject is scarcely one on which to linger. An eminent Scots critic of the nineteenth century says of Buchanan that " his works exhibit a rare union of philosophical dignity and research with the finer susceptibilities and imagination of the poet." " Research " and " imagination " are rather good (54).

As far as vernacular literature is concerned, John Knox is a more considerable figure, and not nearly such a liar as Buchanan, for that eminent scholar knew a true phrase from a false one, while Knox all his life had a power that was almost sublime of believing what his emotions found convenient. It shows amusingly in his attitude to the two most famous murders of the day. When a servant of the Queen, unarmed, is murdered by a whole gang of armed men, with every circumstance of violent brutality, deliberately before a woman six months with child, the lawful sovereign of all the murderers,

Knox's comment on the affair, in considered print, is
that it was " most worthy of all praise." But when
eleven months later the ring-leader of the murderers
is murdered in his turn, the death of Mary's late-
espoused saint rouses Knox to a perfect frenzy of
Christian horror. And there does not seem to be any
doubt as to his complete sincerity over both. It was
this sheer sincerity in the man, in whatever attitude
suited him at the moment, that gave drive to the
shrill east-windy vehemence that intoxicated the
Edinburgh mob and was one of Moray's most valuable
tools.

Knox, indeed, is a most interesting study. It is
probable that the remembrance of his early, re-
pudiated, vows may have been partly responsible for
the queer pathological twist in him over sex that
colours so much of his conduct and opinions, including his political opinions in an age when women were
not only conspicuous in upper-class society, but rulers,
at one time or other, of most of Europe. It is true
that a violent anti-feminism was common to most of
the Reformers, helped perhaps (and conversely) by
the Orientalism of an Old Testament religion (55) :
it is to them that we owe the vow of unconditional
obedience in the Marriage Office, and such social
details as the enactment of 1597—repeated later—
that though men could still have stools in kirk, women
must " sit laigh " (*i.e.* on the floor), the Kirk Officer
going round with a pole to remove, in spite of St Paul,
the plaids from their heads, " lest they should sleip."
In Knox this rises to a foaming hysteria that is partly,
perhaps, resentment at his extreme dependence upon
women ; a spiritual harem followed him about, both
personally and by correspondence, in a way that

rather reminds one of Shelley's soul-mates, though it is most unlikely, in spite of the annoyance of their husbands, that his relations with them were " improper : " in spite of his marriage at fifty-nine to a girl of fifteen, it is fairly clear that what Knox demanded of women was nothing so decent as mere bodily lust.

That side of him, though hardly pleasant to study, throws a good deal of light on his shrill personal hatred of Marie de Guise—though he could flatter her heavily when it suited him. She had not only tolerated him when he trailed his coat in 1555 and considered him an unimportant accessory to her Chancellor's murder—a fact which a man of his type would resent intensely—but was a beautiful and intelligent Frenchwoman. It explains, too, how his teeth were set on edge by the youth, charm, spirit, and dignity of her daughter (56). It is clear, from his own writing, that he had with women of breeding and intelligence what our age would describe as a painful inferiority-complex. Mary's grace and charm, her refusal to bully him, combined with her refusal to be bullied even when his blustering ill-manners had jarred her nerves to—he says so triumphantly—tears, were so many wounds to his passionate self-esteem. Like so many self-made men, he needed to dominate all opinions about him. If Mary had played mirror to his Narcissus, like the worthy Mrs Locke or Mrs Bowes, if even she had threatened him as a rival power instead of inviting him to polite discussion, he would have hated her a good deal less : Moray made of him a most efficient tool. Since she disturbed that vision of himself which his bourgeoise Egerias had helped to maintain, he was forced to attempt to trample her underfoot : and that he should feel the need of doing so made it the righteous conduct for all the world.

The First Blast of the Trumpet against the Monstrous Regiment (rule) *of Women* was published in 1558 from the safe strategic position of Dieppe, midway between his English friends and that Geneva where Calvin had established a reign of terror and was still on friendly terms with his Scottish follower. It has acquired a vague fame from its picturesque title, but though it reveals a good deal of Knox, it is merely one of many political pamphlets, important less as literature than as determinants of Scottish history, including the history of Scottish culture. His principal work is the *History of the Reformation*, from the early Lollards of the fourteen-thirties to 1564, the year before Darnley's arrival, with a continuation to 1567, the year of Mary's deposition, by another hand, but probably from Knox's notes. It is a lively and readable piece of work, though one might wish that its jests, as broad as Davie Lindsay's, were as witty : its main, and considerable, importance in the history of our literature is that Knox is the first Scotsman who deliberately discards his own speech for that of England. He does it, clearly, of set purpose, for the literary languages had not yet undergone the natural process of assimilation that was brought about not so much, perhaps, by the Union as by the death of Scottish literature and the superb inflorescence that was contemporary with that in English. In Knox's generation we had still a literary tradition, while the great Elizabethan outburst does not begin until seven years after his death, with the publication of *The Shepheardes Calender*. Men both younger than

Knox and far more scholarly—Buchanan, Mont-gomerie, the much-travelled diplomat James Melville, the King himself, half a century Knox's junior—still use a definitely Scottish speech as the regular language for " polite letters." Knox's anglicising, though it tallied with his strong pro-English bent, thus seems less a literary experiment than an indication of the fact that the book was intended mainly for English readers.

To the hot nationalism that—in one party at least —not unnaturally followed the English attempts at intimidation in the fifteen-forties, the innovation was unlikely to commend itself. Ninian Winzet, in fact, takes Knox severely to task for leaving " our auld plane Scottis which your mother lerit yow," and declares that if the process is carried on he himself will be driven to Latin, for " I am not acquaintit with your Sudroun." Winzet himself wrote prose of some merit. He was a Catholic Reformer—that is, one of those who believed that *abusus non tollit usum* : and his *Tractatis for Reformatioun of Doctryne and Maneris* shows a lively nationalism, not only of language, that would have delighted Bishop Gavin Douglas. He was schoolmaster of Linlithgow, lost his job for a Catholic, got away to the Continent after an audacious escape when the Kirk authorities raided his printer, and after lecturing on philosophy at Paris and Douai, died Abbot of the Scots Benedictines at Ratisbon. His many pamphlets show him both a devout reformer of his own Church and a warlike handler of her enemies, and his Scots prose has the vigour that comes from sincerity and scholarship and the clear-cut rhythms that both he and Knox had learned from popular preaching.

Quintin Kennedy, Abbot of Crossraguel, may be mentioned on the Catholic side, with Tyrie, John Hay, John Hamilton, Nicol Burn, Adam King, Professor of Mathematics at Paris, and Arran's brother Archbishop Hamilton, hanged in his vestments in 1571, whose *Catechism* is an excellent piece of clear popular exposition. On the Protestant side there are David Ferguson and Robert Rollock; but Knox, the preachers, and the song-writers like the Wedderburns bore the main controversial weight, and the great outburst of Calvinist pamphleteering did not come until the seventeenth century, after the stimulus of union with the English Puritans. Knox's chief Catholic rival as historian is John Leslie, Bishop of Ross and Professor of Canon Law at Aberdeen, which university held so firmly to the old Church, as it was to do later to the Episcopal Reform, that a second one, a mile away in the New Town, was established in 1593 as a counterweight, remaining separate until 1860. Leslie was one of the Queen's few loyal servants, spent four years in prison for attempting her release, and was exiled after, becoming Bishop of Coutances and dying in 1596 in the Low Countries. His *History of Scotland*, written first in Scots and then in Latin, and translated again by a Scots monk of Ratisbon, is a more scholarly affair than Knox's, but being more dispassionate is much less lively. His chief importance in the history of our letters is that he and his translator are the last historians to use Scots. Spottiswoode, the next historian of note, who was nineteen years younger than Leslie and fifty-one than Knox, shows the change that took place between Montgomerie and Drummond : he uses English.

Besides histories, the time yields a good many

diaries and memoirs, the most interesting being those of the two Melvilles. Those of Sir James (1535-1617) are delightful : he had plenty of material, having travelled widely, seen several courts and a few battles, and come more than once to Whitehall as Ambassador, once of the Elector Palatine and on several other occasions as his own Queen's. He was an honest man with a dry sense of humour and a shrewd eye for human nature, and he writes a prose that is well-bred and quietly racy. Everyone knows one or two patches of him—" The Queen of Scots hath a fair son," and Elizabeth caught accidentally-on-purpose playing on the virginals—but it is a pity that there is no popular edition of the memoirs as a whole, though Scottish publishers being what, alas, they are, it is probably a little too much to hope for.

The other Melville, Andrew (1556-1614), Professor of Oriental Languages at St Andrews, writes rather less well, but has equal liveliness and humanity. He was a minister, nephew and namesake of the famous founder of Presbyterianism in Scotland (57). As a young man he was well acquainted with all the major figures among the Protestant reformers : it is from him that we have the famous picture of Knox going into the pulpit with one foot in the grave, but so fired there by his own oratory that " or he had done his sermont he was sae active and vigorous that he was lyk tae ding the pulpit in blads and fly out of it." Can one not see that portentous bristle of beard ?

Little of the prose has to do with creative letters. James VI, already mentioned as a poet, also wrote an assortment of prose works that include the famous and picturesque treatise on *Demonologie and Witchcraft* in 1587, a *Counterblast to Tobacco* as fiery (or smoky) as anything in the literature of prohibition, and the *Basilikon Doron*, a treatise on statecraft for a son who had little of that quality—as indeed had James in practice, beyond a mixture of not very lofty shrewdness and rather undeserved good luck. George Buchanan's pupil is the least likeable of the Stewarts, but he managed to die peaceably in his bed at fifty-nine, the longest-lived King between Robert III and James VII, who had no occasion to bless their length of days. The theory of the *Basilikon* is better than his practice, however, for the conception of the relation between King and people, though unlikely to commend itself to a Victorian Liberal, is not an ignoble one, and has a strong sense not only of divine right, but of responsibility.

His most notable piece of work from the literary point of view is the first known piece of Scottish literary criticism in the vernacular, *Reulis and Cautelis to be Observit and Eschewit in Scottis Poesie*, published in 1585, when he was only nineteen. (It is worth noticing that thirteen years after the death of the angliciser Knox, the learned young King still calls his language *Scottis*.) For so young an author it is a very creditable piece of work : Dr Saintsbury in his *History of English Prosody* calls it " by far the most exact and precise prosodic handbook that exists in any form of English before Bysshe "—that is to say, before Queen Anne's accession—and adds, justly, that from a critical point of view it is, though rather " sapless and scholastic," much Bysshe's superior. Like the Englishmen Webbe and Puttenham, slightly later, he was fired by his studies of classical and Continental literature to attempt to formulate a standard for the prosody and poetic diction of his own language.

His study of extant practice is both scholarly and careful, though some of his negative restrictions are rather unfortunate. The two most serious—his objection to polysyllables and to the use of any rhythm but the strict iambic—are, however, no more than the regular creed of the time, to which even Spenser subscribed in theory.

William Alexander, Earl of Stirling, already mentioned as a poet, also wrote a short treatise on the principles of poetry, *Anacrisis or Censure (i.e.* valuation) *of Poets Ancient and Modern.* It is the work of a man of taste, and of scholarship in several languages, but it is very slight.

From the literary point of view the most notable Scottish prose of what was, elsewhere, the Renaissance, comes fairly well on in the seventeenth century. Drummond of Hawthornden wrote a *History of the Five Jameses,* and earlier, *The Cypress Grove,* a meditation upon mortality which ranks among the fine things of its kind in a century of great meditative prose. Drummond's is our first creative writing in a prose that shows the change in the literary language ; and the last serious work in a definitely Scots prose—the last, that is, save the pleasant semi-Scots of much of Galt, to use Scots for anything but dialogue—is by his fellow-royalist Sir Thomas Urquhart of Cromarty, who was born in 1605, and died (characteristically, of joy at the Restoration) in 1660. He made out of the last of literary Scots not only a number of rather weird treatises on mathematics and what not, with titles like *Trissotetras* and *Logopandecteision,* but a wildly magnificent translation of Rabelais. (Was it, perhaps, a sort of protest against Presbyterian sacerdotalism ?) It comes late among the great

Renaissance translations, but is well worthy to be of their company, with a superb vocabulary like the most fantastic of the Makaris, and the vast vitality of its original. It is a last gesture of the Auld Alliance in face of the blasts of east wind from Geneva, and our most notable piece of literature in a century whose chief Scottish contribution to the arts was the making of very beautiful steel pistols.

The rest of Scottish prose, until well after the death of the last Stewart sovereign, can be briefly dismissed, though its tradition was never so completely lost as was the poetic between Montrose and James Thomson. From Drummond and Spottiswoode onward all writers save Urquhart show the assimilation of the literary language to that of England, already visible in the last of the verse. Much prose was written, but apart from Drummond, Urquhart, and one or two pieces that come after the Restoration (and were published in England), the greater part is primarily *matériel de guerre* and only secondarily literature. Aberdeen had kept up and enhanced the old tradition of scholarship and culture, but with the deposition and banishment of the brilliant " Aberdeen Doctors," " learning began to be discountenanced, and such as were known in antiquitie, and in the writings of the Fathers, werc had in suspicion as men who smelled of Popery.... For the most part learning was nicknamed human learning, and ministers ... cried it down in their pulpits." There was a good deal of rather notable Latin work, in both verse and prose, with Charles I's physician, Arthur Johnstone (1587-1661), as its leader : but most of it belongs to men in exile, and in any case I am dealing with the vernacular.

In polemic, one may just mention those who made most noise in their day. On the Presbyterian side, George Gillespie (1613-48), one of the Scots delegates to the Westminster Assembly, survives in letters mainly as one of the " rugged names " trounced in a pugnacious sonnet of John Milton's, but was well known in his day for a really magnificent pamphlet-war with Coleman. Dickson (1583-1663), a man of more moderate views—he was a Resolutioner—was one of the group who shared with Cant (1570-1664), a gentleman whose oratorical style gave a very useful word to the English language, in the famous and unsuccessful attempt to convert the " Aberdeen Doctors " from their prelatic opinions. His reputation, in his day, was less than Cant's, but his sermons are more likely to go down with the modern reader at least, and they show an agreeable straightforward prose. The most notable from the literary point of view is perhaps Samuel Rutherford (1600-61), also a delegate to Westminster. Though an ardent controversialist, he was more of a mystic than a theologian, with a devotion to the Person of Our Lord unusual in the intellectual leaders of Calvinism. In spite of a fondness for at times rather startling imagery, erotic and legal (he was devoted to the *Song of Songs*) which can be a rather dangerous book for a preacher, his sermons and letters mount at times to real imaginative beauty and a deep and gracious tenderness, though the latter by no means involved him in toleration for anyone outside his party.

On the Episcopal side, the elder Bishop Forbes (William, of Edinburgh) wrote in Latin, but his junior, Bishop Patrick Forbes of Aberdeen (1564-1635), who shared his learning, and did excellent work in academic reform, used the vernacular, and was known as an exegetist and for his defence of non-Roman orders against Ninian Winzet. His son, the equally learned Patrick, Professor of Divinity at King's, Aberdeen, wrote Latin again, and is consequently less to our purpose than his successor in his chair, Henry Scougal (1650-78), whose *Life of God in the Soul of Man* is still a minor classic of theology. The most notable figure on this side, perhaps, is Robert Leighton, Principal of Edinburgh, Bishop of Dunblane, and Archbishop of Glasgow, a man of vast learning, a sweet and saintly personal religion, and a toleration for those of other doctrines very unusual anywhere at the time : the worst charge that even Wodrow could bring against him was that he had " an over-extensive charity " and that he occasionally wrote to a kinsman who was a priest at Douai, which " made him suspected as very much indifferent to all professions that bear the name of Christian." His point of view is crystallised, to one who knows the times, in a famous story : when still a Presbyterian (he had been brought up in that communion) he was rebuked for not " preaching to the times "—that is to say, holding forth on current politics. " Who does so ? " said he, and was answered, with some truth, " Why, all the brethren," to which his response was, " Then if all of you preach to the times, you may surely allow one poor brother to preach Christ Jesus and eternity." He strove hard for reconciliation between the parties, but the Covenanters wished " not to be tolerated but to be supreme " to the point of abolishing, throughout Great Britain, all communions not of their own views ; and Leighton, having done all he could, resigned his see and died heart-broken in England, having seen but too good reason for the famous prayer in his *Commentary on I Peter*, " Deliver us, O Lord, from the errors of wise men, yea, and of good men."

The major theological documents of the day, on the Presbyterian side, the *Confession of Faith*, the *Longer* and *Shorter Catechism*, with their appurtenances, *The Form of Presbyterial Church Government* and *The Directory for the Public Worship of God*, adopted when Knox's Liturgy was abandoned on the demand of the English Puritans, are still the canonical formularies of the Church of Scotland, and have had an enormous effect on Scots history and culture : but their brilliantly lucid if rather heavy prose can hardly be said to belong to Scottish literature, as they were all composed in England and by Englishmen. It is true that a delegacy of Scottish divines attended the Assembly that gave them birth, but as they were eleven in a gathering of a hundred and fifty-one, and complained, moreover, that their opinions were disregarded, we cannot count any of the Assembly's works even as Scottish as the Authorised Version of the Scriptures, whose translators, in their long and interesting preface (generally omitted) give the credit for its inception to the scholarly King James, who disliked the deliberate mistranslations of the Geneva Bible, which by avoiding the use of all words connected with the Old Religion, endeavoured, with success, to create prejudice against the things which the words signified in ecclesiastical practice. The other great Presbyterian document, the Metrical Psalms (which may perhaps be mentioned here without too much violation of categories) is, in its present version, at least partly Scottish. The early Scots Reformers used that of the

Englishmen Sternhold and Hopkins, whose first instalment was published in 1548. It was reprinted for Scots use several times between 1564 and 1635 : it is interesting to note that in 1587 an edition " For the Kirk of Scotland " was printed in London. King James, who did not like it, attempted revision, incorporating work of his own and of Lord Stirling's. The Westminster Assembly also put forward proposals for a new translation, and in 1641 one was made by an Englishman called Rous. This, with some modifications derived from another English version of 1644, by the Provost of Eton, and from the work of two Scots, Mure of Rowallan and Zachary Boyd—which did not change its essential character, however—was finally authorised, and is still in use. The standard historian of the Scottish Psalter, the Rev. L. M. McMeeken, considered Rous's version, thus modified, " as literal and expressive as the prose," and praises its strength and excellence " and " exquisite sublimity." I should not, myself, go quite as far as this, but some of them, notably the Twenty-third, have a pleasant simplicity, and there is a fine phrase now and then, as in the lines

> Like streams of water in the south
> Thy bounties, Lord, recall.

Their chief aesthetic value, however, is in their association with a number of very noble tunes, though as it happens, many of the best of these are not Scottish either : in fact, of the 118 tunes in a " noted " Psalter of the seventeenth century, only ten are Scots, and although the Scottish work in the present Psalter includes *Coleshill*, *Kilmarnock* and *Martyrdom*, three of the most beautiful pieces of devotional music in existence, these all belong to a much later period, while among their rivals, *Stroudwater* and the haunting *Communion* are English, and those fine fighting things, the *Old Hundredth* and the *Old Hundred and twenty-fourth*, are Genevan-French.

The principal document on the other side, the *Scottish Prayer Book* of 1637, is nearer, at least, to being Scottish literature, since though it is popularly known as Laud's it was in the main the work of two Scottish bishops, Wedderburn of Dunblane and Maxwell of Ross. Even this, however (it is, incidentally, a most noble piece of Scots printing, though its black-letter played into the enemies' hands), derives most of its actual language from the English *Book of Common Prayer*—not that of 1552, adopted in Scotland by the Lords of the Congregation in 1557, but the original version of 1549. It is prose of an extraordinary beauty, the beginning of that magnificent tradition that goes through the Authorised Version to Jeremy Taylor and Sir Thomas Browne : and for most of their actual text, the Scottish adaptors very wisely did not attempt to improve on it. The mention here is perhaps anachronistic, but it is interesting to note that the revision of Maxwell and Wedderburn's work in 1764, by Bishops Falconar and Forbes, was the source of the present American Liturgy, and strongly influenced the African, and that the Scottish debt to the Church of England was repaid when the latter, revising her own Prayer-book under two Scots Archbishops, borrowed much from the Scottish partial revision of 1912 and the then uncompleted one of 1929 (58).

After theology and polemic, the main work of our seventeenth century literature is in history. The two chief names in the early part of the century are those of men of opposite parties, Spottiswoode and Calder-wood. The chief work for letters of the former, John Spottiswoode, Archbishop of Glasgow (1565-1639), was perhaps indirect, but of immense importance, for it was Spottiswoode's Act of 1616, during his Chancellorship, that founded the deservedly famous system of our parish schools, which popular tradition attributes, like Presbyterianism, to John Knox. Knox, in fact, to his great credit, had desired them, to replace the wreckage of the Catholic educational system : but in spite of the famous obituary remark about his never fearing the face of man, he was wiser than to try to extract the wherewithal from his backers. Spottiswoode showed more courage, with disastrous results to the popularity of his church : education-rates have never been endearing (59). Besides this very important service to letters, his actual literary work has a good deal of merit. His *History of the Church of Scotland* (1655) is surprisingly moderate in tone for its date, and shows a gift for vigorous narrative that is not without penetration historically, as may be seen from his well-known summing-up of Queen Mary, not much more than sixty years after the event :

This was the end of Queen Mary's life ; a princess of many rare virtues, but crossed with all the crosses of fortune, which never any did bear with greater courage and magnanimity to the last. Upon her return from France, for the first two or three years, she carried herself most worthily ; but then giving ear to some wicked persons, and transported with the passion of revenge for the indignity done unto her in the murder of David Rizzio her secretary, she fell into a labyrinth of troubles, which forced her to flee to England, where after nineteen years captivity she was put to death in the manner you have heard.

David Calderwood, minister of Crailing (1575-1650), produced a rival *History of the Church of Scotland* in 1678. He has not Spottiswoode's analytic calm, but it is a vigorous piece of work, with an excellent gift of vivid narrative. Less gravely intellectual, it has a quicker emotion and a more rapid and dramatic pace.

These two are considerably the chief, but they have many followers. Robert Baillie (1599-1662), Principal of Glasgow, the most learned of all the Presbyterian divines—he is said to have known a dozen languages —was also, or perhaps therefore, about the most tolerant, being one of those men who like Leighton on the other side would have saved Scotland much blood and tears if their counsels could have prevailed. His formal history and polemic are less notable than the delightful *Journals and Correspondence*. They cover 1637-62, and are a most valuable first-hand record. Several other writers of history and memoirs come in this time, but most of them are of more importance to history than to letters, though one may just mention, for its endearing qualities, the *Relation* of Father Blakhall, a Catholic priest and chaplain to Lady Aboyne : it is a quite unpretentious but most exciting narrative of his adventures in the service of her family. The reverend gentleman was sincerely devout, but a born and nourished fighter, who was obviously in his element when circumstances thrust upon him the captaincy of the defence in a small but lively siege ; and as he was in Scotland at the peril of his life, his adventures in ministering to a large district of wild country were not to seek. He once had the enjoyable experience of congratulating an ardent Presbyterian who claimed to have killed him, and—though other sources confirm it as sober fact—a good deal of his

story reads very like Dumas. Incidentally, it explains
why although (to their everlasting credit) there were
many Catholics in Scotland, Scots Catholic literature
in that century is practically non-existent.

Approaching the end of the century, we come to a
rather heterogeneous group, of whom the first is
Gilbert Burnet (1643-1715), Bishop of Salisbury—
though a Scotsman, one of those Whig bishops of the
English Church who looked on at the bitter persecution, aided by the English Government, of their sister
communion in the other kingdom. His chief work is a
stately *History of the Reformation* to 1714, and two short
biographies of Rochester and Hale.

The chief literary quality of the other historians
whom it is possibly worth while to mention here is
nothing more than a racy quaintness and one aspect
of the social mind of the age : but they have so
much of that as really to deserve their traditional
fame, which has outlasted that of more reputable
figures. James Kirkton's (?-1699) *Secret and True
History of the Kirk of Scotland* is less useful as history
than as an astonishing source-book for demonology,
in which it ranks with the famous *Satan's Invisible
World Discovered* (1685) of George Sinclair (1618-87)
and the even more celebrated *Secret Commonwealth of
Elves, Fauns and Fairies* (1691) of Robert Kirk (1641-
92), minister of Aberfoyle. It was, of course, the great
age of witchcraft, the death penalty for which, enacted
on biblical authority as one of the first acts of the established Reformation, was not actually repealed until
1736, though the last witch to suffer in Scotland was
burnt in 1722. The craze, of course, was not peculiar
to Scotland : some 3000 English witches are said to
have been put to death under the Long Parliament,

o

and the exploits of the New England Puritans are well known. Kirkton, Kirk, and Sinclair, are among its classics.

The collection of lives of leading Covenanters, by Patrick Walker (166?-1745), falls just outside our period of time, *Peden* having been published in 1724 ; but may be said to belong to it in spirit. Walker's eulogies are perfectly sincere, but there is truth in the remark that he shatters his own idols with some completeness : this, however, is a matter of the reader's taste, as within this present century they were reprinted, as edifying, by a Presbyterian divine, though I do not know whether he included Walker's tales of miraculous showers of hats and weapons. If he is less than judicious as eulogist, his work is one of the raciest documents of his age, and among the most revealing of the popular mind. His companion-in-arms, the enormous Robert Wodrow (1679-1734), also overlaps our period, but like Walker he has his spiritual home there. His chief work, the *History of the Sufferings of the Church of Scotland from the Restoration to the Revolution* (1721-2), had such a powerful effect on future social history—an effect, indeed, which is not yet at an end—that it is hardly surprising the new and precarious Hanoverian Government should have seen fit to give it a handsome subsidy. It was the *Fox's Martyrs* of the Covenant, and one of the most popular books of the early eighteenth century : indeed much later, popular fiction, such as Crockett's, drew from it largely, and popular tradition, journalism, and even seriously intended history are still in its debt. He tells with much gusto and racy detail of the sufferings of the Covenanters, and he and Walker are in fact the authorities for most of the best-known stories, such as the commonly current version of the death of John Brown (though Macaulay also took a hand there), as well as for such picturesque though less frequently quoted episodes as that of the Episcopalian cleric in whose chapel Satan administered the Communion, and that of the lady who rose in the air and flew up and down the garden, a tale that ends gravely with " the matter of fact is certain." His *Analecta or Materials for a History of Remarkable Providences*, unpublished till 1842, is a perfect treasure-house of oddities.

Outwith history, the later century has very little. One must mention two men, however—Mackenzie of Rosehaugh and Fletcher of Saltoun, both men of uncommon personality who have left a lively (though in Rosehaugh's case a somewhat unjust) tradition. Sir George Mackenzie of Rosehaugh (1636-91) was King's Advocate, a man of great learning, and the founder of our National Library, whose inauguration, in a stately Latin speech, was his last public function before the Revolution sent him into exile. Like most Scots of his day, he held his convictions with vigour, and they led him into the writing of a considerable number of pamphlets upon social and political questions. The chief of these, perhaps, are the *Religio Stoici* of 1663, and that on *Moral Gallantry*, of 1667. Both, like everything else in the two superb folios of his *Collected Works*, are full of personality—a personality almost laughably unlike the traditional portrait of their author—and show a prose style of a terse and stately vigour, curiously French, though rather in *netteté* and the lucid turn of thought than in actual phrasing : indeed, in the essay on forensic style in the *Pleadings* of 1673, he has a lively appreciation of

" the Scottish idiom of the British tongue," as " fiery, abrupt, sprightly, and bold " and " more massy and significant " than English, affirming that " the Scots are thought the nation under Heaven who do with most ease learn to pronounce best . . . foreign languages, and all nations acknowledge that they speak the Latin with the most intelligible accent," though he is no *farouche* Scotomaniac, adding " I speak this not to asperse the English (they are a nation I honour) but to reprove the petulancy and malice of some among them who think they do their country good service when they reproach ours."

Of the pamphlets I have mentioned, the *Religio* includes an interesting plea for religious toleration, addressed to the extreme Covenanters who were claiming not freedom to worship according to their consciences, of which they already had precisely as much as the present-day Kirk of Scotland, but freedom to prevent the rest of the Three Kingdoms from worshipping according to theirs. He sums up the point of view on which he was afterwards to act, saying :

If Laws and Law-givers did not make Hereticks vain, by taking too much notice of their extravagancies, the world should be no more troubled with these than with the Chimeras of Alchemists and Philosophers. And it fairs with them as with Tops, which how long they are scourged, keep foot and run pleasantly, but fall how soon they are neglected and left to themselves.

As a lawyer, however, he is bound to add :

Albeit, I confess, that when these not only recede from the canonised Creed of the Church, but likeways intrude upon the Laws of the State, then, as of all other they are the most dangerous, so of all other they should be most severely punished.

The implied dilemma not only wrecked Mackenzie, but was to ruin his country for nearly three centuries, and she has not yet got over its results.

Moral Gallantry, on the thesis that the point of honour obliges a man to be virtuous and that " there is nothing so mean (or unworthy of a gentleman) as vice," is a piece of vigorous and plain-spoken practical ethics, clear-headed and generous, that must have required considerable social courage to publish in the first flush of the wild reaction to licence that had succeeded the Commonwealth repressions—as much courage as the same thesis would need to-day, with " intellectual " substituted for " gentleman." That was a quality, however, that he did not lack, and both it and the verbal sword-play that could back it show in what he probably considered his *magnum opus*, *The Laws and Customs of Scotland in Matters Criminal*, of 1678, overshadowed as lawbook by the *Institutions* of his chief opponent, the execrated Stair, three years later, but worth reading for the light it throws on both the age and a notable figure in it. It is a formal digest of legal principles, closely reasoned in a strong straightforward prose touched with dry wit, as in the opening of the section on treason :

Unhappy Man retains in nothing so much a desire to be like his Maker, as in that he would be Supreme.

—a sentence that holds a good deal of our history. The whole section, by the way (and it was violently topical at the time) shows his quality as a lawyer. He knew, and as a Highlander had painful reason to know, the vital necessity for Scotland of a stable central power, that could prevent oppression by any sort of oligarchy : but he takes a very strong line against panic administration and the vindictiveness that springs from panic, smiting those who claimed that a charge of treason might be tried in the absence of the pannel, and those who would inflict torture at death in the manner that for another century was to disgrace the English treason laws. The section on witchcraft is perhaps the most revealing, alike of the man and of the age : he does not doubt the actuality of the crime, nor that there is more to it than the witch's delusion, but how unlike common seventeenth century practice is this :

From the horridness of the Crime I do conclude that of all Crimes it requires the closest Relevancy and most convincing Probation.

—this at a time when witches were quite frequently burnt on the evidence of small children, and without any more than the most farcical form of law. He gives instances of legal malpractice with regard to this crime, showing a sanity and pity, and an absence of panic, very unusual when " scarce any who were accused before a Country Assise of Neighbours did escape," and there were few who shared his obvious nausea at the loathsome figure of the witch-pricker. The picture drawn in his calm legal prose is a ghastly one, but there is plenty of evidence to show its accuracy, though if all lawyers had acted on his principles one flaming sore in seventeenth century civilisation would have been cleaner.

There is not space to speak of his learned and delightful treatise on heraldry, for long an authoritative classic : but although it is a minor work published when he was twenty-four, one must mention *Aretina or The Serious Romance* (1660), since it is the first in

time of all Scots novels, unless one is to go back to
Squyer Meldrum and *Wallace*. Like most first novels, it
is very much in the fashionable mode, for in everything but length—it is not a long book—it follows the
Scudéry tradition of the Full-bottomed or Heroick
Romance, with a heroine who is daughter of Monan-
thropos Chancellor of Egypt, a not ineffective borrow-
ing from Marina's adventures in *Pericles*, and a prose
that oscillates a little oddly between eighteenth century and Jacobean *novelle*. Its stately gallantry has a
dedication " To all the Ladies of the Nation" followed
not only by poems on the Restoration and the death
of the Duke of Gloucester, but by an *Apologia for
Romances*, on the thesis that they are *not* bad for morals,
since by setting a high standard in " objects of
affection " they make the reader less inclined to fall
in love with any merely ordinary human being !

David Crawford, Anne's Historiographer Royal,
has already been mentioned for his lively comedies :
he also is one of the pioneers of our novel, for he is
said to have written three. But I have not even been
able to learn their names.

Andrew Fletcher of Saltoun (1665-1716), with
whom this record may very fitly close, was, like
Mackenzie, a politician and a personality, though he
has had better luck, for his tradition is much nearer
the man. Although he was a very considerable
scholar, at home in Latin, Greek, French, and Italian—
in which latter tongue he wrote a political discourse
—as well as in history and in the law, he was not, any
more than most of the men in this chapter, a professional man of letters, his writing being all a side-issue
to his interest in public affairs. He refused, in an age
of passionate partisanship, to take sides in religion, or

to call himself Whig or Tory : in his later years, after his disappointment by the Revolution, he was a frank republican, but characteristically declared the High Tories were " the best countrymen, of most honour, integrity, and ingenuity." In spite of this anomaly in opinion, he was as far as possible from a pococurante, as his record shows. M.P. for Lothian under Charles II, he was put to the horn in the troubles over the Exclusion Bill, went to Holland, served as a soldier in Hungary, came over with Monmouth, but escaped to return with William of Orange, and having helped to establish a new Government, found, like many successful revolutionaries, from Brutus on, that the Kingdom of Heaven had not materialised and that Scotland had only changed King Log for King Stork, and unburdened his soul in a series of pamphlets and speeches that are curiously suggestive of one side of intellectual France a lifetime later, of that most tragical group, the aristocratic revolutionaries like La Fayette and—there is some personal likeness—Mirabeau. He and Mackenzie, indeed, are really men of the eighteenth century, Mackenzie of the " Augustan " side of it, and Fletcher of that which made the Revolution.

Have I made his story sound a little absurd ? Indeed, he made himself ridiculous more than once, and some of his views are wild enough. But there was nothing absurd in the man himself, nor even pitiful, though he failed, and tragically, in the thing that was nearest his heart. This is how a contemporary describes him :

He is a gentleman steady in his principles, of nice honour, with abundance of learning : brave as the sword he wears and bold as a lion : a sure friend and an irreconcilable enemy : would lose his life readily to serve his country, and would not do a base thing to save it. . . . His notions of government, however, are too fine spun, and can hardly be lived up to by men subject to the common frailties of nature : neither will he give allowance for extraordinary emergencies.

In fact, he was difficult. " In his private conversations affable to his friends, he could not endure to converse with those he thought enemies to his country." But I need not describe him further : Mr G. M. Thomson, in a little sketch that is like one of Tassie's heads, has drawn an unforgettable portrait. He loved Scotland burningly, and fought, with a desperate back-to-the-wall devotion, against the perils to her national being he foresaw as a result of the terms of the new Union of 1707. The eighteenth century over-rode him : the nineteenth laughed at him : the twentieth has found out that if many of his remedies for social ills are wild enough, most of his prophecies as to facts have come to pass, and that his demand for a Federal Union might have more to be said for it than Queensberry and the text-quoting Marchmont admitted. His prose is the man's— debater's prose, passionate, stately, and intensely human : he reminds one, turn by turn, of Mirabeau (though morally he was a better man) and of Sir Richard Maitland. He is the museum specimen of a type we have bred often enough, and as constantly wasted : their graves are scattered over the face of the world, for the flag under which they died was seldom their own, and many foreign nations are in their debt. He is not the last of them, for their tale is not over : but he is the end of the age that began with Flodden.

VIII

EPILOGUE

The Gulf—The Risorgimento—The last century

SCOTTISH civilisation perished, though rather slowly. The brilliant promise of 1500 had been disappointed even by 1600. By 1700, Scotland, as a nation, was much where she had been under David II —and that, too, absolutely, not relatively. Relatively, indeed, she was worse off than she had been then. Instead of Bruce, for her immediate past, she had Cromwell. Her navy had disappeared, her trade had perished, even her agriculture was razed by war. Economically, she was at her last gasp : it was computed in 1695 that the total coin in the country worked out at 15s. sterling per head. " Indigence crippled her at every point, sold her statesmen to English purses, starved her industries and seats of learning, drove the flower of her youth to foreign countries, and depressed her influence in the counsels of her neighbours "—as was shown very practically by the strangling (one can call it nothing else) of the Company of Scotland, her first attempt to get on her feet again. Her scholars were driven from their last hold, Aberdeen. Her science was negligible, and her arts, letters dead with the rest. In the generation of Shakespeare she had already little : in the generation of Milton, of Corneille, almost nothing : in the generation of Dryden, of Racine, of Molière, nothing —nothing at least but a little prose, not of the first

218

importance, and a thin underground trickle of the forbidden tradition of song and ballad. Then suddenly, as she drew near the middle of the eighteenth century and the end of two hundred years of religious wars, she seemed to rise to her feet, turn her face to daylight. The roots of her life had been stirring in the darkness : of the two men who were to restore her poetic tradition, Thomson was born in the last years of William II, and Ramsay actually under James VII. Hutcheson's *Inquiry* in 1724, James Thomson's *Winter*, the next year, show the dawn, and though *Winter* had to be published in London, Lady Grizel Baillie, daughter of a Covenanter (and very plucky heroine of his escape), was Thomson's patron, and even ventured to write a song herself, the charming and pitiful *Werena my hert licht, I wad dee*. The ice of the long grim winter began to melt.

The movement was slow at first. Smollett, the next outstanding figure, does not come till 1748, and like Thomson had to publish in England. But throughout the second half of that century, the first third of the next, there is an astonishing revitalisation. It was, indeed, our Renaissance, late but fruitful, for though its chief glories were less in art than in science and philosophy, even in art it is not without high distinction. The little shattered kingdom came back to life, took her place in Europe again—we have allowed ourselves to forget how fully, how many of the roots of modern Europe, for good and evil, lead to those noble streets and squares of old New Edinburgh : the realisation is in fact made difficult even to ourselves by the courteous and endemic English habit of calling " English," even at times " characteristically English," anything Scottish that happens to take the fancy, from Adam Smith to Adams architecture. It is cheaper, certainly, and in both senses, than an army of annexation : but the Whitehall Department that plastered Scotland with the initials *E.R. VII* would be ill with horror if a Balkan princelet were described as Boris VIII instead of IX, while if an eminent Oxford scholar were to call, say, John Huss a Slovak instead of a Czech, what a stir there would be in the *Times* correspondence columns ! Perhaps it is merely the English theory that a man has a right to all his wife's possessions, and does not need to be civil towards her ? But this attitude is a little out of date. And why should gross historical inaccuracy be permissible with regard to one country alone ?

Trade and agriculture awakened : the people had again the machinery of civilised life, and some leisure to live it, some margin beyond bare subsistence. The result was an outburst of intellectual activity that surpasses even that of the fifteenth century. It extended into every department of thought, although as has been said, the artistic side of it is the least notable and the last to develop : the spirit of the age, in fact, was in Scotland, as everywhere, utilitarian, and although it cultivated " sensibility " it had a not inexplicable horror of the more powerful emotions, that are necessary to the greatest kinds of art. It had had enough of " the thunder of the captains and the shouting " of enthusiasts of one kind and another : it wanted to leave its wars to professionals, to sit down and work quietly in counting-house and study, unaware that in both it was creating explosives, to take its leisure in comfort and *cultiver son jardin*.

A good deal of both the explosives and the gardening tools were of Scottish manufacture. James Watt did not invent steam-power, but he did more than anybody else to make it the factor that altered civilisation. He, Adam Smith's new science of economics, and perhaps some help from the spirit of John Knox, founded between them the Industrial Revolution in Europe. I do not consider the fact to our national credit, but it does show that we were alive again. In mechanics we made other, less dubious, gifts. The world's first practicable steamship sailed Scottish waters, devised and built by Miller, Taylor, and Symington (60). Macadam and Telford laid the foundations of the third branch of modern transport, and made the internal-combustion engine feasible by recreating the roads that had been shattered a thousand years before, when the Empire ended.

In other departments of thought, Hume's destructive analysis of current systems of belief was one of the bases of the French, and therefore ultimately of the Russian, Revolution : it is odd to think that that dapper little *bon viveur* should be one of the forces that, quite possibly, may plunge Europe again in another Fifth Century. Hume again and Hutton, the founder of geology, avenged the blight of the Reformation by overthrowing the foundations of the Reformers' religion, the doctrine of the verbal infallibility of Scripture. Joseph Black made chemistry a modern science, and a whole dynasty of brilliant medical men took their full share in establishing modern medicine. The nation showed, as she had always done, as much activity furth of Scotland as within. I need hardly touch on Scotland's share in the development of the Empire, on the work of explorers like Mungo Park and Alexander Mackenzie, of admirals like Duncan and " Cochrane the Dauntless," of soldiers and administrators innumerable : I have not the figures for the eighteenth century and the earlier Revolutionary wars, but in the forty years after 1797, *Skye alone* gave the British Army 21 lieutenant-generals and major-generals, 48 lieutenant-colonels, 600 majors, captains, and subalterns, and ten thousand private soldiers, and to the Civil Service in the same time, one Governor-general of India, four Governors of colonies, a Chief Baron of England, and a Lord of Session.

This quickening of spirit had issue in the arts. In music there is no more than the revival, the return to light, of the old songs, the interest in them enhanced, through the influence of Henry Mackenzie and of Scott, by a fashion for Gaelic music that just saved it. In painting there is again not very much but the gracious portraits of the younger Allan Ramsay and one very great figure, Alexander Raeburn : in sculpture little—it was no age of it anywhere—but the exquisite miniature talent of James Tassie. In the two great arts of the time, however, Scotland was brilliant, and in one for a while pretty nearly supreme. In architecture there is Gibbs—too soon, however, to do much in Scotland—the Swedish-Scot Chambers, Milne, of old Blackfriars Bridge, " Athenian " Stuart, the Adams (61), father and sons, and Gillespie Graham, who built much of that magnificent Edinburgh whose streets and squares, marred as they are by a hundred small squalors of modern carelessness and the sloppy individualism that weak minds mistake for individuality, are even yet among the noblest in Europe, and worthy of their incomparable setting.

Against this background comes the revival of letters. Smollett ranks among the four founders of the modern novel in English, and though his successor Mackenzie is out of date, he was famous through polite Europe in his day, had a good deal of influence on French fiction, and as a critic did enduring service to greater men. Boswell early in the time and Lockhart at its end are among the supreme biographers. Thomson, so early that all his work was published, and most of it written, in England ; the revival of the ballads ; Ramsay's of the old songs ; and Burns, their heir and Ferguson's, between them stirred the great British movement in letters that rose so superbly at the end of the century, and had the great English Victorians as its children. The founders of the French Romantic movement, that inflamed all Europe, are Macpherson, however we may scoff at him now ; Byron, half Scot by blood and (since he never knew it) far more than was good for him a Scot by temperament ; and Walter Scott, whose great work, obscured for a time by the indiscriminate worship of his feebler, stands as secure as Shakespeare's.

Scott is the culmination of that great age. All the old strands of our letters join in him, fused in the magnificent series of the nine great Scottish novels that cover the time from the late seventeenth century to his own, from *Old Mortality* to *St Ronan's Well*, in such a panorama of the writer's country as can only be paralleled—and then incompletely—by Balzac. The folk-strain whose climax is in Burns is the source, in Scott, of *The Heart of Midlothian*, of such things as Edie Ochiltree, Meg Dods, Bailie Jarvie, the Mucklebackits : the darker and loftier side of it that is in the ballads, of *The Bride of Lammermoor*, of Lady Glenallan, of Redgauntlet, of Clara Mowbray's story before a publisher's prudery ruined it. *Wandering*

Willie's Tale goes back, with a glance at True Thomas, through *The Droichis Part of the Play* and *The Friar of Tungland*, to the grotesque ghost of the Tarne Watheling, as surely as Claverhouse or Fergus Macivor are in line of descent from Barbour's Good Lord James. The delight in pageantry recalls the Makaris, as the frame and setting sums up the lettered and scholarly work of the Scots eighteenth century that, urbane as it was, had not lost, even in douce little Jamie Thomson, Gavin Douglas' eye for the zest of a wild landscape, the tang of the old cramped and bickering Edinburgh, that is underneath Scott's superb eye for a crowd, or the memory of old and stately loyalties that fills, and with their own salt of a dry humour, the opening of *The Chronicles of the Canongate*, one of the finest things he ever wrote. Add that Scott was a most lively (if before 1680 a most inaccurate) historian, a great editor, a critic of high quality, a good poet and by instants more than a good one, and always a magnificent personality. . . . He sums up all the rich life of that generation, fusing in himself what seem to a foreigner its antinomies, speaking for his time to his country, and for his country to Time.

Scott died in 1832, as we are busily reminding ourselves. And since then . . . It may have been a coincidence that the revival of Evangelicalism was accompanied by another period of extinction in the arts, at a time when literature at least was flourishing vigorously in the neighbouring kingdom, with which Scott had done so much to improve our relations, and when the eighteenth century activity in the sciences and (though to a less extent) in pure scholarship was still maintained. There was certainly a collapse. Was it that the eighteenth century lacked deep roots, pushed too high from a shallow spiritual soil ? It had broken the bondage of the ministers, but they had left it with nothing to put in place of the Calvinistic Demon-Deity, except a sort of well-meaning Good Influence and the last remembrance, in the code of a gentleman's conduct, of so much as breeding and tradition could carry of the chivalric scheme of personal ethics. The inevitable reaction from the Kettledrummles and Pedens and Macbriars might on the one hand be Muckle John Gibb, but in the more intelligent it was a polite scepticism, or a religion that was " a thing of social decency and private virtues," where enthusiasm was a major vice. Those might shake off the yoke, but they could not hold it off. As the renewal of prosperity made for a powerful middle-class, and—added to the Anglomania which Scott had, perhaps unwittingly, fostered—too often an absentee aristocracy, whose education and social life were all non-Scottish, the negative side at least of Calvinism returned to power, with a hatred of beauty, a loathing, in the Creator's name, of creative art, that were as active as ever. The Scottish Sabbath of the nineteenth century, the religious attitude which it typifies, were a by-word in Europe.

The effects were what might have been expected. We were a proverbially drunken nation, had some of the worst slums in Europe in our wealthy cities, and an illegitimacy-rate that is even now half as high again as that of England and a good deal higher than that of Italy, though in fact it has gone down : in the pious 'eighties of last century it was 10 per cent. in the great towns, and in the shires of Kirkcudbright and Wigtown, where the Covenanting tradition had always been strongest, it was 15 per cent. and 17 per cent.

respectively. The godly had not coped with these social problems, and could not stifle science, but they did succeed in strangling the arts again. Save for the brilliant Glasgow School of painters, what there is of Scottish art between Scott's death and the War is almost all of it the work of exiles.

There was, to be sure, much sentimental lip-service to a Burns and Scott who being decently dead could be enhaloed with all the middle-class virtues. Carlyle was a force among the Victorians, and his influence can hardly be called extinct, for in Germany a volume of selections from his work has sold 300,000 copies since 1926 ; Italian translations are said to have greatly helped the Fascist movement, while the anti-democratic side of his teaching, that was generally disapproved in his own age, begins to commend itself pretty generally. Even he, however, for all the Peden in him, had to shout his gospel of silence from a London suburb, and his fellow-prophet Ruskin was born and bred in England, and seems to have thought of himself as an Englishman. John Galt was neglected, even by himself. Mrs Oliphant's exquisite best lies buried in a wilderness of hackwork. Perhaps more Scotsmen have read the one great Scottish poem of the age, the superb and terrible *City of Dreadful Night*, than have read the Covenants they are bred to reverence : but not many more. It again was written in exile. Stevenson, who with Kipling (half a Scot) founded the whole technique of modern narrative that has life in it apart from merely noise, was idolised into a sentimental cult, until the name of him is nauseating to writers who owe him the very tools of their trade. His pupil, Neil Munro, wrote historical novels of the Highlands, whose handling of narrative and character has great merit. In substance, indeed, they are far above Stevenson : but all save the last of them are spoilt as literature by the restless self-consciousness of their prose style. William Archer created a dramatic revolution . . . in England. W. P. Ker was a great teacher of the humanities, Andrew Lang a delightful critic and *belles-lettriste* : neither was a creative writer in the technical sense, but they were of those men who do much, wherever they are, to create a germinal atmosphere for the arts. Dr. H. J. C. Grierson, of whom that also may be said, is still among living men in his own country. There were other great scholars, some of whom, like Sir William Mitchell Ramsay, did not have to emigrate. In directly creative work there was a thin but pleasant trickle of Scots, in the work of such people as Violet Jacob and Charles Murray, whose best ranks with the eighteenth-century songs. Besides that, there was a poet or two of merit, such as Ronald Campbell Macfie, and a very small number of notable names in prose—the thin but real brilliance of H. H. Munro, the imaginative satire of Mr. Norman Douglas, and the fine horseman's prose of Mr. Cunninghame Graham, all three of whom belong to the " Cavalier " side of Scotland, of Charlotte Square rather than Craigenputtock. Most successful of all was Sir James Barrie, a dramatist of some originality and uncommon technical skill, who unfortunately found his public too soon. Save for the last, and those who wrote in Scots, their own country has never regarded them very maternally. There was a popular fashion for kailyard and whimsy—for the English market, but it found purchasers nearer—that caused a reaction to inverted-kailyard, with the emphasis not on the briarbush but on the midden, that was to become as wearisome a convention.

The popularity of a kailyardie wherein the leeks were all well and tidily laid, and the owner was never but the civil breeks, the libations of golden syrup poured to a Burns who would have been the first to scunner at them, and the apotheosis in chocolate of Stevenson are an odd phenomenon, but not without precedent. In an interesting study of that most amusing, and disconcerting, subject, fashion in literature, Mr E. E. Kellet remarks that " the master of all sentimentalists is Rousseau, born and brought up among harsh and matter-of-fact Calvinists, and wielding his influence mainly among a people distinguished, as a rule, by a remarkable combination of logic and practicality." To starve the emotions of generous nourishment is apt to produce alarming effects on the reason, especially in a hot-blooded race.

Since the War, at least, there are many signs of revival, if its life is not smothered in the gush of little self-admiring coteries, New Lichts and Wee Frees and Seceders of the arts, or choked by a false conception of nationalism. God knows it is time, if we are to survive as anything but a fading phrase of geography. Yet if 1800 were possible after 1700, if 1500 were possible after 1300, to despair is a sin against the Holy Ghost. The life of our barren, small, tormented country has been bled from her veins so many times already, and the worst of her wounds have been at her own hand. And yet she has lived, and can live yet . . . if we choose, if we seek those things that belong unto our peace, raise up again the former desolations. One can see everywhere the sun and stars, except among the cities of modern Progress :

but is there any country in the world where earth and sky have more beauty than our own, have bred a more splendid recklessness of devotion? What have we done, this last century, to deserve it? War and science? A country needs something more than that, or to be an expensive playground for foreigners. Certainly, now, when a man sets his face to Scotland, *tendens Venafranos in agros, aut Lacedaemonium Tarentum,* he will find less of Athens under Arthur's Seat than he would have done a hundred and twenty years since . . . or—perhaps—than he may before this generation are old. That plant of formal and sharp-pointed beauty that is our national emblem has a tough life. *Mais il nous faut cultiver notre chardon.* A generation has the art it deserves.

NOTES

CHAPTER I. PROLOGUE

1. Little more than a dozen Gaelic MSS. of a date earlier than the tenth century have been found in the British Isles, but over 200 are preserved in Germany and Austria.

2. David's nieces, by the way, both the Queen and the Empress, are distinguished in the mediaeval tradition of fighting princesses that includes Agnes of Dunbar and Christina Bruce, Marguerite d'Anjou and Jeanne de Montfort.

3. Forty-six years after the Reformation, the institution was revived, in an act empowering masters of coalpits and saltpits to seize vagabonds and put them to forced labour. It was not until 1799 that this disgraceful institution of " bound colliers " (men and women) came to an end.

4. Scots Catholics in special had terrible difficulties to contend with in education—indeed in everything else, since for example in 1640 it was made illegal to sell anything to Catholics, or buy anything of them ; and at a much later time they could not legally inherit, dispone by will or acquire any annual rent. It was illegal, under penalty of death, to take the children of Catholic parents out of the kingdom in order to have them educated in their own faith. As late as 1701 it was enacted that " the children of Catholics, being minors, shall be taken from their parents and committed to Protestant teachers, who are to educate them at their parents' expense."

5. It is worth noting that when I, a Scot, taught in the University of London in the nineteen-twenties, the sequence of my immediate superiors—the head of my Department, the Principal of the College, its President, and the Chancellor of the University —were all Scotsmen. My college had its ancestry in Glasgow, and the University itself was founded by a Scotsman and on the Scottish model.

6. This tradition did not cease with the Middle Ages : the civil wars of the sixteenth, seventeenth and eighteenth centuries did much to strengthen it. A full account, even in outline, would need a largish book, but I think it is worth while to give one or two points. The most famous instance, after the Garde

écossaise, is the Scots troops of Gustavus Adolphus. He had 34 Scots colonels and 50 lieutenant-colonels in his service, with Scots commands, and like the King of France had a Scots body-guard, while he was said to have made over 60 Scotsmen gover-nors of castles and towns in the conquered provinces of Germany. At the taking of Frankfurt in 1632, Lumsden's Regiment alone captured nine stands of colours from the enemy, and at the great victory of Leipzig, one of the decisive battles of the world, it was the Scots Brigade who led the advance. The Swedish connection lasted for some time : after the 'Forty-Five, the son of that Lord Cromartie who had led my own clan went into Swedish service and rose to be general—to return after the amnesty and die in 1789 a British Major-general and founder of that distinguished corps the Highland Light Infantry, who wear our tartan. As late as 1857, the Marshal of the Kingdom of Sweden was a Hamilton.

Gustavus showed himself none too grateful, however, and the most brilliant of his Scots captains, Sir John Hepburn, called in his day " the best soldier in Christendom," carried his command into French service, where as the Régiment d'Hébron they fought gallantly under Turenne and le grand Condé, and were given the right of the line, in perpetuity, by Louis XIII. Later, Dundee's officers formed a corps in France, the first of many Jacobites : Napoleon's Marshal Macdonald was the son of an Uist refugee. The family of the famous banker Law produced brilliant soldiers, who were associated specially with India, though one of them, Law de Lauriston, was Napoleon's senior A.D.C. in Egypt and subsequently commanded the guns at Wagram—where he saved the day—and distinguished himself with the rear-guard in the Retreat from Moscow. Even in 1870, a Scots Captain Ogilvie did notable service in the siege of Paris. Neither Scotland nor France, at any rate, have yet lost the memory of later service, or of the Border man who shared with Foch the glory of that last great drive to the East that broke a menace that is now forgotten.

France and Sweden are the best-known theatres of Scots foreign service, but not the only ones. Gustavus' troops, in the service of a recently-formed kingdom, had their ancestors in that of Denmark from which Sweden had broken off : Christian II in 1518 had 1000 Highlanders in his army. In the Low Countries—where Bruges for long had a Scots quarter—the famous Scots-Dutch Regiment, Mackay's, existed from 1570, one of their founders being no less than the Bauld Buccleuch of *Kinmont Willie*. With such parentage, it is not surprising that they were bonny fechters : after Bois-le-Duc in 1629, the Prince of Orange called them the Bulwark of the Republic. In 1782 they were still Scots enough to mutiny at the tactless attempt to change their words of command from Scots to Dutch : the breeze blew over, and they remained embodied till 1818. The first " Dutch " governor of Surinam was a Scotsman.

Scots services in Russia are less well known, but from the late sixteenth century they were considerable. There is a Douglas-berg in Esthonia, and seventeenth century Moscow had a Scots quarter. The Russian artillery was founded by James Bruce, and his grandson was Peter the Great's Master-General of the Ordnance. (That Emperor's mother, by the way, had two Scots ladies-in-waiting, married to Russian nobles, and had herself been brought up by a Scotswoman.) The Russian navy was created by a group of Scots, and in the eighteenth century had several Scots admirals, one of them a clansman of my own, who gave his name to Khonter Mackenzie in the Crimea, a planta-tion he established to grow ships' timber. Admiral Elphinstone destroyed the Turkish fleet in 1770, with three Scots officers in command of his fireships. Admiral Greig defeated the Swedes in 1788. As late as 1877 an English traveller in the Caucasus came on a Schottlandskaya Koloneya there, and was addressed in broad Scots by a man of pure Russian blood.

The soldier, like the scholar, passed from country to country. The Earl Marischal who fought in the 'Fifteen and shared with Seaforth in the Glenshiel affair was successively a colonel in the Spanish army, Governor of the Ukraine for Catherine II, and Frederick the Great's Ambassador to Madrid, while his brother was Frederick's most distinguished marshal. . . But this note must end !

7. Barbour has a little picture of King Robert reading *Fiera-bras* to his draggled staff to help them to forget short rations, and telling tales of Oliver and Roland. It does not seem to surprise even a writer of the later fourteenth century that he should choose French literature for recreation on a campaign. Napoleon, after all, reciprocated with *Ossian*.

8. The use of *Scots* as the common name for all these races comes from the royal title of King of Scots, inherited from Alpin. It should be noted, by the way, that the " English " inhabitants of Scotland were often Flemings, who were so called, apparently, because the first of the numerous Flemish immigrants came via England. Many of these were absorbed into their adopted country : the great house of Fleming in the

south, and in the Highlands the chiefs of the Murrays and the Frasers are of Flemish origin.

9. The fact that between 1200 and 1600 the most turbulent country in Europe was governed for 127 years by kings under 20, and for 36 more by absentees or scrambling usurpations, probably had some effect on our history. Between David I in 1124 and Charles I in 1625 only four sovereigns of Scotland, out of twenty-one, had passed 16 at accession. Of the eight Stewarts between 1406 and 1648/9, only four lived beyond 40 (one of them ceasing to reign at 24), and of these two died on the scaffold at 44 and 48, and the third was murdered at 42. Their ages at accession were 11, 6, 7, 15, 2, a few days, 1, and 25.

10. Not quite all, in fact, but the only two exceptions are Florent of Holland, whom the genealogical table shows to have been an optimist, and Eirik II of Norway, claiming in right of his wife, who would have been Queen of Scots in her own right if she had outlived her father. The Scoto-Scandinavian coalition that would have ensued might have been an interesting factor in the politics of Europe.

11. Edward imprisoned two Scots bishops and was very anxious to lay hands on the rest, most of whom had at one time or another taken the field against him, although the Pope was backing his claim. When it came to a question of national independence, the old Church in Scotland was decidedly " gallican."

CHAPTER II. THE MEDIAEVALS

12. " Lingua Scotica " originally meant Gaelic, and this usage lasted into the fifteenth century. We do not find " Scottis " with the modern meaning until the sixteenth.

13. I am told that the biographers of Mikhail Lermontov, one of the greatest of Russian poets, claim for him a connection with this gentleman. He undoubtedly was the descendant of a seventeenth century Lermont, who emigrated first to Poland and then to Russia, and in his poems he several times refers to his Scots descent.

14. It has been gravely advanced as an argument that *The Pearl* cannot be Scots because it shows a knowledge of Dante! As Scots were teaching in Palermo and Toulouse a hundred years before Dante, it is difficult to see why a Scot fifty years after him should not have known him as well as Chaucer did.

15. I do not ask anyone to take this as serious evidence. But I may add that when I read Mrs Mitchison's *The Conquered*,

which deals with Gaul under Julius Caesar, I recognised it as a Scotswoman's work, though I knew nothing of the author.

16. No one who has had to read much criticism of Shakespeare will call this unjust.

17. Spotless, *sine macula*, Dunbar's *bot macle* of the *Ballat to Our Lady*.

18. *Erbere* is a little turfed pleasance (*herbe*) not necessarily roofed.

19. I say "so far as we know," for so much has perished. *The Pearl* itself exists in a single MS., that might easily have followed Barbour's *History of the Stewarts*.

20. History is shorter than it looks. Henry Mackenzie was born on the day Prince Charles set up his standard, and lived to see the last *Waverlies*. I am not even elderly, but I can remember a lady born before Waterloo.

21. As a matter of fact, the King was the seventh Robert de Brus from the original immigrant to England from Normandy (also a Robert) and the fifth from the Robert who arrived in Scotland early in the twelfth century.

22. It is a rather little interesting *differentia* that to get anything out of a Scot or a Frenchman you have at least to begin by being civil, whereas with an Englishman or a German it is generally necessary to snub him before one can afford to be polite.

CHAPTER III. THE LAST OF THE MIDDLE AGES

23. Nothing in "literary" literature, that is, except the noble prose of Malory, who stands alone, strayed out of another age, as does Berners in his translation of Froissart. There is a thin but lively and sometimes lovely stream of "popular" song, from the enchanting *Nut-brown Maid* to the satanic *carillonade* of the mock dirge for Suffolk : but it is rather the equivalent, in its country, of our ballad. And though there is plenty of "literary" work, it is, with the very late exception of Skelton, irredeemable, not least in pure deliquescence of prosodic form. It is cheering to read Hawes, and remember the Elizabethans came after *that*.

24. This question of "influence" is not always simple. I once made a list of people whose work my own novels have been said, by professional critics, to resemble. It includes, so far, Handel, Debussy, Dickens, Mozart, Mrs Elinor Glyn, Scott, Stendhal, Mrs Annie S. Swan, Mr Hergesheimer, Sardou, Mrs

234

Wharton, Mr Humbert Wolfe, Jane Austen, Maeterlinck, and the Brontës, not to mention "the wild blossom flavour of a pastiche." (I have always wondered if the lady meant *pastille*.) The closest resemblance I can trace myself to any of these is to a writer whom, at the time when the comparison was made, I had never read. None of the three people whose technical devices I was quite frankly copying appear in it, though all of them are universally known : and in fact I should be rather surprised if they did.

25. The younger English universities, with the exception of Durham, are their descendants, as they follow London, which was a deliberate attempt to reproduce the Scots model.

26. The reports of the Scottish Commission for Antiquities give a magnificent series of plans and photographs, though their *terminus ad quem* (1707) has been fixed a full century too early.

27. All philosophy is based ultimately on a conception of the relation of matter and spirit, of the experiend and the experient. There are, in the long run, three such conceptions possible : the materialist, to which matter alone is significant ; the manichaean, which repudiates matter as either insignificant or evil ; and the sacramental, which regards the two as, in human life, inseparable, and sees matter as the normal vehicle of spirit and spirit as normally mediated by matter. This latter is the basis of Catholic metaphysic and practice, and of all the phenomena of creative art.

28. Robert Bruce was born two years after the last, and his great antagonist had actually taken part in one. Both, and their successors for several generations, looked for a renewal : indeed, the idea seems to have glimmered dimly under the consciousness of Europe until at least the death of Adrian VI in 1523 : one can see it as late as Lepanto in 1571. But after that Christendom was nobody's business.

29. St Gilbert, Bishop of Moray, saint, soldier, and statesman, now all but forgotten by his countrymen.

30. *La Divina Commedia* is not, of course—characteristically not —a dream. But it does grow out of the allegorical or semi-allegorical " vision " convention.

31. " The nightshadow darkened ; the north snowed ; frost bound the land ; hail fell on earth, coldest of harvests."

32. I am not forgetting (though some of my betters do) that there was a considerable religious revival in seventeenth-century France. But I am thinking of the Court-Paris whose dominants

were two not very priestly cardinals, not of the France of Père Coton, Madame Acarie, St François de Sales, and the great reforming Abbesses.

33. Another foreign visitor of the time remarks on the gay attire of the common people, whose independent bearing shocked both French and English, though Ayala's Spaniards probably understood it.

34. I have always wondered, not without a shiver, exactly what Villon meant by opening a hymn to the Blessed Virgin with the triple invocation that belongs to Dian-Hecate, Mistress of Witches. One can take it " straight," of course. But how far is it meant to have a second meaning, that links it to the Aix Annunciation ? The witch-cult had not reached the proportions it assumed after the Reformation, but it existed : and though his mother is the last person the average Frenchman would play tricks on, the man who could see himself as Fat Margot's pimp was capable of some queer turns of the mind.

35. My doctor's diploma bestows on me (on the authority of a Borgia pope) the right " legendi, docendi, et commentandi ubique gentium." Four hundred years ago I should have nailed the heads of this study on the doors of the University of London, put on my best gown, and waited for an invitation to have it out with a selected D.Lit. Lond., the loser to stand drinks round. It may be a recollection of this practice that induces the Bidding Prayer of London University to ask separate and specific intercessions for " our doctors " instead of lumping them with " our graduates " generally.

36. Later Countess of Lennox. Henry VIII's niece, Elizabeth Tudor's first cousin, and Darnley's mother, whose life was an alternation of brilliant posts at court and imprisonment with her head loose on her shoulders.

37. Greek itself had as yet made no mark on either Scots or English vernacular, though it was nearly half a century since Tiphernas had brought it to Paris and made it available to a swarm of Scots, and it was taught as far north as Aberdeen in Douglas' youth, a few years after Linacre brought it to Oxford.

CHAPTER IV. WHAT SHOULD HAVE BEEN OUR RENAISSANCE

38. It is an interesting relic of Stewart tastes that the Royal Household in Scotland still includes a King's Sculptor, a King's Limner, and an Historiographer Royal.

39. Calvinism seems to have a considerable attraction for the

Welsh stock : its stronghold in Scotland, outside the burgesses of the capital, was always in the Brython-Celtic South-west.

40. Although I know what the Scots Reformers could do, I should not believe this story if it were not recounted by a contemporary Protestant historian.

41. This point needs no emphasis for a Scots reader, but it is difficult for an Englishman to understand (though a Spaniard would find it perfectly comprehensible) that much Scots verse that looks most authentically " folk-literature " is a good deal less so than the *Daily Mail. Cauld Kail* was written by a duke ; *Tullochgorum* by a very learned dean, famed for theology and Latin verse ; *The Laird of Cockpen* and *Auld Robin Grey* by what the London papers call " titled women " of very blue blood and impeccable breeding. But all these things were (and are) sung by " the people," although the lower middle class thinks them ungenteel. And some of the best modern work in the tradition is by a distinguished colonial administrator.

42. The modern work that has most in it of the Makaris is Mr Linklater's *Juan in America,* which might have been written by Dunbar *redivivus* and off for another of those foreign journeys. I can see traces of them in Mrs Mitchison, who follows Henryson into Asia Minor, and in the landscape of my friend Nan Shepherd, though in both these latter cases it appears less in substance than in accident.

43. I call Jonson a Scot because he called himself one, by descent at least. We have to take his word for it : it is the only external evidence. Of internal there is, I think, a good deal in the very sharp difference in kind and temper between his work and that of the other Jacobeans, as well as in the antinomies of itself. The rather truculent intellectualism of the plays, their inclination, in form, to a classical tightness that anticipates Corneille more than it follows Shakespeare, and the union of their harsh masculine quality with the wit and tenderness, the austerely exquisite grace of the lyrics, have nothing at all like them among his fellows. But to find the author of *Bartholomew Fair* writing the crystal lyric of the masques would surprise no courtier of James the Fourth. I will bow to convention, however, and leave Ben out of our beadroll, the more as I have written of him elsewhere.

44. The penultimate line is almost certainly in need of emendation. Echoes do not relent, even for a powerful preacher.

But if the poet is a French-speaking Scot, they may conceivably *retent* (*retentir*). I am rather sorry, as the *l* sounds better : but I am fairly sure that Drummond wrote *retent*.

CHAPTER V. FOLK-LITERATURE

45. It is a little surprising to find that in the decorous year 1872, the Rev. L. W. McMeeken, in his *History of the Scottish Metrical Psalms*, quotes the most cerulean passages of *Hey Trix*, and adds even worse ones, at length and with approval, as specimens of what happens when " the hearts of an enlightened people, freed from the darkness of Romanism, (find) vent for joy and gratitude in song. . . . They found in (these songs) the *appropriate* expression of their new-born spiritual life and light." (My italics.) I have said some hard things of Presbyterianism, but they come short of that.

46. The last author in the series is sometimes Scott. The Norroway stanza of *Sir Patrick Spens* is his, and " they hadna sailed," and the dying Douglas's speech in *Chevy Chase*. And Burns, who we are told had an eighteenth century incapacity for magic, is responsible for

> About the deid hour o' the nicht
> She heard the bridles ring.

Nor are these pastiche. The two men, for the time, were balladists, and great ones. Indeed, " Proud Maisie," the death-song in *The Pirate* and the Warroch Head snatch in *Guy Mannering* are as genuine ballad as anything you please : the only difference is that we know who wrote them. And most of *Harlaw* would deceive the very elect.

47. In justice, I should add that it was not Adam Gordon, but his lieutenant, Ker of Fawdonsyde, who burnt the house of Lady Forbes of Towie in the year 1571. I do not know if the child's death is historical.

48. Early in 1639, it was proposed to confiscate the means of those who refused to sign.

49. Auvergne is not exactly North France, to be sure. But a scholar recently refused to believe that Mrs Willa Muir's racy Scots translations of Auvergnat songs were not really " sonnets from the Portuguese." And in fact any of them might be included in a Scots anthology without at all appearing to be a stranger.

Chapter VI. Drama

50. On the morning of the day after the draft of this book was finished, it was stated in Parliament that " great numbers of valuable uncodified (Scots) historical records are lying about in garrets and cellars . . . many in a state of hopeless decay." Mr Buchan, a person not given to exaggeration, said " the public records (of Scotland) are in a deplorable condition, and there is great danger that they may be destroyed altogether. . . . They (the Record Office) are hopelessly understaffed. There is not enough money for the mere business of physical preservation, not to mention the reorganisation of the Department to make it properly accessible." For the financial year 1927-8, the latest for which I have figures, the grant to the English Record Office was £24,393, and it had 26 higher officials : the Scottish grant was £2932, with one higher official. This proportion has its parallel elsewhere : the University grants for the year 1929-30 are in respect of each full-time student, for England £45, for Scotland, £29 14s. The English Antarctic Expedition under Shackleton and Scott received over £100,000 : the Scots under Bruce, £3,000. For 1931-32, the Wallace Collection receives £10,585, the London Museum £5757, and the Scottish National Library, £1,201. In 1930-31, the Scottish National Library received £2,600, the Welsh, £25,000. The population of Scotland is 4,842,554, that of Wales 2,593,984. It appears that the resentment of our Senior Partner against our old refusal to be annexed has lasted longer than she cares to admit.

51. The *Scotch Intelligencer* of 1643 was intended to give Scots news to Londoners, and the *Mercurius Criticus* of 1651, the first to be actually printed in Scotland, was to supply London news to Cromwell's army. Sydserf's *Mercurius Caledonius* of 1660 was the first Scottish paper addressed to a Scottish public.

Chapter VII. Prose

52. Those who wish to restrict Scottish creative writing to Scots and Gaelic are reminded of a few figures. Gaelic is the language of 144,218 people in a population of 4,842,554. (The figures are from the current *Whitaker*.) If it were spoken by the whole population of the Highland counties, including Caithness, it would be the language of 370,426—that is to say, of one-twelfth of the population of Scotland, Scots being native to, if not spoken by, the remaining 4,472,228. Outside Scotland,

there are a good many Gaelic speakers in Canada, and there are a considerably larger number of Scots-speaking people scattered over the habitable globe. But English, which is as native to most Highland and all Lowland Scotsmen as either Gaelic or Scots (and the only tongue in which men from Lewis and Buchan can converse), is the language not only of the 41 millions of the United Kingdom, but of an Empire of 422 millions (or leaving out India, of 178), of which Scotland, unless she likes to sink to Dominion status—as some of her young patriots appear to desire—is co-head. It is also the language of a country outside the Empire, with a population of 137 millions. Besides being the speech of 356 millions against less than 5, or well under half a million, it is also the language most commonly taught in countries to which it is not native : Gaelic and Scots are not learned in Italian schools. I think that Scotland will excise a lobe of her brain if she ever abandons either Gaelic or Scots : but speaking as a writer myself, I think she would be acting very absurdly if she could be brought to refuse her inheritance of the language common to Shakespeare and Walter Scott, the most widely spoken of all the tongues of man.

53. *Tales in Complaynt of Scotland.* Sum was in prose and sum was in verse : sum was stories and sum was flet taylis. This war the namis of them as after follows : Tailis of Cantirberrye. Robert le diabil, Duc of Normandie. The Tayl of the volf of the varldis end. Ferrand Erl of Flandirs that mareit the deuyl. The tayl of the reyde Eyttyn with the thre heydis. The tayle quhou Persius savit Andromada fra the cruel monster. The Prophysie of Merlyne. The tayl of the giantes that eit quyk men. On fut by Forth as I culd found. Wallace. The Bruce. Ypomedon. The tail of the thre futtit dog of Norroway. The Tayle quhou Hercules slew the serpent Hidra that had vii heydis. The tail quhou the kyng of Estmureland mareit the kyngis dochtir of Westmureland. Skail Gillenderson the kyngis sone of Skellye. The tayl of the Four sonnis of Aymon. The tail of the brig of the Mantribil. The tail of Syr Euan Arthors knycht. Rauf Collyear. The Seige of Millan. Gauen and Gollagres. Lancelot du Lac. Arthur knycht He raid on nycht With gylten spur and candil lycht. The tail of Floremond of Albanye the sleu the dragon be the see. The tail of Syr Waltir the bauld Leslie. The tail of the Pure Tynt. Claryades and Maliades. Arthur of litil Bretayne. Robene Hude and litil Jone. The Mervallis of Mandivil. The tayl of the yong Tamlane and of the bauld Braband. The ryng of the Roy Robert. Syr Egeir and Syr Gryme. Bevis of Southamtoun. The Goldin

Targe. The Paleis of Honour. The tayl quhou Acteon was transformit in ane hart and syne slane be his awin doggis. The tayl of Pirramus and Tesbe. The tail of the amours of Leander and Hero. The Tail quhou Jupiter transformit his deir love Yo in ane cow. The tail quhou that Jason wan the goldin fleice. Opheis kyng of Portingale. The tayl of the goldin appil. The tayl of the thre Weird Systers. The tayl quhou that Dedalus maid the laborynth to keip the monster Minotaurus. The tail quhou kyng Midas gat twa asseis luggis on his hede because of his avareis.

"*Sangis of natural music of the antiquitie.*" Pastance witht gude cumpanye.[1] The brier byndis me soir. Stil vndir the leuis grene.[2] Cou thou me the raschis grene.[3] Allace, I vyit ʒour tau fayr ene. Gode ʒou gude day, vil boy. Lady help ʒour presoneir. Kyng Villʒamis Note. The lang nonneou. The Cheapel Valk. Faytht is there none. Skald abellis nou. The Abirdenis nou. Brume brume on hil.[1] Allone I veip in grit distres.[2] Trolee lolee lemmen dou. Bille vilt thou cum by a lute and belt the in Sanct Francis cord. The frog cam to the myl dur. The sang of Gilquhiskar. Rycht soirly musing in my minde.[2] God sen the duc had byddin in France and dela bautie hed neuir cum hame. Al musing of meruellis amys hef I gone.[3] Mastres fayr ʒe vil forfayr. O lusty May vitht Flora quene.[3] O myn hart hey this is my sang.[2] The ballet of the Hayrlaw.[3] The huntis of Cheuet.[3] Sal I go vitht ʒow to Rumbelo fayr. Greuit is my sorou.[2] Turne the sueit ville to me. My lufe is lyand seik. Send hym ioy, send hym ioy. Fayr luf lend thou me thy mantyl ioy. The persee and the mongomery met.[3] That day, that day, that gentil day. My luf is laid apon ane knycht. Allace that samyn sueit face.[2] In ane myrthful morou. My hert is leuit on the land.

Dances. (Some of these were probably provided with words, as Gaelic reels still are, to be sung when no instrument is available.) Al Crysten Mennis Dance. The North of Scotland. Huntis up. The Comont Entry. Lang flat fut of Gariau. Robene Hude. Thom of Lyn. Freris al. Ennyrnes. The Loch of Slene. The gosseps dance. Levis grene. Makky. The Speyde. The flail. The lammis wynde. Soutra. Cum kyttil me nakit wantounly. Schayk leg. Fut before gossep. Rank at the rute. Bag, lap, and al. John ermistrangis dance. The Alman haye. The bace of Voragon. Dangeir. The beye. The

---

[1] English [2] Ghost preserved in *Gude and Godlie Ballattis*.
[3] Extant in whole or in part.

dede dance. The dance of Kylrynne. The wod and the wal. Schaik a trot.

54. Sir Edward Parry's *Persecution of Mary Stewart* examines, with the thoroughness of a great lawyer, the evidence for the case against Mary. His enthusiasm goes a little far in endeavouring to paint a spirited Franco-Scot of the sixteenth century as a douce little English girl of the nineteenth : but he does succeed, on cold documentary evidence, in damning Moray, Lethington, and Elizabeth with a very comprehensive thoroughness. It is not a book that an Englishman or a Scot can read with comfort, but it is worth reading, if only as comment on the art of history.

55. Only 36 of the 282 proof-texts of the Shorter Catechism come from the gospels.

56. As I have more than once seen it categorically stated that Knox objected to Mary because she persecuted his religion, I had better add that she did nothing of the sort. She *could* have done so when she came to Scotland : at all events the Catholic North and West were ready to put her into a position where she would certainly have had power to persecute if she had chosen. Instead, she chose to be guided by her brother, the head of Knox's faction, and even, sooner than break with him, permitted the oppression of her own co-religionists. By the time she had seen through Moray, she could not have persecuted if she had wished to do so.

57. Neither Knox nor Calvin was a Presbyterian. The movement comes from the English Puritans, and was established in Scotland by Andrew Melville the elder, the first Scottish Presbytery being set up in 1581, nine years after Knox's death. It is, by the way, a little remarkable that a religious system so intensely Scottish in character and so universally popular as we are constantly informed was the Presbyterian and Calvinist, and from its beginnings so pugnacious, should have taken two hundred years before achieving the armed overthrow of its rivals, have done so then only by the help of a foreign—and non-Presbyterian—power, and have required to persecute for another half-century before it could really feel that it sat secure.

58. It is interesting to note that the Scottish members of Parliament adhered to those clauses of the Solemn League and Covenant by which the Covenanters bound themselves " to endeavour the reformation of religion in the Kingdoms of England and Ireland . . . to bring the Churches of God in these three kingdoms to the nearest conjunction (*sc.* to the model of

the Scots Kirk) " . . . and to " endeavour the extirpation of . . . prelacy, . . . in the three kingdoms." The Church of England was forbidden by them to adopt the revision of one of her major documents approved by her archbishops and by majorities in both her own representative councils and among the English members of Parliament. If English members were to block an ordinance of the General Assembly, affecting Scotland alone, it is possible that there might be some comment.

59. One later episcopal contribution to education is worth noting. After 1688, the rents of the suppressed bishopric of Argyll and the Isles were to be bestowed " upon Erecting of English Schools for rooting out of the Irish (=Gaelic) language and (*sic*) other pious uses." When the Highland Episcopalians objected to paying taxes for this purpose, English soldiers were quartered upon them till the money was paid, no deduction being made for their entertainment. (*Act Parlt. Sc.* ix. 448.)

Chapter VIII. Epilogue

60. In the same year (1788) Fitch in America made a steam-boat which actually sailed, but she was propelled by paddles " like those of an Indian canoe," a method impossible for a vessel of any size, whereas the Scottish experimenters used the rotary paddle-wheel, not superseded by the screw till the mid-nineteenth century. The first steam-boat used as more than an experiment was Symington's *Charlotte Dundas* in 1801.

61. In 1888, the standard *Encyclopaedia of Architecture* remarks in shocked tones, " It is a fact that the depraved compositions of Robert Adam were not only tolerated, but had their admirers." It would be in that very year of grace that the plans of the North British Hotel in Edinburgh were being passed by the approving City Fathers.

GLOSSARY

A GOOD deal of the apparent difficulty of Middle Scots is merely a matter of an unfamiliar system of spelling, and vanishes if the sentence is read aloud. Certain more or less constant differences from modern usage may be noted here. *Quh* = modern *wh* : *quhill* = while. (*Quhair* [noun], however, is an exception, being of Old French origin, cognate with *quire* and *cahier*.) *U* and *v* are more or less interchangeable : *vnseyne* = unseen, *reuir* = river. *Ƶ* = *y*, as in modern *Menzies* : *zeir* = year. *þ* = *th* : *þat* = that. 3 initially, as *z* above : *zow* = you. 3 finally (here only in *Pearl*) = *s* : *stone3* = stones. 3 between vowels (here only in *Pearl*) = *ch* : *ly3t* = licht, light, *lo3e* = loch.

N.B.—To save confusion, the following words are glossed only in the senses they bear in the passages quoted in this book. Words current with slight differences of spelling in Modern Scots are not given.

alkin, alkyn, all kinds of.

amene, gracious.

attour, about.

bedene, also.

beft, beat.

begaried, patterned variously.

bernis, men.

beyn, bien, cosy.

boundis, borders.

bowgaris, beams of wood.

bremys, pebbles.

bruik, enjoy.

bubbis, blasts.

cane, khan.

con (in *Pearl*) has force of *did* or *does*.

contenye, continue.

daseyne, daisy.

dress, redress.

eild, old age.

eird, erd, earth.

feid, (occasion for) feud.

feir, companion.

felloun, dreadful.

fers, fierce.

fetrit, arranged.

fireflawcht, wildfire.

flaw, blast.

flete, float.

foir (*grantschir*), great-grand-sire.

fouth, plenty (*meikle of f.* = " weel-boukit ").

freikis, stout fellows.

frewall, fickle.

frog, frock, gown.

fudder, fother, a weight.

furth-warpit, threw forth.

gest, jest.

geste, res gestae, deeds : common term for story of anyone.

gormaw, cormorant.

gousty, gusty.

graithit, adorned.

haire, hoar.
hegis, hedges.
heynd, man.
hudpykis, misers.
kayis, daws.
kirsp, gauze.
kithit, showed.
largnas, generosity.
lawte, loyalty.
leme, a gleam.
lest, stay.
ligg, lie.
likand, pleasant.
lippar, leper, *lippar-leid*, leper-
    folk.
lyking, *my l.*, my love.
marleyonis, merlin hawks.
mawis, seagulls.
maynful, strong.
meven, move.
meyne, *maen*, to pity.
mo, move, go (in *Murning
    Maiden*).
myttane, a kind of hawk.
oder, *on oder* = on each other.
okkeraris, usurers.
oneath, hardly.
patent, in sense of *letters patent* =
    open, addressed to " whom
    it may concern."
prunye, preen (feathers).
rakit, sauntered.
recure, cure, remedy.

rege (with), rage against.
riggis, backs.
ring, *règne*, kingdom.
rise, see *ryss*.
roch, rock.
rouke, reek, vapour.
rourde, murmur.
ryse, *ryss*, brushwood, under-
    growth.
schene, fair, bright.
scyll, shrill.
schyne, see *schene*.
scuggis, shadows.
shene, see *schene*.
skug, see *scuggis*.
snipand, snell.
souch, sough.
spraings, streaks.
spynist, outspread.
stanneris, stones.
staren, stand.
swyr, breeze.
teyne, sorrow.
tomit, emptied.
vche, each.
wappit, happed, wrapped.
watȝ, was.
warlo, warlock.
widder, wither.
wode, wood, mad.
wylycoat, overcoat.
wysnit, wizened.
ȝeid, went.

INDEX

247

INDEX

PRINTED IN GREAT BRITAIN
BY ROBERT MACLEHOSE AND CO. LTD.
THE UNIVERSITY PRESS, GLASGOW